EDEXCEL
MEDICINE
& HEALTH THROUGH TIME

In order to ensure that this resource offers high quality support for the associated Edexcel qualification, it has been through a review process by the awarding body to confirm that it fully covers the teaching and learning content of the specification or part of a specification at which it is aimed, and demonstrates an appropriate balance between the development of subject skills, knowledge and understanding, in addition to preparation for assessment.

While the publishers have made every attempt to ensure that advice on the qualification and its assessment is accurate, the official specification and associated assessment guidance materials are the only authoritative source of information and should always be referred to for definitive guidance.

Edexcel examiners have not contributed to any sections in this resource relevant to examination papers for which they have responsibility.

No material from an endorsed resource will be used verbatim in any assessment set by Edexcel.

Endorsement of a resource does not mean that the resource is required to achieve this Edexcel qualification, nor does it mean that it is the only suitable material available to support the qualification, and any resource lists produced by the awarding body shall include this and other appropriate resources.

The Schools History Project

Set up in 1972 to bring new life to history for students aged 13–16, the Schools History Project continues to play an innovatory role in secondary history education. From the start, SHP aimed to show how good history has an important contribution to make to the education of a young person. It does this by creating courses and materials which both respect the importance of up-to-date, well-researched history and provide enjoyable learning experiences for students.

Since 1978 the Project has been based at Trinity and All Saints University College Leeds. It continues to support, inspire and challenge teachers through the annual conference, regional courses and website: http://www.schoolshistoryproject.org.uk. The Project is also closely involved with government bodies and awarding bodies in the planning of courses for Key Stage 3, GCSE and A level.

Note: The wording and sentence structure of some written sources have been adapted and simplified to make them accessible to all students, while faithfully preserving the sense of the original.

Thanks to all the Suffolk schools that have trialled our work and in particular to Ian Startup for his input into Section 9 of the book.

Memory map on page 21 courtesy of Hannah Mitcheson.

Although every effort has been made to ensure that website addresses are correct at time of going to press, Hodder Education cannot be held responsible for the content of any website mentioned in this book. It is sometimes possible to find a relocated web page by typing in the address of the home page for a website in the URL window of your browser.

Hachette UK's policy is to use papers that are natural, renewable and recyclable products and made from wood grown in sustainable forests. The logging and manufacturing processes are expected to conform to the environmental regulations of the country of origin.

Orders: please contact Bookpoint Ltd, 130 Milton Park, Abingdon, Oxon OX14 4SB. Telephone: (44) 01235 827720. Fax: (44) 01235 400454. Lines are open 9.00–5.00, Monday to Saturday, with a 24-hour message answering service. Visit our website at www.hoddereducation.co.uk

© Ian Dawson, Dale Banham and Dan Lyndon, 2009
First published in 2009 by
Hodder Education,
An Hachette UK Company
338 Euston Road
London NW1 3BH

Impression number   5
Year   2014

Cover photo: NATIONAL LIBRARY OF MEDICINE/SCIENCE PHOTO LIBRARY
Illustrations by Dylan Gibson, Ian Foulis, Barking Dog, Janet Matysiak, Pat Murray, Peter Lubach, Richard Duszczak, Steve Smith, Tony Randell and Tony Wilkins
Typeset in Palatino Light 11pt on 13pt by Ian Foulis/DC Graphic Design Limited
Printed in Italy

A catalogue record for this title is available from the British Library

ISBN: 978 0340 98670 7

EDEXCEL MEDICINE
& HEALTH THROUGH TIME

Ian Dawson
Dale Banham
Dan Lyndon

HODDER
EDUCATION
AN HACHETTE UK COMPANY

Contents

Before you start using this book here is a guide to help you get the most out of it.

Enquiries

The book is structured around a series of Enquiries, each one focusing on a key aspect of your GCSE course. Each Enquiry helps you understand a particular event, person or breakthrough and then links it to the broader history of medicine.

Banners introduce each Enquiry so you know exactly what you are focusing on from the start.

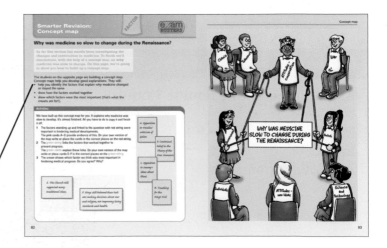

Activities guide you through the material so you build up your knowledge and understanding of the key content of your GCSE course. They also link into the on-going Smarter Revision activities.

Medical Moments in Time

These pages give you an overview of the key features of medicine at five important points in history: AD200, 1347, 1665, 1848 and 1935.

Smarter Revision

These pages help you prepare effectively for your examinations, showing you a variety of ways to build up your knowledge and understanding of the history of medicine. You will be building up your revision material from the very beginning of your course – not waiting until you have completed it. See page 13 for more details on Smarter Revision pages.

Smarter Revision pages give you clear advice on how to use each Smarter Revision strategy.

Exam Busters

These pages explain how to win high marks in your exams. They show you how to:

- answer each type of question in your examinations
- identify exactly what a question is asking
- structure answers and develop the vocabulary to make full use of what you know.

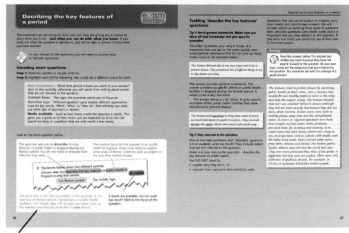

Sample answers help you identify what makes a good answer.

Dynamic Learning

Dynamic Learning resources provide an extensive range of supporting resources. They feature:

- Enquiries developing your knowledge and understanding of key topics within each period
- Thematic investigations helping you understand the development of major themes across time
- Exambuster activities helping you revise and prepare effectively for examinations.

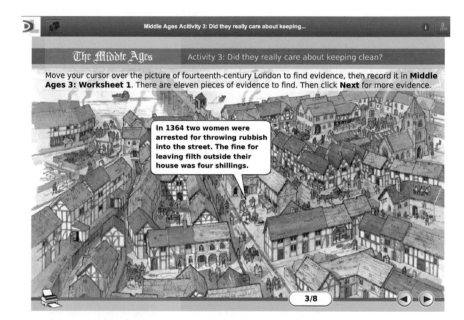

Part 2

Part 2 of this book contains:

Source Enquiry: The transformation of surgery c.1845–c.1918

Full coverage of Unit 3a – the Source Enquiry, providing all of the required content and detailed guidance on using sources within an overall investigation into which surgical breakthrough was the most important.

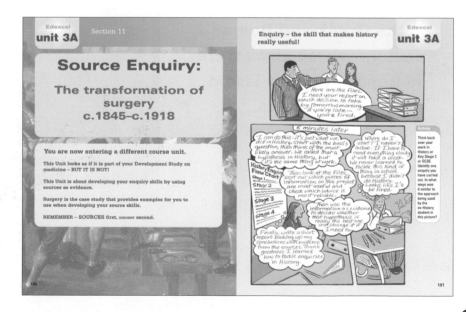

1

Development Study

Medicine and treatment through time

Welcome to the Development Study!

You are going to discover ...

... the Greek and Roman doctors whose ideas were so important they lasted thousands of years. ▶

... why the Black Death was so devastating in the Middle Ages. ▶

... why we should all be grateful to a Frenchman and his test ◀ tubes.

... which letters of the alphabet are revolutionising medicine today and how could they have helped this man walk again. ▶

And much more!

This section helps you build up an outline picture of the history of medicine in your mind and on paper. We'll start by getting you to think! Which period of history do you think each of the clues comes from?

Activity

The history of medicine can be surprising. Sometimes what seems to be a modern idea turns out to be thousands of years old. Sometimes a treatment we take for granted only began quite recently.

Read Clues A–J. Think about what each one tells you about medical ideas or treatments. Then draw your own version of the timeline at the foot of these pages and pencil in each clue heading where you think it belongs on the timeline.

Clue A Home remedies – herbal medicine

'Medicine for dimness of the eyes: take the juice of the celandine plant, mix with bumblebees' honey, put in a brass container then warm until it is cooked and apply to the eyes.'

Clue B Penicillin – the first antibiotic

'We had an enormous number of wounded with infections; terrible burn cases among the crews of armoured cars. The usual medicines had absolutely no effect. The last thing I tried was penicillin. The first man was a young man called Newton. He had been in bed for six months with fractures of both legs. His sheets were soaked with pus. Normally he would have died in a short time. I gave three injections of penicillin a day and studied the effects under a microscope. The thing seemed like a miracle. In ten days' time the leg was cured and in a month's time the young fellow was back on his feet. I had enough penicillin for ten cases. Nine were complete cures.'

Clue C Explaining disease – the four humours

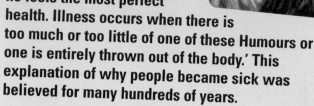

Hippocrates wrote: 'Man's body contains Four Humours – blood, phlegm, yellow bile and melancholy (black) bile. When all these Humours are truly balanced, he feels the most perfect health. Illness occurs when there is too much or too little of one of these Humours or one is entirely thrown out of the body.' This explanation of why people became sick was believed for many hundreds of years.

Clue D 'Cure-alls' patent medicines

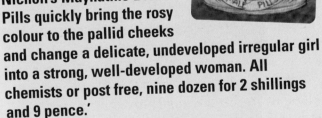

From an advertisement for Nicholl's Mayhatine Blood Pills: 'If your daughters have Pale Faces, Weakness, Palpitation, Bloodlessness, Nicholl's Mayhatine Blood Pills quickly bring the rosy colour to the pallid cheeks and change a delicate, undeveloped irregular girl into a strong, well-developed woman. All chemists or post free, nine dozen for 2 shillings and 9 pence.'

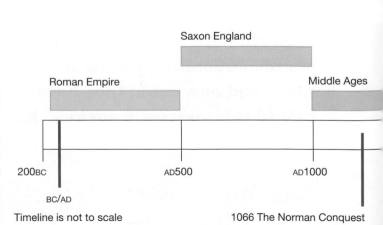

Saxon England

Roman Empire

Middle Ages

200BC

AD500

AD1000

BC/AD

Timeline is not to scale

1066 The Norman Conquest

Clue E Better hospitals, better nursing

Florence Nightingale became a national heroine during the Crimean War. This helped her raise money to set up nursing schools in Britain and all over the world. Her schools focused on hygiene and cleanliness to prevent diseases spreading. In 1859, she wrote her book *Notes on Nursing* and in 1863, *Notes on Hospitals*. These books provided the basis for training nurses and for hospital design world-wide.

Clue H No sick people in hospitals

From the rules of the hospital of St John, Bridgwater in the south of England: 'No lepers, lunatics or persons having the falling sickness or other contagious disease, and no pregnant women, or sucking infants and no intolerable persons, even though they be poor and infirm, are to be admitted. If any such be admitted by mistake they are to be expelled as soon as possible.'

Clue F NHS – free treatments for all

'On the first day of free treatment on the NHS, Mother went and got tested for new glasses. Then she went further down the road to the chiropodist and had her feet done. Then she went back to the doctor's because she'd been having trouble with her ears and the doctor said he would fix her up with a hearing aid.'

Clue I Explaining disease – God sends diseases

'Terrible is God towards men. He sends plagues of disease and uses them to terrify and torment men and drive out their sins. That is why the realm of England is struck by plagues – because of the sins of the people.'

Clue J Explaining disease – Pasteur and germ theory

Louis Pasteur, a French scientist, published his 'germ theory' suggesting that bacteria or 'germs' were the true cause of diseases. His germ theory replaced all previous ideas about the causes of disease.

Clue G Treatments – the black cat remedy

'The stye on my right eyelid was still swollen and inflamed very much. It is commonly said that rubbing the eyelid with the tail of a black cat will do it much good so, having a black cat, a little before dinner I tried it and very soon after dinner the swelling on my eyelid was much reduced and almost free of pain.'

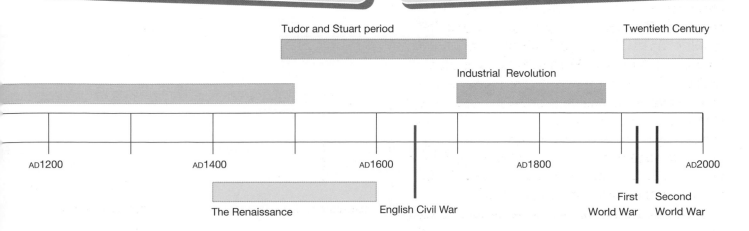

Tudor and Stuart period

Twentieth Century

Industrial Revolution

AD1200   AD1400   AD1600   AD1800   AD2000

The Renaissance

English Civil War

First World War

Second World War

The Big Story of medicine and health through time

Activities

1 Work in a group of three.
You have one minute to tell the outline story of medicine.
Your story needs to answer the question: 'Why do people today have better health and live longer lives than people in the past?'

Spend ten minutes preparing your story. Include each of these:
- continuity
- change
- turning point
- progress.

2 One of the most important skills in history is asking questions.
a What questions do you want to ask to fill in the gaps in the story?
b Look at the blue and red lines on the graph. What questions do you want to ask about the shapes of these lines?

Information

Life expectancy
These graphs show the life expectancy of men and women throughout history. The life expectancy age is the average age that people lived to.
Until the 1900s around 20 per cent of babies died before their first birthday and this therefore reduced the average life expectancy.

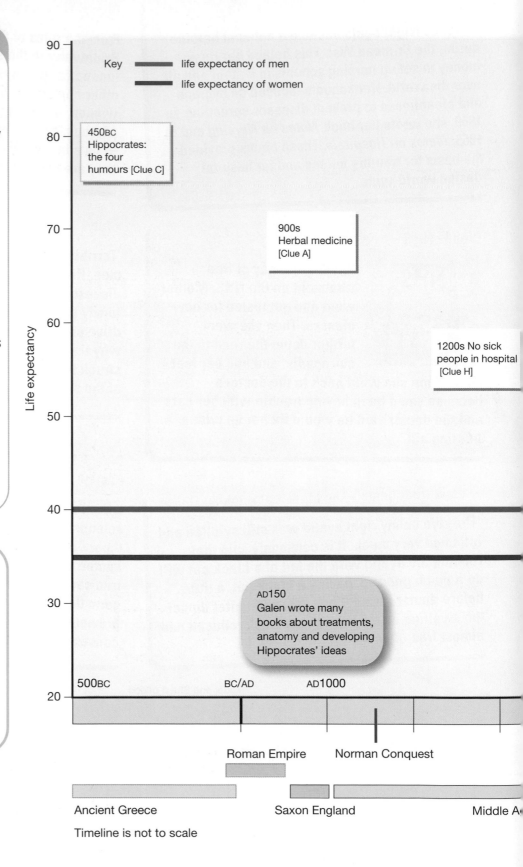

Key ▬▬ life expectancy of men
▬▬ life expectancy of women

450BC
Hippocrates:
the four
humours [Clue C]

900s
Herbal medicine
[Clue A]

1200s No sick
people in hospital
[Clue H]

AD150
Galen wrote many
books about treatments,
anatomy and developing
Hippocrates' ideas

Life expectancy

500BC   BC/AD   AD1000

Roman Empire   Norman Conquest

Ancient Greece   Saxon England   Middle A

Timeline is not to scale

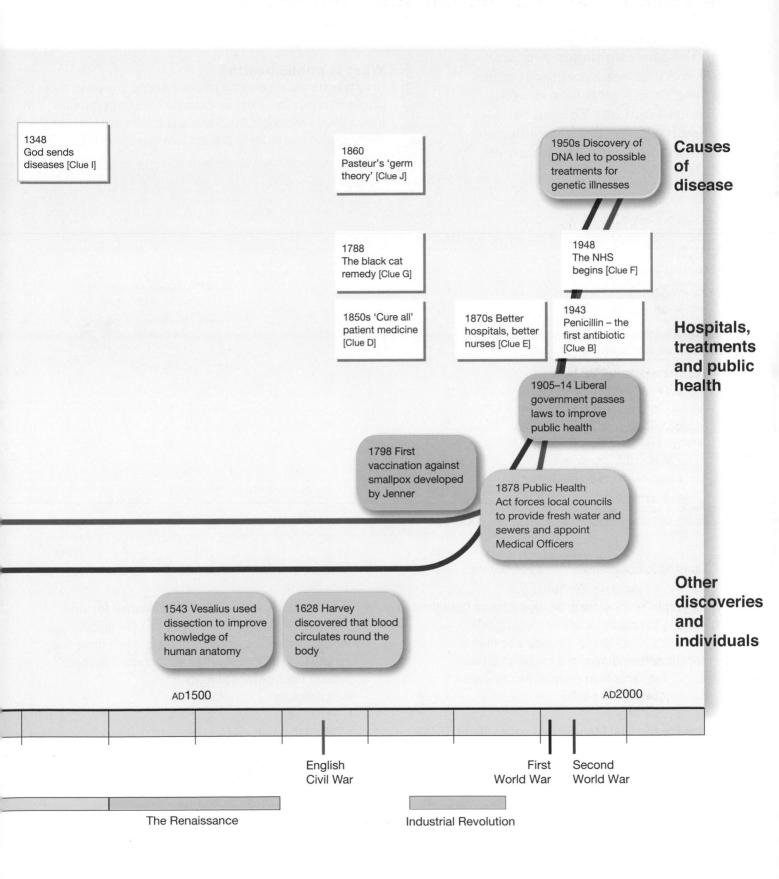

1348
God sends
diseases [Clue I]

1860
Pasteur's 'germ
theory' [Clue J]

1950s Discovery of
DNA led to possible
treatments for
genetic illnesses

**Causes
of
disease**

1788
The black cat
remedy [Clue G]

1948
The NHS
begins [Clue F]

1850s 'Cure all'
patient medicine
[Clue D]

1870s Better
hospitals, better
nurses [Clue E]

1943
Penicillin – the
first antibiotic
[Clue B]

**Hospitals,
treatments
and public
health**

1905–14 Liberal
government passes
laws to improve
public health

1798 First
vaccination against
smallpox developed
by Jenner

1878 Public Health
Act forces local councils
to provide fresh water and
sewers and appoint
Medical Officers

**Other
discoveries
and
individuals**

1543 Vesalius used
dissection to improve
knowledge of
human anatomy

1628 Harvey
discovered that blood
circulates round the
body

AD1500

AD2000

English
Civil War

First
World War

Second
World War

The Renaissance

Industrial Revolution

Smarter Revision: Living graph

On the last two pages you saw the story of life expectancy right across time – all in one graph. Graphs are really helpful for following the story of medicine across time so it's important to start early – NOW!

What is public health?
Governments organise public health systems to protect their people from disease. This, for example, includes providing fresh water, sewers and hospitals, and making laws to force towns and people to try to prevent diseases spreading.

Activities

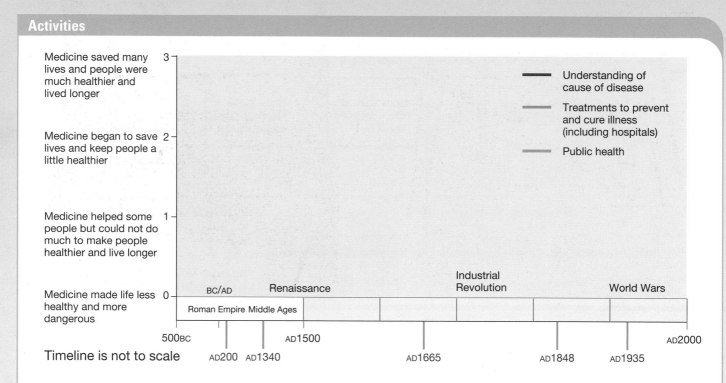

Medicine saved many lives and people were much healthier and lived longer — 3

Medicine began to save lives and keep people a little healthier — 2

Medicine helped some people but could not do much to make people healthier and live longer — 1

Medicine made life less healthy and more dangerous — 0

— Understanding of cause of disease
— Treatments to prevent and cure illness (including hospitals)
— Public health

BC/AD   Renaissance   Industrial Revolution   World Wars
Roman Empire   Middle Ages

500BC   AD1500   AD2000
AD200   AD1340   AD1665   AD1848   AD1935

Timeline is not to scale

Living graph: You are going on an evidence hunt through the book to create three lines on your graph.

1 Work in a small group. Choose one theme:
   a Understanding of the cause of disease
   b Treatments to prevent and cure illness (including hospitals)
   c Public health

2 Use the Medical Moments on pages 16, 18, 66, 86 and 88.
   a Pick out from each picture the evidence about your theme. Decide for each date where to place your theme on the graph.
   (For example if you think public health in AD200 made life less healthy and more dangerous put a cross at level 0 above AD200.)

   b Use sticky notes to list the evidence for your choice of level. Stick these on your graph.

3 When your outline graph is complete you have one minute to explain it aloud to your class. You must include each of these words:
   • continuity
   • change
   • turning point
   • progress.

4 Compare the lines for each theme. What similarities and differences can you see between the shapes of the three lines?

5 Look back at the life-expectancy graph on pages 6–7. What have you learned from your new graphs that helps to explain the shape of the life-expectancy graph?

Why is this page really important?

To be successful in your examination you need to have an overview of the history of medicine in your mind. You will remember this outline better if you build it up from the beginning, filling in the detail as you go through the course. The best way to build up this outline knowledge is to see it as a graph. You can do this in different ways:

1 Draw the graph on A3 paper and add notes to explain the lines going up or down. Use sticky notes for the Activity opposite when suggesting first ideas. Then copy the notes onto the graph as you feel more certain about the patterns of changes and continuities.

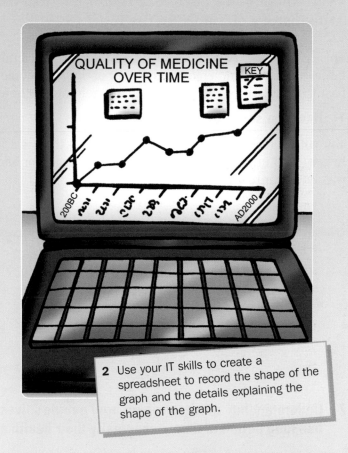

2 Use your IT skills to create a spreadsheet to record the shape of the graph and the details explaining the shape of the graph.

3 Turn the graphs into living graphs with a group of friends. Create a graph on the floor, then choose a theme such as understanding of the causes of disease. Each person is a period in history and you have to decide where on the graph you stand. Then each person has 30 seconds to explain why they are in that place on the graph. Turning your ideas into more precise spoken words and sentences is an effective way of revising. Doing this physically is an excellent way of remembering the patterns of changes and continuities.

Why are you studying the history of medicine?

Your course will stretch back at least 700 years and possibly 2000 years, all the way to Roman times. Why are we going so far back? Why are you studying the history of medicine? Pages 10–13 help you understand how your History course links together and where the history of medicine fits in.

This course isn't trying to turn you into doctors. It's aiming to help you get better at History and enjoy finding out about the people who lived in the past. Here are three things that you are going to become a lot better at.

1 Having a sense of chronology

You will increase your knowledge of some of the most important events in history, and understand better how they fit together and why each period was important.

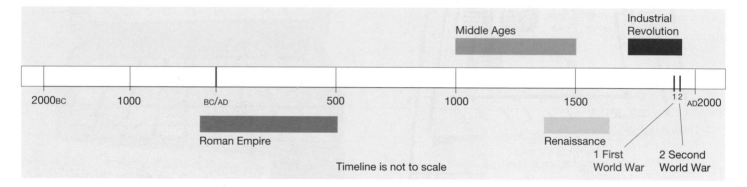

Middle Ages

Industrial Revolution

2000BC   1000   BC/AD   500   1000   1500   AD2000

Roman Empire

Renaissance

Timeline is not to scale

1 First World War   2 Second World War

2 Understanding and describing how people's lives developed over this long period of time – especially their health and medicine

Your core question is 'Why are we healthier and why do we live longer lives than people in the past?', but by the end of the course you will be able to answer this question and many more!

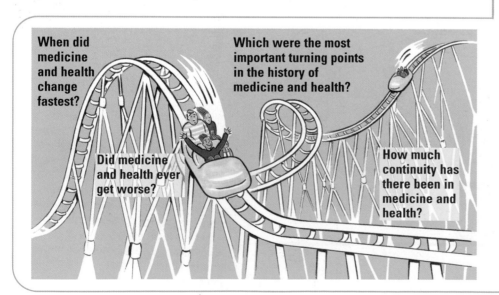

When did medicine and health change fastest?

Which were the most important turning points in the history of medicine and health?

Did medicine and health ever get worse?

How much continuity has there been in medicine and health?

Activities

1 Think back to your KS3 History and what you learned about different periods.
   a Do you think the Middle Ages was a time of many improvements in medicine?
   b How might the Industrial Revolution have affected people's health?
   c When do you think changes in medicine have been fastest?
2 Now use your answers to question 1 to suggest answers to the questions on the rollercoaster.

3 Explaining why changes happened – and why they didn't happen

You are going to describe the continuities and changes in medicine and why they happened. The people shown below will help you a lot with your explanations. They are the reasons, the factors, which explain the changes and continuities in medicine.

Activities

3 Can you suggest how any of the factors shown in the cartoon below improved medicine and so helped to save lives?

4 How might any of the factors have hindered (stopped or slowed down) the development of medicine?

(Don't worry if you can't suggest any ideas right now. You will be able to give really good answers at the end of the course.)

How does your GCSE History course all fit together?

Your GCSE History course is special.
Here are three good reasons why.

Reason 1: different types, topics and periods

Your course might look like a random set of topics, but it's not like that at all. This course was designed to let you investigate different types, topics and periods of history. This is much more varied and interesting than sticking to one period throughout your course.

Reason 2: concepts and processes

It's not just about topics such as the history of medicine. It is developing your ability to use all the concepts and processes you used in KS3. The people, topics and periods we study change but we always use the same concepts and processes to study that content.

**Interpretations
Diversity
Sources and evidence
Chronological understanding
Significance
Cause and consequence
Enquiry
Change and continuity**

Reason 3: understand events today

It will help you see how knowledge of history helps us understand events today. It's really satisfying to appreciate how past events and people have led to items in the news today – and knowing that events are complicated stops us leaping to simple conclusions.

D E V E L O P M E N T

Medicine and treatment shows the value of developing a long overview of the development of a topic

S T U D Y

(25%)

Source Enquiry (25%)
This unit develops your ability to follow an enquiry by using sources, developing skills essential to being successful in History.

Depth Study (25%)
This investigation of a short period of time allows you to understand the ideas and attitudes of a period and contrasts with the much longer Development Study.

Representations of History (25%)
An enquiry chosen by your school in which you investigate a topic, then analyse and evaluate representations of events, people or places from the past.

Activities

1 Which topics are you studying and where do they fit into this diagram?
2 Can you suggest how any part of your History course helps you understand the world today?

What are the best ways to prepare for your GCSE exams?

Good revision and planning will help you do well at GCSE. We will help you with the two important features below.

smarter revision

The Smarter Revision toolkit

The toolkit helps you prepare your revision notes thoroughly and intelligently. Each tool helps you with a different aspect of your revision.

Factors chart – helps you record how different factors affected the development of medicine. See page 115.

Concept map – helps you to link factors to improve your explanation. See page 80.

Living graph – helps you see the pattern of change and continuity in each medical theme. See page 9.

SMARTER REVISION TOOLKIT

Photo revision – find out more on page 34.

Memory map – helps you remember the key medical developments in each period. See page 20.

'Role of the individual' chart – helps you record the impact of key people. See page 35.

exam busters

These features will show you how to answer source-based questions in the exam.

Examine that question – analyses each kind of question you will face. See page 36, for example.

Improve that answer – gives you sample answers and asks you to mark them or improve them. See page 37, for example.

How to – takes you step by step through the process of answering each kind of question. See page 200, for example.

Warning – helps you avoid the most common mistakes. See page 164, for example.

Introducing the Development Study exam

By now you should have a good overview of the content of the Medicine course. However, simply knowing a lot of content is not enough to achieve a good grade in your GCSE exam. Exam Busters are ready to help you.

Unit 1: Development Study – medicine and treatment

This unit is assessed by a 1 hour and 15 minute exam.

The exam paper below gives you an idea what the exam for Unit 1 looks like. We have not included the Sources for Questions 1 and 3.

**Unit 1: Development Study
Medicine and public health in Britain, c.AD50 to the present day
Time: 1 hour 15 minutes**

Answer Questions 1, 2 and 3, **EITHER** Question 4 **OR** 5 and then EITHER Question 6 **OR** 7. The total mark for this paper is 53.

Answer Questions 1, 2 AND 3

1 What do Sources A and B show about changes in the way doctors find out about a patient's health? **[8 marks]**

2 The boxes below show two different periods.

Choose one and describe the key features of hospitals during that period. **[6 marks]**

The late Middle Ages	The late nineteenth century, after the work of Florence Nightingale

3 Study Source C.

How useful is this cartoon to a historian who is investigating public health problems in Britain in the early nineteenth century?

Use Source C and your own knowledge to explain your answer. **[8 marks]**

Answer EITHER Question 4 or Question 5

EITHER

4 Why did the discoveries of the Renaissance have so little impact on medical treatments in Britain between 1500 and 1750? **[12 marks]**

OR

5 Why have ways of preventing and treating illness improved since 1750? **[12 marks]**

**Answer EITHER Question 6 or 7.
Spelling, punctuation and grammar will be assessed in this question.**

EITHER

*6 How far was the progress made by the Romans continued in the Middle Ages in England? **[16 marks]**

(Total for spelling, punctuation and grammar = 3 marks)

(Total for Question 6 = 19 marks)

OR

*7 How important was the role played by Edwin Chadwick in improving public health services in towns in nineteenth century England? **[16 marks]**

(Total for spelling, punctuation and grammar = 3 marks)

(Total for Question 7 = 19 marks)

Thinking for success

TIMING AND MARKS

The marks for **each** question are shown in brackets. Use this as a guide as to how much time to spend on each question.

It is important to time yourself carefully. Some students run out of time because they spend too long on the first three questions. These questions are worth a total of 22 marks. The last two questions are worth a total of 31 marks so stick to a time plan:
- Questions 1, 2 and 3: approx. 30 minutes
- Questions 4 OR 5: approx. 15 minutes
- Questions 6 OR 7: 25 minutes

This leaves 5 minutes to check your answers.

FOLLOW INSTRUCTIONS CAREFULLY

Read the instructions very carefully. You must answer Questions 1, 2 and 3, but notice that for Question 2 you choose **one period** to write about. If you write about both periods you will not gain extra marks, but you will waste valuable time!

THINK CAREFULLY ABOUT WHICH QUESTION YOU CHOOSE

After Questions 1, 2 and 3, you need to make TWO important choices.

You need to decide whether to answer Question 4 OR Question 5.

Do not rush your decision. Think carefully about which question you will perform best on. Plan your answer and check that you will be able to fully answer the question.

You then need to decide just as carefully whether to answer Question 6 OR Question 7.

Types of questions

1 DEVELOPING INFERENCES
The first question will usually be an inference question. You will need to use both sources AND your own knowledge to answer the question. You will find advice on this type of question on pages 110–11.

2 DESCRIBING KEY FEATURES
This question asks you to describe the key features and characteristics of a period you have studied. The Exam Busters on pages 36–37 help you answer this type of question effectively.

3 EVALUATING THE USEFULNESS OF A SOURCE
The third question on the exam paper tests your ability to evaluate how useful a source is for a historian investigating a particular issue. You must refer to the source and use your own knowledge of the period. The Exam Buster on pages 164–65 explains how to approach this type of question.

4 THE 12-MARK QUESTION
This question needs to be planned as it carries a lot of marks. Look at the question carefully. You may be asked to make comparisons or analyse change. The questions here ask you to

explain why something happened. For this type of question you need to analyse the factors involved. You have been introduced to the factors which explain changes and continuities in medicine on page 11. The Exam Busters on pages 82–83 and 124–125 help you to tackle 'factors' style questions effectively.

5 THE 16-MARK QUESTION
This question carries the most marks and requires a longer answer that also needs to be carefully planned. It is important that you break down the question so that you know exactly what you are being asked to do. You may be asked to evaluate the extent of change and continuity across a period or to explain the causes or consequences of a particular development. Pages 52–53, 108–109 and 178–181 provide advice on answering 16-mark questions.

6 QUALITY OF WRITTEN COMMUNICATION
Questions marked with an **asterisk (*)** are ones where the quality of your written communication will be assessed. Make sure you check your answer to this question carefully as 3 marks are awarded for your spelling, punctuation and grammar.

Being sick in the past must have been grim. There were no effective painkillers, for a start. But were some periods better at preventing and healing sickness than others? Your task is to compare Roman Britain with Medieval Britain: Which was better at medicine and public health? We'll begin with two snapshots on this page and the next. What clues can you find to help with the comparison?

Medical Moments in Time: Roman Londinium, AD200

Water came from aqueducts which brought water from the hills.

Public toilets emptied into stone sewers flushed by rainwater or by water from the bath-house.

Keep the bleeding cup steady. I also have something to clear your stomach out. That will sort out the other humours.

Best price! My potion cures any sickness! Rare ingredients from Asia blessed by the gods. Only three pennies.

I learned to amputate legs as a surgeon in an army hospital. It's a pity there are n[o] hospitals for ordinary people.

Water flowed along streets in wooden and lead pipes.

Most towns had a bath-house where people washed and exercised for a small price.

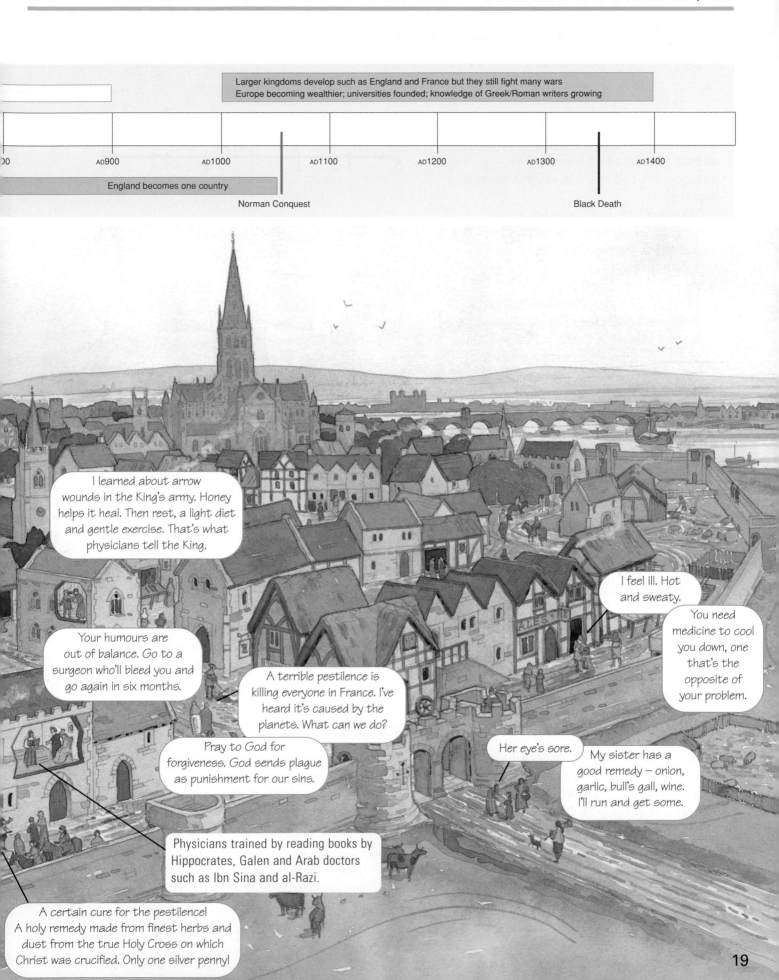

Comparing medicine and public health in Roman and Medieval Britain – creating your hypothesis

Activities

You have already learned a lot about medicine in Roman and Medieval Britain – enough to build a first answer to your question. We call this first, rough answer a hypothesis.

1 **Washing line:** From what you know already, where on the 'washing line' would you put the six topics? If you're not sure or haven't got any evidence yet, leave them to one side.

2 Were medicine and public health better in Roman or Medieval Britain? Now write a short answer in rough, including what you think is the strongest evidence to support your answer. When you have completed this section you can use this as the basis for a fuller answer.

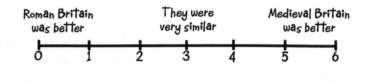

Smarter Revision: Memory map

You're only just starting the course but we're thinking about helping you revise already. Revision isn't something you tack onto the end of a course. It's something you build up as you go – that makes it a lot easier. You are going to build two memory maps as your main activities in this section, ready made to revise later in the course. How about that for saving time?

How can a map save you time and boost your memory?

- Memory maps encourage you to link pieces of information together. You learn more by making links, because it makes you think!

- You are actively involved with your revision. This is much better than simply reading, hoping your brain will act as a sponge and soak up the information!

- Your own images, colours and acronyms will help your memory.

- Memory maps are a flexible tool for revision. You can produce a memory map from memory, check it against the original, then add in what you have missed.

- Finally, and perhaps most importantly, memory maps make revision a lot more interesting!

How to build your Roman Britain medicine memory map

Step 1: Use plain A4 or, even better, A3 paper (landscape). Space is important. The end result should not look too busy or cramped.

Step 2: The memory map below shows how you could start, but the important thing about a memory map is that you do it **your own way** so you remember it better!

Step 3: As you work on pages 22–33 add more information to the map. Use pencil so that you can make corrections later if necessary. Remember:

- Use key words or phrases. Do not write full sentences.
- Use pictures/images/diagrams to replace or emphasise words. Lots of you will find it easier to remember visual images than words.
- PRINT words to make them stand out.

Step 4: Decide how successful people in Roman Britain were at each topic. Give each topic a mark out of 3 as follows:

3 marks – they were very good at this topic and it helped the sick a great deal

2 marks – they were quite good at this and it helped the sick a little

1 marks – they were very poor at this topic and it did not help the sick at all.

Step 5: When you have finished:

- redraft your map to make sure everything is clear
- draw your own central picture which sums up the topic for you.

Step 6: Now create a memory map for medieval medicine using pages 38–51.

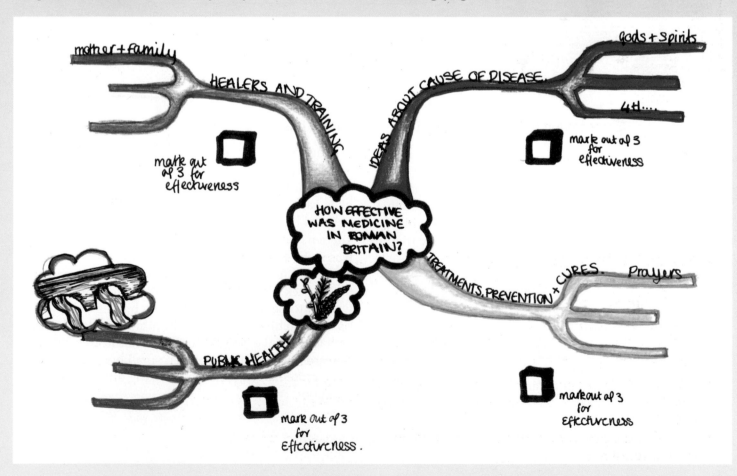

2.1 How effective was medicine and public health in Roman Britain?

The Romans are famous for living comfortably. They built public baths and central heating. They had trained doctors with detailed theories about the causes of disease and treatments. But did any of this help them stay healthy? Use pages 22–33 to find out and complete your memory map for Roman Britain.

Public health – the Romans' big idea

I am Frontinus, the Water Commissioner of Rome. We Romans have built reservoirs, fountains, water basins. Compare such an array of useful buildings with the idle Pyramids or the useless though famous works of the Greeks.

Public health

Activities

1 Why was public health so important to the Romans?
2 Make two lists:
   a the strengths, and
   b the weaknesses of the system.
3 Do you think the Roman public health system would help:
   a everyone
   b small groups of people
   c no one at all?
   What evidence would you use to support your answer?

Why did the Romans want to protect the public's health?

Roman rulers needed healthy soldiers to control the Empire. Healthy workers and merchants were needed to keep the Empire fed and prosperous. Therefore they built their towns, villas or army forts in healthy places, away from marshland and polluted water. They tried to keep army forts and cities clean and make sure people had fresh water.

Their public health schemes (see opposite page) used their great skills as builders and engineers. Engineers, often from the army, kept everything running and dealt with repairs.

Roman public health schemes were the best there had been – and better than anything in Europe for the next 1500 years. But they were not perfect. They could not stop plagues spreading, partly because soldiers carried diseases wherever they were sent to fight or defend the Empire.

Roman hospitals

Hospitals

Roman forts had hospitals for soldiers. They had small wards, often of four beds each, and the hospital had its own kitchen, baths and dispensary for making remedies. It was staffed by a surgeon and his assistants. Roman towns did not have hospitals as we know them, caring for the sick. People who could afford to pay a doctor wanted to be treated in their own homes rather than risking catching illnesses from other people. However, archaeological evidence suggests that from c.200AD onwards there may have been small hospitals that were more like care-homes, looking after the elderly and poor.

The key features of Roman public health schemes in towns

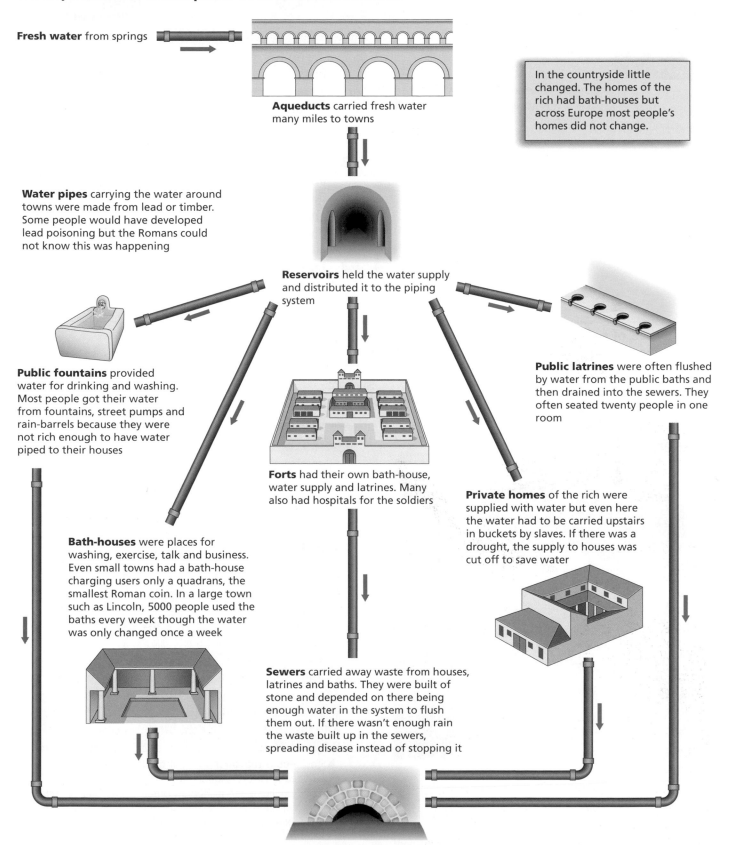

Fresh water from springs

Aqueducts carried fresh water many miles to towns

In the countryside little changed. The homes of the rich had bath-houses but across Europe most people's homes did not change.

Water pipes carrying the water around towns were made from lead or timber. Some people would have developed lead poisoning but the Romans could not know this was happening

Reservoirs held the water supply and distributed it to the piping system

Public fountains provided water for drinking and washing. Most people got their water from fountains, street pumps and rain-barrels because they were not rich enough to have water piped to their houses

Public latrines were often flushed by water from the public baths and then drained into the sewers. They often seated twenty people in one room

Forts had their own bath-house, water supply and latrines. Many also had hospitals for the soldiers

Private homes of the rich were supplied with water but even here the water had to be carried upstairs in buckets by slaves. If there was a drought, the supply to houses was cut off to save water

Bath-houses were places for washing, exercise, talk and business. Even small towns had a bath-house charging users only a quadrans, the smallest Roman coin. In a large town such as Lincoln, 5000 people used the baths every week though the water was only changed once a week

Sewers carried away waste from houses, latrines and baths. They were built of stone and depended on there being enough water in the system to flush them out. If there wasn't enough rain the waste built up in the sewers, spreading disease instead of stopping it

The sewers emptied into rivers, which were used to wash clothes and also for washing and drinking water

Did public health facilities in Roman Britain really protect people's health?

Public health

Source 1

From Lindsay Allason-Jones, *Women in Roman Britain*, 1989. Dr Allason-Jones is a historian and archaeologist, an expert on life in Roman Britain.

'The impression given by most descriptions of town life in the Roman empire is of spacious, well-organized streets, water on tap, an efficient sewerage system; but this may not be the whole picture or even an accurate one. The great civic bath-houses, unless kept scrupulously clean, would have been hotbeds of disease. Housewives had to carry water from public water tanks or draw it from a well. Sewers were often open or built very close to the surface, leading to unpleasant smells and disease.'

Activities

1 Read Source 1. What does the author say:
   a is our usual image of public health in Romans towns
   b was the reality of public health in Roman towns?
2 Complete the table below, collecting evidence of the effectiveness of public health in Roman Britain.
3 Did public health facilities in Roman Britain really protect people's health?
   Give your verdict and list the key pieces of evidence that support your view.
4 **Memory map:** Add information to your memory map from page 21.

Evidence of public health helping people stay healthy	Problems of public health facilities

Source 2 — Away from the towns

▲ Before the Roman invasion in AD43, there were no towns in Britain. Britons lived in roundhouses like this in small farming communities. After AD43, this way of life continued for the majority of Britons. Only a minority lived in towns or villas with baths and heating. Keeping clean, collecting water and being hygienic was up to families and individuals, not organised by local rulers.

Source 3 — The impact of the army

▲ This reconstruction drawing of the latrine at Housesteads Fort on Hadrian's Wall is typical of our usual ideas of public health in Roman Britain. Forts had sewers, good water supplies, hospitals and toilet blocks (equipped with washing sponges, not toilet paper). However, they were only for soldiers and they were not perfect. Poor water flow through sewers if there was little rain led to diseases spreading.

Source 4 Public health in towns

▲ The bath-house at Wroxeter in Shropshire was one of the best in Britain with a large outdoor exercise yard and pool, as well as indoor facilities.

Water supply – Clay-lined channels were dug to bring fresh water to towns. The channel at Dorchester was 8 miles (13 km) long, 5 feet (1.6m) wide and 3 feet (1m) deep. Two million gallons of fresh water flowed into Wroxeter each day and was distributed around the town through lead and timber pipes. Water supplies mostly went to baths and water tanks for public use. Few houses received their own water supplies.

Baths – Public baths have been discovered by archaeologists in most Roman towns. In a large town like Lincoln, 5000 people used the baths every week. However, this wasn't as wonderful as it sounds. The water was only changed once a week. Archaeologists have also discovered that the baths in Exeter and Wroxeter were demolished long before the end of Roman Britain. Using the baths may not have been as popular as we assume – but we can't be certain.

Sewers and toilets – Every town needed public toilets as few homes had toilets that emptied directly into sewers. At home, people used pots that they emptied into sewers or rivers. Most towns had timber or open sewers with only the largest towns, such as York, having stone sewers. However, even stone caused problems. In York the sewers were too large so water did not flow through quickly enough to clear sewage in the bottom of the sewers. This led to bad smells and helped to spread disease.

Despite these facilities, towns could still be dirty places. People had to carry water upstairs. If they did not want to carry it down again they might just heave it out of a window. The poet Juvenal warned, 'Each open window may be a death trap. So hope and pray, poor man, that the local housewives drop nothing worse on your head than a bedpan full of slops!'

Source 5 The impact of disease

◄ Roman towns suffered from regular outbreaks of plague and other diseases despite their public health schemes. This mass grave in Gloucester contains victims of 'Galen's plague' in the AD160s. There were many more outbreaks of epidemic disease that killed hundreds of people or more in towns.

Who could you get medical help from?

Imagine you were living in Roman Britain and woke up one morning feeling sick. Your head hurts and you are sweating. You feel as if you might be sick at any moment. What can you do?

a) Home remedies

Most asked their mothers for help. Many women had a vast knowledge of medical treatments handed down from one generation to another. Many specialised in herbal remedies, mainly made from plants, but also including animal fats and minerals. Many of these remedies helped or people would not have kept using them. To make you feel better your mother might give you a mixture of onion juice, honey and valerian or poppy juice. We now know honey can kill infections. The plant valerian worked as a sedative and pain reliever and the poppy plant was used for pain relief in general as well as for toothache and coughs. The Romans brought new plants to Britain to use in medicines.

However, if you came from a wealthy family, your father (the head of the household, the *paterfamilias*) would look up treatments in a medical book, such as the huge compendium of herbal cures collected by Dioscorides. Modern scientific tests have shown that

at least 20 per cent of these remedies contained ingredients, such as honey or garlic, which helped patients by killing bacteria in infections.

The books might also advise you what to do once you recover. One medical encyclopaedia was *Artes*, 'The Sciences', by Celsus, a wealthy landowner who built up his knowledge partly by treating his own family and friends. Celsus stressed the importance of exercise for avoiding illness:

'He who has been busy during the day, whether in domestic or public affairs, ought to put aside some part of the day for the care of the body. The most important way to care for the body is through exercise, which ought to come to an end with sweating.'

Of course, this was only for the wealthy. You will probably have to get back to working on the family farm as soon as you feel better!

b) Gods and their priests

When you were sick, you wouldn't just take your medicine. You might wear a charm to ward off evil spirits. You would certainly pray to your household gods for good health and a cure. You would also pray to the gods of healing. The greatest of these gods was Asclepius.

People who couldn't shake off an illness often went to a temple to see the god's priests and seek help. They sometimes left small carvings of the sick part of the body. At the temple in Lydney in Gloucestershire, people prayed to the god Nodens. A carving of a hand with deformed fingernails has been found there. The temple at Lydney contained a large bath-house, a guesthouse with a covered courtyard and an *abaton* where people slept and were visited by the god in their dreams. The priests probably also encouraged patients to take exercise, cleanse themselves in the baths and build up their strength by eating regular meals and having plenty of rest.

Source 1

▲ A carving of the god Asclepius treating a patient while another patient lies down. The god was helped by his daughters, Panacea and Hygieia, and by his snake, which could cure blindness by licking the patient's eyelids. Asclepius is usually shown with his snake twined around his staff. Snakes were symbols of health because they could shed their skins and so appear younger and healthier.

Source 2

Inscriptions from Roman altars found in Britain. Even trained doctors prayed to the gods.

'To the holy god Asclepius and to Hygeia, Julius Saturninus set this [altar] up. To the mighty saviour gods, I, Hermogenes, a doctor, set up this altar. To Asclepius and Salus for the welfare of the cavalry regiment.'

c) Trained doctors

Training of doctors

If your mother's herbal remedies and your prayers had still not helped then you could see a trained doctor. This would probably cost you money, although many towns in the Roman Empire employed doctors to treat the poor and this may have happened in Britain. Some of these doctors were women. One woman, Antiochus, was so successful that her home town erected a statue in 'recognition of her skill as a medical practitioner'. You will find out more about the kinds of treatments doctors provided later.

Doctors mostly trained by acting as apprentices to experienced doctors. This was not always a good thing. One writer complained 'I was sickening but you came to me at once, Symmachus, followed by a hundred apprentices. A hundred hands frosted by the north wind have pawed me. I had no fever before, Symmachus, now I have.' They also read the medical books by the Greek doctor Hippocrates and the great Roman writer, Galen. However, medical training was not compulsory. Anyone could call himself a doctor!

Activity

Memory map: Read this page and add details to your memory map from page 21. Use these questions to help you:

a Who treated most illnesses and who did they learn from?

b What kinds of remedies were used in the home and how effective were they?

c Who looked after women having babies and how helpful were they?

d What did people do to avoid illness?

e How important were gods in medicine?

f How were doctors trained?

Information

Having a baby

Women looked after each other in childbirth. Many became very experienced and often acted as midwives. According to the medical writer Soranus, the best midwives were intelligent, robust, respectable and literate and experienced in nutrition, pharmacy and surgery. Handbooks on midwifery emphasised the importance of cleanliness, listing the need for oil and hot water for cleansing, sponges, wool coverings and bandages. However, midwives had no technical methods of helping if there were problems during a birth. One piece of advice was for four people to take hold of the mother and shake her violently ten times to speed the birth. Pliny the elder suggested reducing labour pains by hurling a projectile, preferably a cavalry spear, three times over the roof of the house!

Trained doctors – their theories and treatments

On the last page you discovered that there were trained doctors in the Roman Empire, including in Britain. The most important books used by these doctors were written by Hippocrates and Galen, who were among the most influential men in the whole history of medicine. Pages 28–33 help you find out about these two key figures.

Training of doctors

Activities

1 Use the information on pages 28–33 to complete this table.

	The work of	
	Hippocrates	Galen
How should doctors behave?		
How to diagnose illnesses?		
What causes illnesses?		
How to treat illnesses?		
How to stay healthy?		
How to learn more about the body?		

2 **Memory map:** When you have finished your table, use the details to add to your memory map from page 21.
3 Work in a small group and devise a way of explaining the theory of the four humours to people who do not understand it. You could use props, physical movement, labels or tabards to help you.

Hippocrates

Hippocrates was born c.460BC on the island of Cos where he worked as a doctor and teacher of doctors. Very little else is known about him. He died c.370BC.

The Hippocratic Oath

This oath was created by Hippocrates to give people confidence in doctors. It makes clear that doctors are not magicians. They have to keep high standards of treatment and behaviour and work for the benefit of their patients, not to make themselves wealthy.

'I will swear by Apollo, Asclepius and by all the gods that I will carry out this oath. I will use treatment to help the sick according to my ability and judgement but never with a view to injury or wrongdoing. I will not give poison to anybody. Whatever I see or hear professionally will be kept secret.'

The Hippocratic Collection of Books

Hippocrates probably wrote some of the books known as The Hippocratic Collection, but many were written by other doctors. This collection is important because it is the first detailed list of symptoms and treatments. Doctors continued to use the theories and methods in these books for many centuries.

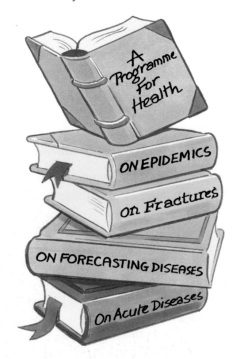

A Programme for Health

ON EPIDEMICS

On Fractures

ON FORECASTING DISEASES

On Acute Diseases

Observing and recording

Hippocrates showed that it was very important to observe and record carefully the symptoms and development of diseases. This had two advantages. Doctors were more likely to choose the right cure if they took care to find the cause of the problem. These notes could then be used to help with diagnosis and treatment of future patients.

Training of doctors

First look at the patient's face. The following are bad signs – a sharp, pointed nose, hollow eyes, dry skin on the forehead, strange face colour such as green, black, red or lead coloured. If the face is like this at the beginning of the illness, the doctor must ask the patient if he has lost sleep or had diarrhoea, or not eaten. Then record how his condition changes each day.

Natural treatments

Hippocrates encouraged doctors to look for natural treatments for illnesses rather than praying to the gods for help.

Treatments

We must use natural treatments because illnesses have natural causes. For example, many illnesses can be treated by rest and a change in diet. Then, when you feel stronger, take regular exercise. If this does not work then we can bleed or purge you to remove excess humours.

Keeping healthy

Hippocrates also emphasised the importance of helping people stay healthy. He recommended a light diet, gentle exercise and rest to keep the body's humours balanced.

Staying healthy

The four humours – the cause of disease

The body contains four humours or liquids: blood, phlegm, yellow bile and black bile. When we are healthy these four humours are perfectly balanced in our bodies but we fall sick when they become unbalanced and we have too much or too little of one humour.

Look at how our bodies naturally try to get rid of excess humours:

▲ Blood

▲ Black bile

▲ Yellow bile

▲ Phlegm

Why was Galen so important?

Claudius Galen was born in Pergamum in Greece in AD129, the son of an architect. Galen's father had a dream in which Asclepius said that his son would become a physician. Galen began studying medicine when he was 16, even travelling to study at the great medical school in Alexandria. He also became a surgeon at a gladiators' school, gaining experience treating wounds and increasing his knowledge of anatomy.

Age 20, Galen moved to Rome. He was a great showman and put on public performances, dissecting animals and giving talks. He also had a terrible temper, inherited from his mother, whom he said 'bit her maids and was always shouting at my father'. When plague broke out, the Emperor Marcus Aurelius summoned Galen to take care of the royal family and he remained doctor to the emperors for the rest of his life.

The work of Claudius Galen

What really made Galen famous were the books he wrote. They combined Greek ideas with what he learned from his own work in Alexandria and Rome, and presented it all so convincingly that they became the basis for medical teaching and learning for the next 1500 years. For most of that time nobody dared to say that Galen was wrong!

Careful observation

The four humours
• Hippocrates' ideas
• His own ideas about 'opposites'

Dissection and surgery
Knowledge of anatomy

Galen wrote over 350 books on medicine. They were the main books used by medical students for over 1500 years.

Diagnosis and the four humours

Galen's work was built on the key ideas in the Hippocratic collection:

Four humours – Like Hippocrates, he believed that illness was caused by imbalances in the four humours.

Observation – Like Hippocrates, Galen told doctors to observe and examine patients carefully, taking the pulse and detailed notes of symptoms. In AD167 Galen made detailed notes on the plague sweeping across the empire, recording how his patients had fever, thirst, diarrhoea, skin rash and spat blood. His notes were so thorough this plague became known as 'Galen's plague.'

Treatments

Galen followed Hippocrates in giving advice on diet and exercise to prevent illness. His most common treatment was bleeding patients to restore the balance of the humours. He used bleeding

far more than Hippocrates, who had preferred to interfere with the body as little as possible. Galen also developed the idea of using 'Opposites' to balance the humours. For example, if a patient's symptom was too much phlegm then the illness was caused by cold. Galen's treatment was the opposite of cold – heat! He treated the patient by using hot ingredients such as peppers in his cures. If a disease was caused by heat, then the patient would need a cooling cure, perhaps treating this with cucumber in the medicine or diet.

You have too much phlegm, which is cold and wet. You must take something that is hot and fiery – try a pepper.

Anatomy and dissection

Hippocrates had not done much work on anatomy and had not said that dissection was important. Galen disagreed. He believed that physicians should find out as much as possible about the structure and workings of the body, if possible dissecting human bodies themselves. If this was not possible, he advised doctors to dissect apes because they were most like humans.

Source 1

From Galen's book *On Anatomy*, written c.AD190:
'Human bones are the subjects that you should first get to know. You cannot just read about bones in books but you must also acquaint yourself with the appearance of each of the bones, by the use of your own eye, handling each bone by itself. At Alexandria this is very easy because the doctors there let their students inspect human bodies. If you cannot get to Alexandria it is not impossible to see human bones. I have often done this where tombs have been broken. On one occasion a river carried a corpse downstream before depositing it on the riverbank. Here it lay, as though prepared by a doctor for his pupils' lesson. Once I examined the skeleton of a robber lying on a mountain-side. If you do not have the luck to do this you can still dissect an ape. Choose apes which most resemble men, which walk and run on two legs, where you will find other parts as in man.'

Although he often had to dissect animals, not humans, some of Galen's discoveries were important. He proved that the brain, not the heart, controlled speech and that the arteries, and not just the veins, carried blood around the body. Inevitably, he made mistakes because the bodies of apes and pigs are not the same as those of humans, but it was to be well over a thousand years before anyone dared to challenge Galen's findings.

New discoveries

Galen demonstrated his discoveries about the workings of the nervous system by dissecting a pig. As the pig squealed on the table, Galen cut into its neck, finding the nerves. He could have cut through the right nerve immediately to stop the pig squealing but that did not appeal to Galen's showmanship. Instead he announced 'I will cut this nerve but the pig will keep squealing'. He cut, and the pig kept squealing. He cut again, building up the tension, and again the pig kept squealing. Then he announced, 'When I cut this nerve, the pig will stop squealing.' He cut and the pig was silent!

Activities

1 How does Source 1 show that Galen was respected at the time?
2 How does it also show that he was respected for a long time after his death?

Source 1

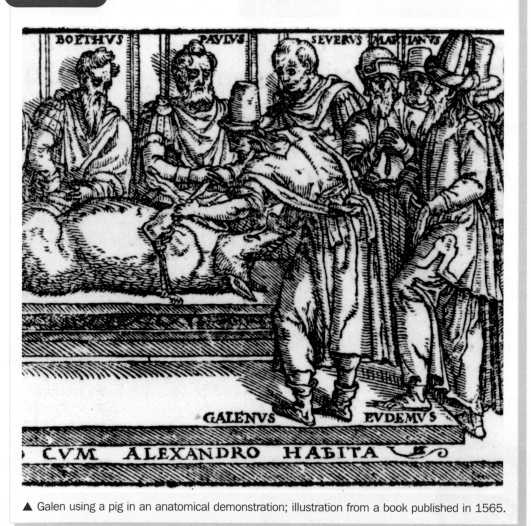

▲ Galen using a pig in an anatomical demonstration; illustration from a book published in 1565.

Clue

Note the date that the source was produced.

What difference did Galen make?

I have done as much for medicine as the Emperor Trajan did for the Roman Empire when he built bridges and roads through Italy. It must be admitted that Hippocrates prepared the way but he made mistakes. It is I, and I alone, who have revealed the true methods of treating diseases.

Activities

1 Read Galen's speech bubble to the left. Choose two words to summarise his assessment of his own work.
2 Read the text on this page and look at the wall painting below. What was Galen's contribution to:
   a the understanding and treatment of diseases
   b knowledge of anatomy?
3 How would you revise or add to Galen's assessment of his own work to sum up his long-term importance?

Galen's influence

Galen wrote hundreds of books, covering every aspect of medicine in an extremely detailed and well-organised way. He included the work of earlier doctors such as Hippocrates, but also added his own work on treatments and on the structure and workings of the body. It seemed that Galen had covered everything so people believed that his books had all the answers. That was one reason why Galen's books became the basis for medical training for over a thousand years.

A second reason why so many people believed Galen was always right was that his ideas fitted in with the ideas of the Christian Church, which controlled education in Europe in the Middle Ages. Although Galen was not a Christian, he believed that the body had been created by one god who had made all the parts of the body fit together perfectly. This matched the Christian belief that God had created human beings so for centuries Christians did not dare to question Galen's ideas.

You see how well each part of the body fits together. Each organ has a role to play. The body is wonderfully designed.

Source 2

▲ A wall painting in an Italian church showing Galen (left) and Hippocrates. The painting dates from the 1200s, 900 years after Galen died.

Smarter Revision: Photo revision

Revision can be fun. You probably don't believe this but here's how to enjoy revision by thinking hard and being creative. This class wanted to sum up why Galen was so important so they created this picture.

1 They investigated Galen's work. Then they started thinking creatively – how could they turn this information into a picture they could revise from? In this photo each feature they have included in the photo tells you something important about Galen's work.

2 The class took the picture and annotated it – writing in a short explanation of what each object tells us about Galen.

3 They added two think bubbles to sum up Galen's thoughts – but we've taken off those notes and thought bubbles!

Activities

Either
Annotate your own copy of this picture. All the information is on pages 28–33.
Or
You could even produce your own summary picture of Galen's work. Have fun!

Smarter Revision: 'Role of the individual' chart

You will need to record the achievements of a number of key individuals – Galen, Harvey, Pasteur and others. It will be much easier to work out why each person was important if you use the same chart for each of them. That way you will be able to recall the pattern of the chart in your mind if you need it in an examination.

Activity

4 **'Role of the individual' chart:** This chart on Galen is not quite complete. Use the information on the opposite page to complete it.

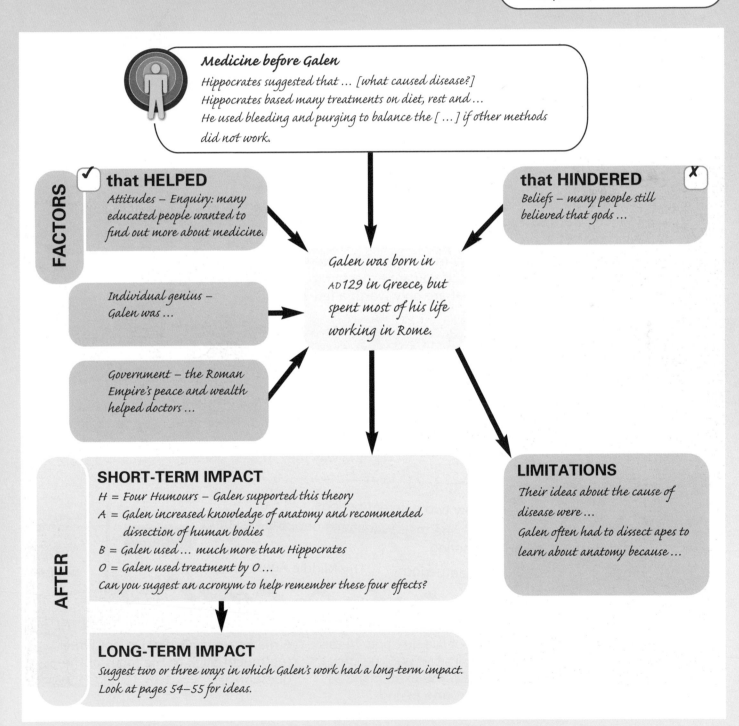

Medicine before Galen

Hippocrates suggested that … [what caused disease?]
Hippocrates based many treatments on diet, rest and …
He used bleeding and purging to balance the […] if other methods did not work.

FACTORS

✓ **that HELPED**

Attitudes – Enquiry: many educated people wanted to find out more about medicine.

Individual genius – Galen was …

Government – the Roman Empire's peace and wealth helped doctors …

Galen was born in AD129 in Greece, but spent most of his life working in Rome.

✗ **that HINDERED**

Beliefs – many people still believed that gods …

AFTER

SHORT-TERM IMPACT

H = Four Humours – Galen supported this theory
A = Galen increased knowledge of anatomy and recommended dissection of human bodies
B = Galen used … much more than Hippocrates
O = Galen used treatment by O …
Can you suggest an acronym to help remember these four effects?

LIMITATIONS

Their ideas about the cause of disease were …
Galen often had to dissect apes to learn about anatomy because …

LONG-TERM IMPACT

Suggest two or three ways in which Galen's work had a long-term impact.
Look at pages 54–55 for ideas.

The examiners are not trying to catch you out: they are giving you a chance to show what you know – **and what you can do with what you know**. If you work out what the question is getting at, you will be able to answer it from what you have learned.

 To stay relevant to the questions you will need to practise how to 'decode' questions.

Decoding exam questions

Step 1: Read the question a couple of times.

Step 2: Highlight each of the following. You could use a different colour for each.

> **Date boundaries** – What time period should you cover in your answer? Stick to this carefully, otherwise you will waste time writing about events that are not relevant to the question.
>
> **Content focus** – The topic the examiner wants you to focus on.
>
> **Question type** – Different question types require different approaches. Look for key words, 'What', 'Why', or 'How far', that will help you work out what type of approach is needed.
>
> **Marks available** – Look at how many marks the question is worth. This gives you a guide as to how much you are expected to write. Do not spend too long on questions that are only worth a few marks.

Look at the exam question below.

The question asks you to **describe** the key features of public health in England during the Roman period. You do not need to evaluate how effective they were.

The content focus for this question is on public health in England. There is no need to explore other areas of Roman medicine such as surgery or the way they treated disease.

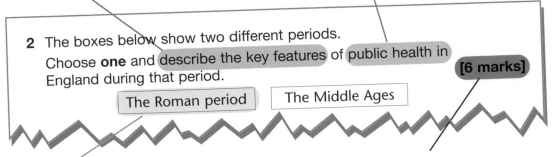

2 The boxes below show two different periods. Choose **one** and describe the key features of public health in England during that period.

The Roman period   The Middle Ages   [6 marks]

You must stick to the date boundaries of the question. In this case it is the Roman period. Comparisons to public health facilities in the Middle Ages will not gain you extra marks as the question says that you must stick to **one** period.

6 marks are available. Do not write too much! Stick to the focus of the question.

Tackling 'describe the key features' questions

Tip 1: Avoid general statements. Make sure you show off your knowledge and give specific examples.

'Describe' questions only carry 6 marks. It is important that you get to the point quickly and avoid general statements that do not pick up many marks. A good way to approach the question is to produce a quick plan before you start to write your answer. Jot down the key features you can remember then add relevant information to describe this feature. Look at the example below:

> *The Romans believed that it was very important to try to prevent disease. They introduced lots of different things to try to stop disease spreading.*

This answer contains general statements. The answer provides no specific details of public health facilities in England during the Roman period. It would score a very low mark.

The answer below is a lot better. It gives specific examples of the public health facilities that were introduced to prevent disease.

> *The Romans used <u>aqueducts</u> to bring clean water to towns and built bath houses for people to wash in. They also built <u>latrines</u> and <u>sewers</u>, which were used to take waste away.*

Tip 2: Stay relevant to the question.

One of the main problems with 'Describe' questions is that students write too much! They include details that are not relevant to the question.

Make sure you stick to the question – describe the key features of public health.

You DO NOT need to:

*   **explain** why they did it, or
*   **evaluate** how successful their methods were.

Questions that ask you to explain or evaluate carry more marks and need longer answers. We will provide advice on tackling these types of questions later. Describe questions carry fewer marks and it is important that you stay relevant to the question. If you write too much you could run out of time later in the exam paper.

Activity

 Read the answer below. The student has written too much because they have not stayed relevant to the question. On your own copy, cross out the sentences that are irrelevant to the question. You should be left with the makings of a good answer!

> *The Romans tried to prevent disease by improving public health in their towns. This is because they needed fit and healthy people to serve in the army and keep the Empire strong. The Romans thought that dirt was somehow linked to disease although they did not know exactly how because they did not know about bacteria. Roman towns were built in healthy places, away from marshes and polluted water. In towns in England aqueducts were built that brought in fresh water. Public fountains provided water for drinking and washing. Even small towns had bath-houses which were cheap to use. In large towns such as Lincoln 5000 people used the baths every week. Sewers carried away waste from baths, latrines and houses. The Roman public health schemes were the best the world had seen. They were more advanced than those of the Greeks or Egyptians but they were not perfect. There were still outbreaks of epidemic disease. For example, in AD165, an epidemic killed five million people.*

2.2 Why was there so little progress in the Middle Ages?

The Roman legions left Britain c.AD410. They took their engineering skills and the security they had given against invaders. Your task is now to describe and explain what happened to medicine over the next 1000 years, revising the answer you gave to the question on page 20.

After the Roman army left

After the Roman army left, life in Britain changed. Towns were slowly abandoned. Public health systems gradually stopped working without the engineering skills of the Roman army. By AD500, a hundred years after the Roman army had left, the towns looked like Canterbury in Source 1. Britain had gone back to being a country without towns in which everyone lived in small villages and lived as farmers.

Activity

1 **Washing line:** Your task for pages 38–49 is to complete the 'washing line' opposite, placing each of the six topic boxes on your own copy of the line and adding brief notes to each box to justify your choice of positioning.

   Begin by looking back to page 18 at the features of medicine in 1347. Use this evidence to pencil in the boxes onto your own copy of this line.

Source 1

▲ A reconstruction drawing of Canterbury in the fifth century.

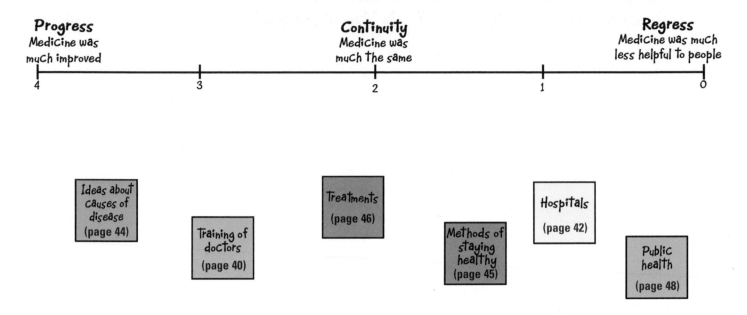

Progress
Medicine was
much improved

Continuity
Medicine was
much the same

Regress
Medicine was much
less helpful to people

4   3   2   1   0

Ideas about causes of disease (page 44)

Training of doctors (page 40)

Treatments (page 46)

Methods of staying healthy (page 45)

Hospitals (page 42)

Public health (page 48)

The end of the Roman Empire

After the Roman Empire collapsed, Britain split into many small kingdoms, frequently invading and fighting each other. During the fifth and sixth centuries, Britain was taken over by tribes of Angles and Saxons who couldn't read and were not interested in Galen, baths or sewer systems. You can see the impact of all this war and destruction below.

Activities

2   List the effects of Roman withdrawal from Britain on medicine and public health.
3   Look at the timeline on pages 18–19.
   a   Which later events do you think affected medicine?
   b   How do you think they affected medicine?

1 Without the Roman army there were **no engineers** with the technological knowledge to keep public baths, sewers and aqueducts working effectively.

6 All these wars meant there was plenty of **practice for surgeons.**

5 Wars made **travel more dangerous** so doctors travelled much less to gain experience and education.

2 Invading tribes **destroyed or neglected public health** systems.

3 Invasions and wars **destroyed libraries** and books in monasteries.

4 The attitudes of rulers were different. **Kings spent their money on wars**, not on sewers and baths. They were illiterate so had no interest in education.

The training of doctors

The disappearance of trained doctors c.AD400–c.1000

There had been trained doctors in Roman Britain because:

- the towns were wealthy. There were plenty of people who could read and there were rich people who could afford to pay to see doctors.
- Britain was fairly peaceful so people who wanted to be doctors could get Galen's books and travel to learn from other doctors.

Now think back to the picture of Canterbury on page 38. With no towns and no wealth there were soon no trained doctors in Britain. For hundreds of years people who were sick got help from the family, local wisewomen and 'leeches' – men who built up their knowledge through practice. Many of these healers were probably just as good – or better – than the trained doctors of Roman times, but knowledge of the work of Hippocrates and Galen had almost disappeared completely.

The rise of universities and the return of physicians

Between 1000 and 1300, landowners grew rich from good harvests on their land. The wealthiest landowners were the bishops and abbots of the Christian Church. They spent their profits on building grand cathedrals and on founding universities such as Paris in 1110, Oxford in 1167 and Cambridge in 1209.

These universities trained physicians – the highest-ranking of all healers. Very few people could afford the training which took seven years so there were never a lot of physicians. In the 1300s there were still fewer than 100 physicians in England. However, qualified physicians could charge high fees to kings, nobles and wealthy merchants.

Training physicians

Medical students attended lectures and read books by Galen and other Greek and Roman writers. They also read translations of Arab scholars such as Ibn Sina (known as Avicenna in Europe) and al-Razi (known as Rhazes in Europe). Students were expected to memorise what these great doctors had written. They were not expected to challenge their ideas. When the English scientist Roger Bacon suggested that doctors should do their own research instead of just reading Galen he was thrown into prison by church leaders.

Another crucial part of medical education was astrology. Students learned how each part of the body was affected by the movements of the planets and stars. People believed the planets and stars affected the balance of the humours in the body and so could cause illness, so a doctor needed to know the position of the planets before making his diagnosis and deciding on a treatment.

Source 1

▲ A picture of a physician from c.1400.

Source 2

In *The Canterbury Tales*, Geoffrey Chaucer described a physician as:
'Well read was he in Asculapius, Hippocrates, and Hali, and Galen, Serapion, Rhazes, and Avicen …'

Understanding the human body

Source 3

Physicians learned about anatomy by dissecting human bodies as Galen had recommended. However, nothing new was learned from these dissections because dissections were *not* part of a search for new knowledge. Physicians believed that Galen's books contained everything that needed to be learned about the human body. So dissections were demonstrations that Galen's descriptions of the human body were correct, not investigations to make new discoveries.

The physician (in the red robe on the right) was in charge, but he did not do the dissection himself. He told the surgeon which parts of the body to dissect.

He also told his assistant (middle right) which important passages from Galen to read out to illustrate the dissection.

The students had to listen to Galen's words and watch the dissection. They weren't allowed to do anything!

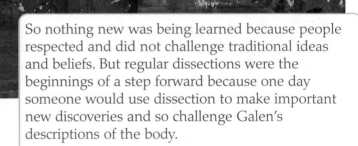

So nothing new was being learned because people respected and did not challenge traditional ideas and beliefs. But regular dissections were the beginnings of a step forward because one day someone would use dissection to make important new discoveries and so challenge Galen's descriptions of the body.

Activities

1. Would you describe the development of the training of physicians as:
   a. steadily improving throughout the Middle Ages
   b. steadily getting worse throughout the Middle Ages
   c. rapidly getting worse then slowly improving?
2. What evidence would you use to support your answer to Question 1?
3. a. Which clue in Source 1 opposite tells us the man is a physician? (Look at page 46 to see if you are right.)
   b. How does Chaucer (Source 2) show that the physician was well-qualified?
4. Why did physicians not learn more about anatomy?
5. **Washing line:** Complete the 'washing line' (page 39) for this topic.

Could you go to hospitals for help?

Activities

1 **a** Who did hospitals look after?
  b What kinds of help did hospitals provide?
2 **Washing line:** Complete the 'washing line' (page 39) for this topic.

Source 1

From the rules of the hospital of St John, Bridgwater in the south of England, 1219:
'No lepers, lunatics or persons having the falling sickness or other contagious disease, and no pregnant women, or sucking infants and no intolerable persons, even though they be poor and infirm, are to be admitted. If any such be admitted by mistake they are to be expelled as soon as possible. And when the other poor and infirm persons have recovered they are to be let out without delay.'

Who did hospitals look after?

'Care for the sick is of great importance. You must help them as you would help Christ, whom you help in helping the sick.'

This extract from the rules of the Benedictine monks might make you optimistic about going to a hospital if you were ill. Looking after the sick was an important part of the work of the Christian Church and this led to many hospitals being founded by the Church in the Middle Ages. St Bartholomew's Hospital in London was one of the first to be founded, in 1123. By 1400 there were over 500 hospitals in England, although many had only five or six beds. St Leonard's in York was unusually large with over 200 beds.

However, hospitals were very careful about whom they took in, as Source 1 shows.

So you could not get into hospital if you had a disease that other people might catch! Occasionally, hospitals were set up to care for particular cases. In London, Richard Whittington, the Lord Mayor, paid for an eight-bed hospital for unmarried pregnant women. In Chester there was a hospital for the care of 'poor and silly persons'. Leper houses were built outside towns to separate the victims of the disease leprosy from healthy people. Leprosy was particularly feared because it rotted people's flesh.

Most hospitals were like care-homes today, looking after the poor and elderly. They provided food, rest and, most importantly, prayer. At the end of the hall (or ward) was an altar where priests said mass seven times each day. People believed that God sent sickness to punish them for their sins so they joined in the prayers, hoping that God would realise they were sorry for their sins. Nursing care was provided by nuns who had a good knowledge of herbal and other remedies, often drawn from the books in their library.

Source 2

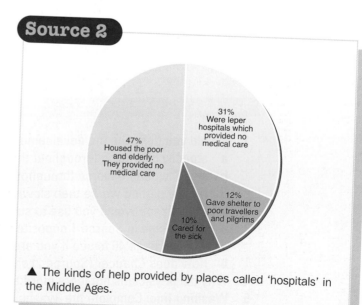

47% Housed the poor and elderly. They provided no medical care

31% Were leper hospitals which provided no medical care

12% Gave shelter to poor travellers and pilgrims

10% Cared for the sick

▲ The kinds of help provided by places called 'hospitals' in the Middle Ages.

Source 3

▲ The Hôtel Dieu in Paris. The King's doctors worked there so this was not typical, but it is one of the few illustrations of the inside of a medieval hospital. What evidence can you see of **a)** religion and **b)** medical help?

Who else could you go to for help?

So you are sick but you can't afford to see a physician and the hospital won't take you in case you infect the elderly people living there. Who would you see? For nearly everyone except the wealthy, illnesses were taken to the women of the household. Just as in Roman Britain, women treated the vast majority of illnesses in the Middle Ages. Mothers and wives had a wide range of remedies at their fingertips, although sometimes the local wise-woman was called in to use her skills and knowledge. Women also acted as midwives. In some towns, midwives had to be apprenticed and gain licences and were then paid for their expertise. Women could qualify as surgeons by working as apprentices. Family links played an important part in giving women this opportunity. Records list Katherine, a surgeon in London around 1250, whose father and brothers were surgeons. However, women were not allowed to become physicians and they certainly were not allowed to attend university.

What did they think caused disease?

Activities

1 Look at Explanations 1–3 below.
   a Which idea do you think was most common among ordinary people?
   b Which idea do you think was most common among educated and rich people?

2 Why didn't they develop new ideas about the causes of disease? (Look back to page 40 on the training of physicians.)

3 Look at Explanation 4. Why do you think so many desperate ideas were common around 1349?

4 **Washing line:** Complete the 'washing line' (page 39) for this topic.

1 God or the Devil

The most common belief was that God sent illnesses such as the Black Death to punish people for their sins. The Anglo-Saxons also believed that elves and spirits, the Devil's helpers, shot invisible arrows, known as elf-shot, to cause everyday illnesses such as headaches.

2 The four humours

Physicians followed the theories of Hippocrates and Galen and said that illness was caused when the body's humours were out of balance. Greek books were at the centre of university medical training. Many people accepted this theory because physicians were respected for their university training. Islamic doctors also believed in the importance of the four humours because of their studies of Galen.

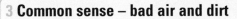
Ideas about the causes of disease

3 Common sense – bad air and dirt

A common explanation was that bad air caused illness. At the time of the Black Death many people said that earthquakes had infected the air. Some people did link the bad air to dirt and filth in the streets but could not explain exactly what the link was. Another common-sense belief was that worms caused illness. This sounds strange but archaeological discoveries show that many people suffered from worms in their stomachs and they would have seen these worms in their faeces.

4 Desperate explanations

As the Black Death killed millions, a wide range of other desperate and bizarre explanations were put forward:

- An English monk blamed the outrageous fashions that people had been wearing in recent years.

- When another outbreak of plague in 1361 killed many children, another churchman said God was punishing children who did not respect or look after their parents.

- Minority groups were blamed. Jews were said to have poisoned water supplies and in some places they were burned as people looked for someone to blame.

How did they try to stay healthy?

Physicians gave their wealthy clients plenty of advice on how to stay healthy. After all, making someone better when they were ill was very difficult, so it was better to avoid becoming ill in the first place. Physicians wrote guides on how to stay healthy for individual clients, tailoring their advice to the individual person. The suggestions below are all taken from guides written in the Middle Ages.

A GUIDE TO HEALTHY LIVING

1. EAT LIGHT MEALS SO THAT YOU DIGEST YOUR FOOD EASILY.

2. TAKE PLENTY OF GENTLE EXERCISE IN THE FRESH AIR.

3. RELAX AS MUCH AS POSSIBLE.

4. STAY ON GOOD TERMS WITH YOUR NEIGHBOURS AND THE PEOPLE YOU WORK WITH.

5. AVOID STRESSFUL NOISE SUCH AS BARKING DOGS AND STREET BRAWLS.

6. REGULARLY SEND SAMPLES OF YOUR URINE TO YOUR PHYSICIAN SO HE CAN LOOK FOR SIGNS OF ILLNESS DEVELOPING.

7. AVOID EVIL HUMOURS BUILDING UP IN YOUR BODY BY TAKING POTIONS TO PURGE YOUR STOMACH OR GOING REGULARLY TO A SURGEON TO BE BLED.

8. BUILD YOUR HOUSE AND GARDEN IN FRESH AIR WHERE THE WINDS CAN TAKE AWAY BAD SMELLS.

9. BATHE IN HOT WATER TO SOOTHE YOUR BODY.

Bleeding was one of the most common ways of trying to avoid illness. In some monasteries, monks were bled between seven and twelve times a year to prevent illness. On occasion, this was carried out until the monk was on the point of unconsciousness, which means he lost three or four pints of blood! Careless bleeding by surgeons did sometimes kill people.

Of course this was advice for the wealthy. Most people had to get on with work and had to put up with the stress of earning a living. However, simple hand-copied versions of the 'Guides to Healthy Living' were very popular and were sold in towns and carried round the country by peddlars.

Activities

5. Which of the ideas above had been recommended by Hippocrates (see pages 28–29)?
6. Why was advice on avoiding illness such an important part of the physician's work?
7. **Washing line:** Complete the 'washing line' (page 39) for this topic.

How did they treat the sick?

Activities

1 What were the most important parts of a physician's equipment and what did he use them for?

2 Why was bleeding such a common treatment?

3 How effective were herbal remedies?

4 **Washing line:** Complete the 'washing line' (page 39) for this topic.

The work of the physician

Diagnosing the illness

Timing the treatment

Source 1

▲ A urine chart

The physician's most important piece of equipment was his urine chart. The physician matched the patient's urine against the colours, smell and density shown on the chart. He might also taste the urine to check it was normal.

Wealthy patients sent their urine to their physician to make sure that they were not falling ill. This method of diagnosis (called uroscopy) fitted the Theory of the Four Humours. For example, very white urine was a sign of too much phlegm in the body.

Physicians also followed Hippocrates and Galen by making careful observations of symptoms. This led the Arab doctor, al-Razi, to describe for the first time the difference between smallpox and measles. Until then, all infections with rashes had been put together as one illness.

Source 2

Once the physician had decided on the treatment he then chose the best time to carry it out. This required knowledge of astrology because they believed that parts of the body were linked to signs of the zodiac and the planets. The Zodiac man showed the doctor when to avoid treating each part of the body. When the moon was in Pisces, for example, the feet should not be treated.

▲ A Zodiac man

Bleeding

Source 3

This kind of chart showed the surgeon where to take blood from. Bleeding, urine and zodiac charts were the three most common illustrations in medical books.

Treatments such as bleeding were usually carried out by a surgeon. Bleeding was done by warming a bleeding cup, placing it over a small cut and letting the warmth draw blood out of the cut. Alternatively, leeches were used to sink their jaws into the patient and draw off blood, a method still used in the nineteenth century.

One medical book said that bleeding 'clears the mind, strengthens the memory, cleanses the guts, sharpens the hearing, curbs tears, promotes digestion, produces a musical voice, dispels sleepiness, drives away anxiety, feeds the blood and rids it of poisonous matter and gives long life, cures pains, fevers and various sicknesses and makes urine clear and clean.'

Bleeding was carried out as a cure to restore the balance of the humours. Purging the stomach was another way of getting rid of evil humours. This could mean swallowing a mixture of herbs and animal fat to make the person sick or taking a laxative to empty their bowels. Both methods were commonly used, and often at the same time!

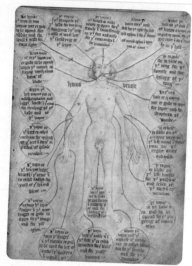

▲ A bleeding chart

Home remedies

Source 4

The medieval remedy

1 Take onions and garlic
2 Pound them together
3 Take wine and bull's gall
4 Stand for nine nights in a brass vessel
5 Strain mixture through a cloth
6 Apply to stye with a feather

The modern verdict: Onion and garlic kill bacteria | Bull's gall also attacks bacteria | Wine contains acetic acid which reacts with copper in the brass vessel to form copper salts which also kill bacteria | The result: a practical cure

This cure for a stye comes from *Bald's Leechbook*, a tenth-century collection of treatments. Many ingredients in such remedies were helpful. Honey and plantain, both very common ingredients for problems such as cuts, wounds and dog-bites, acted like modern antibiotics in fighting infection.

Common remedies were based on plants or herbs, minerals and animal parts. Most women knew these by heart but increasingly they were written down in commonplace books or 'herbals', books illustrating each plant and other ingredients, the exact quantities required and how to mix up the potion. They also included prayers to say while collecting the herbs to increase the effectiveness of the remedy.

Some cures combined all kinds of ideas, a mixture of prayer, magic and folklore, such as this Anglo-Saxon cure written down c.AD900: '[scratch] the neck after the setting of the sun and silently pour the blood into running water. After that, spit three times, then say: Have thou this unheal and depart with it.'

An example of a cure that was less likely to work was for treating quinsy (an abscess in the throat):

'Take a fat cat, flay it well and draw out the guts. Take the grease of a hedgehog, the fat of a bear, resins, fenugreek, sage, honeysuckle gum and virgin wax and crumble this and stuff the cat with it. Then roast the cat and gather the dripping and anoint the sufferer with it.'

Why did public health deteriorate?

Medieval towns were much dirtier than Roman towns. Viking Jorvik (York) was a filthy place around AD1000. Water for drinking and cooking was collected from the river or storage pits, which were often next to the cesspits people used as toilets. Pigs and chickens roamed the streets. Rats, mice and hawks scavenged in streets full of rotting fish bones, animal dung, food waste and even human faeces.

Animals were always a problem. People used horses for transport. Cattle, sheep and geese constantly arrived to be butchered for food. But conditions did start to improve a little. By 1200, many houses in cities like London and York had stone foundations. A few were built entirely of stone. Cesspits were lined with brick or stone and so were less likely to leak into drinking water supplies.

However, the problems were always greater than the solutions. Medieval towns were dirtier than Roman towns, but the Romans had army engineers with good technological knowledge, the wealth to afford aqueducts and public baths and slaves to do at least some of the building. Even so, the Romans had been no better at stopping plague than people were in the Middle Ages.

Solutions
A small number of rakers employed to clean streets.
Building public latrines and regulations about where to build private latrines.
Laws to punish throwing waste.
A small number of officials tried to enforce laws.

Problems
People dropping waste and litter – and worse!
Open sewers.
Butchers throwing out waste.
Animals in streets.
Streets were often muddy with open drains along the middle.
Contents of cesspits emptied into streams and rivers used for washing and drinking water.

Why didn't people's efforts work?

People expect me to lead my army and defend them – against the French, not against disease. I collect taxes to pay for wars, not to clean the streets or build sewers.

▲ King Edward III

We do not have enough officials to punish all the people who break the laws. Londoners will not pay the taxes we need to employ more officials.

▲ Lord Mayor of London

Why should I worry about dirt? God sends the diseases we suffer from. What's illness got to do with dirty streets?

▲ Londoner in 1300s

Activities

1 Was public health always really bad in medieval towns?
2 a What was good about the monastery's public health system?
  b Why was the monastery's public health system better than London's?
  c Compare Canterbury Abbey with a Roman fort. Which had the better public health system? Explain the reason for your choice.
3 The Romans were no better at stopping plague than people in the Middle Ages. Why?
4 **Washing line:** Complete the 'washing line' (page 37) for this topic.

The best public health facilities were in monasteries because they could afford them. Monks were better fed than most people, did less physical work and had the advantages you can see in this plan.

▼ A plan of the water system at Canterbury Abbey, drawn by the engineer who designed it in the 1100s.

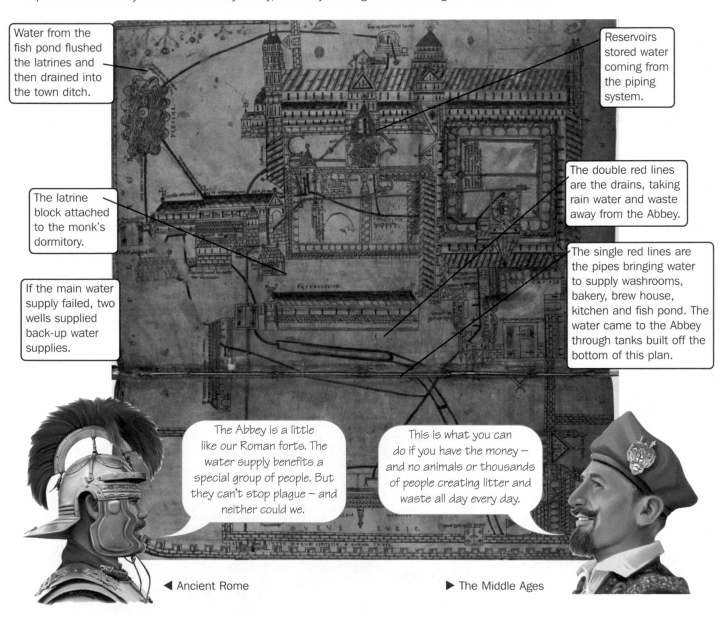

Water from the fish pond flushed the latrines and then drained into the town ditch.

Reservoirs stored water coming from the piping system.

The latrine block attached to the monk's dormitory.

The double red lines are the drains, taking rain water and waste away from the Abbey.

If the main water supply failed, two wells supplied back-up water supplies.

The single red lines are the pipes bringing water to supply washrooms, bakery, brew house, kitchen and fish pond. The water came to the Abbey through tanks built off the bottom of this plan.

The Abbey is a little like our Roman forts. The water supply benefits a special group of people. But they can't stop plague – and neither could we.

This is what you can do if you have the money – and no animals or thousands of people creating litter and waste all day every day.

◀ Ancient Rome   ▶ The Middle Ages

Why were they still reading Galen in 1350?

Roman doctors used the books of Galen. They believed that his ideas were correct and that it was nearly impossible to improve on his work.

Look across to the bottom of page 51 and you can see that 1000 years later Galen was still the unchallenged authority on medicine! This spread explains why.

We have divided the period into three phases, although the phases obviously overlap with each other.

Phase 2: The growing power of the Christian Church

Christianity was the religion of the Roman Empire. Surprisingly, it did not decline when the Roman Empire fell apart. Instead it grew stronger. The Church sent missionaries all around Europe converting the pagan tribes to Christianity. Within a few centuries there were thousands of churches and monasteries all over Europe.

The Christian Church was the only strong, centralised organisation to survive the collapse of the Roman Empire. It was very powerful throughout the Middle Ages. Galen's books survived in monasteries. When universities began to train doctors, Galen's books were there for them to read.

Phase 1: Chaos in Western Europe

After the collapse of the Roman Empire, Western Europe was gradually split into many, much smaller countries and tribes. The following factors destroyed a great deal of old knowledge and made it impossible to build up new medical knowledge:

- These countries and tribes were often at war with each other.
- Wars destroyed the Roman public health systems. War also destroyed medical libraries.
- The rulers of the small kingdoms built up defences and armies rather than improving medical skills or public health.
- War disrupted trade so countries became poorer.
- Travel became more dangerous, thus reducing communication between doctors.
- Education and the development of technology was disrupted.
- In Europe, the training of doctors was abandoned. Copies of Galen's books were either lost, or hidden away for safety.

War
War destroyed many of the Romans' achievements.

Government
Central government collapsed. Small kingdoms fought with each other.

Trade
Trade and travel decreased.

Churches
Each village had its church and priest who told people what to believe and how to behave.

Education
The Church controlled education. Priests and monks were often the only people who learned to read in this period. The Church monasteries also controlled what people read. The Church sometimes banned books which they did not want people to read.

Conservatism
People respected what was written in the Bible and other ancient books. People were not encouraged to think for themselves or challenge old ideas in case new ideas challenged the power of the Church. This included ideas about medicine. Bodies were sometimes dissected to teach students about anatomy, but this was done to show Galen was right, not to question his descriptions of the body.

Superstition
The ancient Greeks had looked for rational explanations. The Church taught the opposite – that there were supernatural explanations for everything. People believed that God controlled their lives, including their health.

Phase 3: Things start to change in the late Middle Ages

After about 1000, Europe had begun to recover from the period of chaos:

- harvests improved
- trade increased
- scholars travelled more freely
- there was more money around
- the Church became very rich.

By the 1300s:

- the Church had set up universities where doctors could be trained
- rulers were again taking measures to clean up towns, although they were not very effective
- merchants and scholars were again travelling around Europe, spreading ideas.

Still reading Galen!

Doctors in 1350 were still reading the books of Galen. They believed that his ideas were correct and that it was impossible to improve on his work. Church leaders also believed that Galen's works fitted in with Christian ideas so it was very difficult to challenge or question Galen.

Activities

1 Explain how each of the following factors affected medicine in the Middle Ages.

 Think about whether each one helped or hindered the development of medicine – or both.
 - War
 - Government
 - Beliefs – religion

2 Which factor do you think was the most important in explaining why doctors in 1350 were still reading Galen?

Evaluating progress

The last question on the exam paper carries the most marks and requires a carefully planned, detailed answer. You may be required to evaluate how important an individual or specific discovery was in improving medicine. On other occasions you may be asked to evaluate the extent to which medicine progressed during a period.

Look at the question below:

> *6 How far was the progress made by the Romans continued in the Middle Ages in England? **[16 marks]**
>
> **(Total for spelling, punctuation and grammar = 3 marks)**
>
> **(Total for Question 6 = 19 marks)**

This type of question presents a new challenge. It requires you to compare two periods that span over 1000 years of history! You can use your memory maps (see page 20) to help you. There is a lot of information that you could include, so you need to make sure that you <u>keep focused on the question</u>. Follow the tips to tackle the question effectively.

APPROACH A

Look at the plan below.

Paragraph 1 – Medicine in the Roman period	Paragraph 2 – Medicine in the Middle Ages
Describe:	Describe:
· Ideas about the cause of disease	· Ideas about the cause of disease
· Treatments	· Treatments
· Hospitals	· Hospitals
· Training	· Training
· Methods of keeping healthy	· Methods of keeping healthy
· Public health	· Public health
	Paragraph 3 – Conclusion Sum up the changes in each period.

- It is good to see that the student is planning to **cover both periods** in the question. Some students spend far too long writing about the Romans and forget to go into detail about the Middle Ages!

- It is good that this student **covers a range of topics**. The question asks you to evaluate medicine as a whole during both periods. Do not write in detail about one topic, like public health, and ignore other important topics such as treatments.

STOP

Re-plan this question

However, overall the student has taken the wrong approach. He will **describe** medicine in both periods **rather than evaluating** how far progress continued. As a result he will struggle to get more than half marks. Approach B is better – each paragraph focuses on the question and the answer builds up to a final conclusion.

APPROACH B

Paragraph 1 – Evidence that progress did continue

Look at your 'washing line' and the information on your memory map. Select one or two examples that you can use as evidence to prove that there was progress in medicine (for example – hospitals set up by the Church). You can use this as the basis for your first paragraph.

> **Tip A: Select information that you can use to support an argument.**
>
> Selection is important. In the exam, you will not have time to write everything down. You will only have about 25 minutes to answer this type of question.

Paragraph 2 – Evidence of stagnation

Follow the same steps as paragraph 1. Select and use examples of continuity to show that progress slowed down (for example – ideas about the cause of disease, treatments).

> **Tip B: Try to avoid making general points without fully explaining them and backing them up with a specific example.**

Look at the following answer.

> There was a great deal of continuity during the Middle Ages. The same ideas about what caused illness continued and treatments changed little.

The student starts by making a general point. They would score just 1 mark if they stopped here. They are simply saying something; they are not proving anything!

Do not stop here

> During the Roman period doctors believed that many illnesses had natural causes. They followed Hippocrates' and Galen's theories that illness was caused when the body's humours were out of balance. In the Middle Ages, people continued to follow this theory. Therefore they continued to use bleeding and purging to correct the balance.

However, the student goes on to score extra marks by proving their point. They compare ideas about the cause of disease in Roman times with the Middle Ages.

Paragraph 3 – Evidence that things got worse

Follow the same steps to prove that in some areas of medicine things got worse, not better (for example – the collapse of the Roman public health system).

Paragraph 4 – Weigh the evidence and come to a clear conclusion

The conclusion is a crucial part of your answer. It is usually the part that pupils forget or answer poorly. A good conclusion is not a 'summing up' of everything that has already been said. You should be aiming to weigh the evidence carefully and to come to a clear conclusion that answers the question.

> **Tip C: Keep focused on the question during your conclusion.**

You have been asked to **evaluate** how far progress made by the Romans continued in the Middle Ages. You need to be confident and **reach an overall judgement** about the extent of progress. Which of these conclusions do you agree with? Does everyone in your class agree with you?

53

The horror of the Black Death!

This section investigates one of the most significant events in medical history. The Black Death killed over 40 per cent of the population. Why was it so devastating? What does it tell us about what medicine was like in the late Middle Ages?

The Black Death was one of the most frightening outbreaks of disease in history. The epidemic began in China, spread to India and across Europe. In Britain people heard stories of the disease spreading through France. At the time they simply called it 'the pestilence'. What happened next was described by a monk writing at a monastery in Wiltshire:

> In 1348 the cruel pestilence arrived at a port called Melcombe in Dorset. It killed numberless people in Dorset, Devon and Somerset and then it came to Bristol where very few were left alive.
>
> It then travelled northwards, leaving not a town, a village or even, except rarely, a house, without killing most or all of the people there. There was such a shortage of people that there were hardly enough living to bury the dead.

Historians now estimate that at least 40 per cent of the population died, with towns and ports being even harder hit. It killed everyone who caught it, rich and poor, and they died quickly and painfully. Only remote villages and farms high up on the hills were likely to be safe.

What was the Black Death?

Even now historians are not completely certain what the pestilence was but it was probably bubonic plague. Bubonic plague is carried by rats and spread by fleas. A flea becomes infected when it bites an infected rat, then it passes the disease on to other rats and to humans when it bites them. People bitten by infected fleas suddenly felt cold and tired and then discovered painful swellings called buboes in their armpits and groins. Blisters appeared all over their bodies, followed by high fever, severe headaches, unconsciousness for several days and then death.

The impact of the plague was probably made worse by a second disease called pneumonic plague. This was spread by people coughing over others. The victims coughed up blood because the disease attacked their lungs, causing breathing problems. They died more quickly, in a day or two at most.

Activities

1 Information speed test! How quickly can you find the answers to these questions?
  a When did the Black Death arrive in England?
  b Which two diseases do historians think were involved?
  c Which two creatures probably spread the disease?
  d What percentage of people in Britain died?
  e What were buboes?

2 Use Sources 2–6.
  a Choose three words to describe people's reactions to the Black Death.
  b Why do you think they reacted in these ways?

3 Look back at the 'Medical Moments in Time': London, 1347 (on pages 18–19). What evidence can you find that helps explain why the Black Death was so devastating?

Source 1

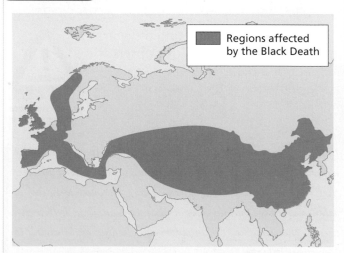

Regions affected by the Black Death

▲ The Black Death spread throughout Asia and Europe, probably carried by rats and fleas on trading ships and in packs of goods carried by merchants.

Source 2

An Irish monk, Brother John Clynn, wrote an account of the plague and concluded:

'I, waiting among the dead for death to come, leave parchment for continuing the work, in case anyone should still be alive in the future and any son of Adam can escape this pestilence and continue my work.'

Source 3

The Italian writer, Petrarch, wrote this letter to a friend in 1350:

'Where are our dear friends now? Where are the beloved faces? Where are the affectionate words, the relaxed and enjoyable conversations? What lightning bolt devoured them? What earthquake topped them? There was crowd of us, now we are almost alone. We should make new friends, but how, when the human race is almost wiped out; and why, when it looks to me as if the end of the world is at hand?'

Source 4

▲ King Death, an illustration in a French book of prayers from the early fifteenth century. The scroll he is holding reads: 'Remember man that you are ash [and] into ash you shall return'.

Source 5

▲ Black Death graves at Hereford cathedral. A chronicler wrote that in London 'they dug broad, deep pits and buried the bodies together, treating everyone alike, except the most eminent'.

Source 6

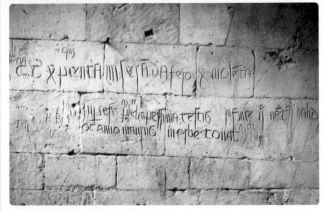

▲ Words scratched on the church wall in Ashwell, Hertfordshire:

'1349 the pestilence 1350 pitiless, wild, violent, the dregs of the people live to tell the tale'.

What did people think caused the Black Death?

Physicians believed that people became ill when their humours were out of balance. They still believed this during the Black Death, but there were also plenty of other ideas about why such a terrible disease had started. What can you work out about people's explanations for the Black Death from these sources?

Activities

1 Which of Sources 1–5 would you use to support each of these statements?
   a The Theory of the Four Humours was still followed by physicians.
   b Some people connected the Black Death to dirt and bad air.
   c In some places, people took the chance to blame and attack outsiders.
   d There was strong belief that God sent diseases as a punishment.
2 How do these statements help to explain why the Black Death killed so many people?

Source 1

A Swedish bishop who had read work by John Jacobus, a French physician, suggested:

'Sometimes the pestilence comes from a privy toilet next to a chamber or some other thing that corrupts the air. Sometimes it comes from dead flesh or from standing water in ditches.'

Source 2

In September 1348 the Prior of Christchurch Abbey, Canterbury wrote to the Bishop of London:

'Terrible is God towards the sons of men … He uses plagues, miserable famines, wars and other suffering to arise and to terrify and torment men and so drive out their sins. Thus England is struck by the pestilence because of the increasing pride and numberless sins of the people.'

Source 3

▲ By the 1400s the science of astrology was an important part of medicine. Physicians believed the stars and planets affected people's bodies because both were made of the same four elements – air, earth, fire and water. Guy de Chauliac, a French surgeon, blamed the Black Death on two things. One was 'the state of each victim's body – bad digestion, weakness and blockage'. The other was 'the close position of Saturn, Jupiter and Mars in 1345 … always a sign of wonderful, terrible or violent things to come'. This fifteenth-century illustration shows the planet Saturn eating his children.

Source 4

▲ A German woodcut showing the burning of Jews in Germany. Minority groups were blamed for the Black Death in many countries. Jews were said to have poisoned water supplies and in some places were burned as people looked for someone to blame.

Source 5

In 1365 a physician called John of Burgundy wrote:

'Many people have been killed by the plague, especially those stuffed with evil humours. As Galen says, the body does not become sick unless it contains evil humours.'

What impact did the Christian Church have on medicine?

One of the things you can learn from the sources on the opposite page is that many people believed that God had sent the Black Death as a punishment for their sins. This was because the Christian Church dominated people's lives. It influenced ordinary people's everyday lives and it also controlled how doctors were educated and trained.

The Church controlled the universities where physicians were trained, and believed that ancient writings, such as those of Galen, should not be questioned for two reasons. Firstly, if people started questioning Galen they might question the Bible, so questioning was not a good idea! Therefore, when Roger Bacon said that doctors should do their own research instead of just reading Galen, he was thrown into prison by church leaders.

Secondly, the Church supported Galen's ideas because they fitted in with its own ideas. Although Galen was not a Christian, he believed that the body had been created by one god who had made all the parts of the body fit together perfectly. This matched the Christian belief that God had created human beings, so Christians were happy to support Galen's ideas.

Here are some other effects of Christianity on medicine in the Middle Ages:

Activities

3 Why was the Church so keen for people to believe the writings of Galen?

4 In what ways did the Church make it difficult for medicine to improve?

5 What advice do you think the Church would have given people about how to save themselves from the Black Death?

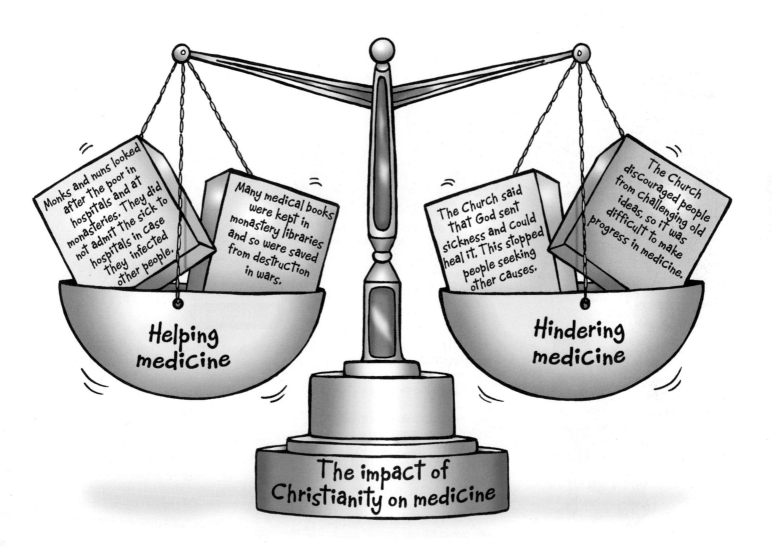

Monks and nuns looked after the poor in hospitals and at monasteries. They did not admit the sick to hospitals in case they infected other people.

Many medical books were kept in monastery libraries and so were saved from destruction in wars.

The Church said that God sent sickness and could heal it. This stopped people seeking other causes.

The Church discouraged people from challenging old ideas, so it was difficult to make progress in medicine.

Helping medicine

Hindering medicine

The impact of Christianity on medicine

How did people try to treat or stop the Black Death?

Activities

1 Which of Sources 1–5 provide evidence of:
  a methods based on the belief that God had sent the pestilence
  b methods following Galen's use of treatments by Opposites
  c doctors being helpless to stop the Black Death
  d methods based on the belief that bad air caused the disease?
2 Why were there no effective methods of dealing with the Black Death?

Source 3

▲ Flagellants walked through towns as the plague spread, whipping themselves to show God that they had repented their sins and asking God to be merciful.

Source 1

▲ One physician takes the victim's pulse while the other examines his urine, but even they cannot stop 'Death' taking the victim. This warning was in a fifteenth-century French manuscript.

Source 4

This advice comes from John of Burgundy, author of one of the first books about the plague, written in 1365:

'Avoid too much eating and drinking and avoid baths which open the pores, for the pores are doorways through which poisonous air can enter the body. In cold or rainy weather, light fires in your room. In foggy or windy weather, inhale perfumes every morning before leaving home. If the plague arrives during hot weather, eat cold things rather than hot and drink more than you eat. Be sparing with hot substances such as pepper, garlic, onions and everything else that generates excessive heat and instead use cucumbers, fennel and spinach.'

Source 2

◄ King Edward III of England and his bishops ordered that services and processions be held in every church at least once a day, in which people prayed for forgiveness and asked God to put an end to the disease. Some people went further and made candles their own height and lit them in church as offerings to God. In Barcelona, the citizens made a candle 7 kilometres long that they hoped would encircle and protect the city.

Source 5

One fourteenth-century writer reported people using this method of avoiding the Black Death:

'I have heard of a certain way to defeat this pestilence. It is caused by stinking air so my plan is to surround myself with an even more terrible smell which will ward off the bad air that carries the pestilence. Every night and morning my servants will fill a bucket with waste from our toilet and I will put my head in the bucket and breathe in the fumes for half an hour. That will keep the pestilence away.'

Review: Medicine in 1350

The way people responded to the Black Death tells us a lot about medicine at the time. Use your knowledge of the Black Death to help you produce a Memory Map summarising the key features of medieval medicine.

Activities

3   List three reasons why you think the Black Death killed so many people. Which of these reasons do you think was the most important?

4   **Memory map:** Create a memory map for medicine in 1350. On the left is the outline. How would you complete it?

5   **Living graph:** On pages 8–9, you began to create living graphs that record developments across time. Now fill out your graphs for the Middle Ages up to 1350.

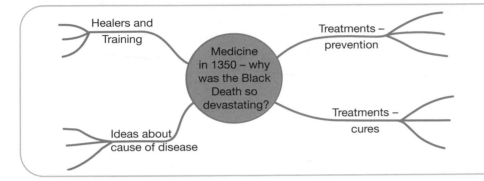

Healers and training

a   Mothers and family members treated most illnesses. Women with skills and experience were often called to help, e.g. childbirth.

b   Priests said prayers to help the sick and protect from illness.

c   Physicians trained at universities by reading the books by Hippocrates and Galen and some Arab medical writers. In the 1300s, there were fewer than 100 physicians in England.

Treatments – prevention

a   Diet, rest, exercise in fresh air

b   Bleeding and purging to stop evil humours building up

Medicine in 1350

Treatments – cures

a   Remedies made up from herbs, minerals and animal parts

b   Prayers, charms and rhymes

c   Bleeding, purging and other methods to restore the proper balance of the humours

d   There were many small hospitals all around England. Their main work was taking care of the elderly and others who could not look after themselves. They were run by monks and nuns who provided food, warmth and lots of prayers. They rarely admitted the sick in case they spread infection.

Ideas about causes of disease

a   Many believed that illnesses were sent by God.

b   Physicians (doctors who had trained at universities) said that many illnesses had natural causes. They followed the theory of the Greek writer Hippocrates, who said that illness was caused when the body's humours were out of balance.

c   Some people linked disease to bad air and dirt.

Section 4: Why were the medical Renaissance and Scientific Revolution so important when they didn't make anyone healthier?

The Renaissance is the period of European history between around 1400 and 1600. It is famous for discoveries in science, geography and art, and led onto the Scientific Revolution and breakthroughs in medicine. However, by 1750, people were no healthier than in the Middle Ages. So, if they weren't any healthier, why was this period in medical history so important?

Read all about it! Great medical discoveries! Nobody will notice for centuries!

Activities

1   Sources 1–3 were all important developments in the period of the Renaissance. How do you think each development influenced medicine?
2   Which breakthroughs do you think each of the two medical pioneers shown on page 61 made use of in his work?
3   Think about the medical discoveries made by these pioneers. Why do you think they did not immediately lead to people being healthier and living longer?

Renaissance breakthroughs

Source 1

▲ Drawings of parts of the body by Leonardo da Vinci (1452–1519). Da Vinci gave this advice to young artists: 'The painter who has knowledge of sinews, muscles and tendons will know exactly which sinew causes the movement of a limb. He will be able to show the various muscles in the different attitudes of his figures. You will need three dissections to have a complete knowledge of the arteries, three more for the membranes, three for the nerves, muscles and ligaments, three for the bones and cartilages. Three must also be devoted to the female body.'

Source 2

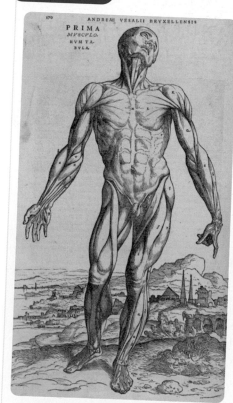

◄ The printing press was invented by Johannes Gutenberg in the 1450s. By 1500 printing presses were being used throughout western Europe. Some books were highly illustrated such as this page from Andreas Vesalius' book on anatomy, *The Fabric of the Human Body* (1543).

Source 3

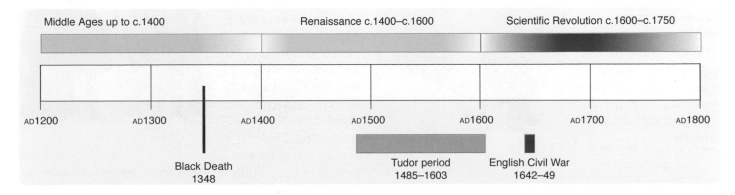

◀ The first effective microscopes were developed in the 1600s by instrument makers including Robert Hooke in England and Antoni van Leeuwenhoek in Holland. They allowed people to see things they could not see with the naked eye.

Medical pioneers and their discoveries

▲ Andreas Vesalius made new discoveries about the anatomy of the human body.

▲ William Harvey discovered that the blood circulates around the body.

Middle Ages up to c.1400	Renaissance c.1400–c.1600	Scientific Revolution c.1600–c.1750

AD1200   AD1300   AD1400   AD1500   AD1600   AD1700   AD1800

Black Death
1348

Tudor period
1485–1603

English Civil War
1642–49

4.1 What was re-born in the medical Renaissance?

Renaissance means 're-birth'. The Renaissance period was a time of 're-born' interest in all things Greek and Roman: their books and ideas, buildings and sculptures. But, in medicine, interest in the Greeks and Romans had never gone away because physicians had kept reading and relying on Galen. So what exactly was being re-born in the medical Renaissance?

The Renaissance struggle: conservatism versus enquiry

In the Big Fight of the Middle Ages, conservatism beat enquiry.
This wasn't surprising as conservatism had the experienced and powerful Christian Church in his corner. What happened next?

Then came the Black Death. Afterwards many of the survivors were better-off because employers had to pay higher wages to attract workers. Many people had spare time and spare money and they spent some of this time and money on education.

Wealth and education helped trigger the Renaissance, the re-birth of interest in the Greeks and the Romans. Educated people during the Renaissance thought that the Greeks and Romans were just like them – intelligent and thoughtful. They looked down on the people of the Middle Ages as ignorant.

They made new translations of Galen. Greeks and Romans, like Galen, had never gone away in medicine. Medieval doctors had studied them in detail. In universities in the 1500s scholars were still reading translations of Galen but now they were worried. The translations had been made in the Middle Ages. What if they were wrong? What if vital knowledge had been missed out or misunderstood by ignorant people in the Middle Ages? They decided to make new translations to make sure they were right. They published new editions of Greek and Roman books, including nearly 600 editions of Galen's books.

> Better make sure this is right. Can't trust those medieval monks to get things right.

This work changed attitudes. In the Middle Ages, people respected traditional ideas and simply copied Greek knowledge and ideas. They did not challenge them. But in the Renaissance, people realised that the Greeks loved enquiry – asking questions, challenging old ideas (like the gods causing disease) and suggesting new ones (the Theory of the Four Humours). If the Greeks could ask questions and challenge old ideas, then so could they, the people of the Renaissance.

> Those Greeks asked questions and challenged old ideas. Maybe enquiry is more important than tradition?

So what was re-born? It was not just interest in Greek and Roman ideas that was re-born but, far more importantly, their love of enquiry and willingness to challenge existing ideas. Once they began to ask questions and look carefully some people began to realise that Galen had not known everything – and had even made mistakes!

> What? Why? Who? Is Galen right?

ENQUIRY

But not everyone agreed. Many people still conservatively stuck to tradition, not daring to think for themselves, still saying it was wrong to challenge Galen. So what developed was a battle between attitudes – between people defending the old ideas and people fighting for new ones.

> We can't let this upstart enquiry win. Old ideas have always been right and we're not going to think differently.

Activities

1 What exactly was being re-born in the Renaissance?
2 Conservatism beat enquiry in the Middle Ages.
   a What kinds of changes in medicine do you think would be needed to change the result and give enquiry a knock-out victory over conservatism?
   b Look at the possible results to the right. Which do you think was the likely result by 1750?

The Big Fight 1400–1700 – how will it end?

So who did win the Big Fight between the attitude twins – conservatism and enquiry? Your task is to create your own commentary on the great conservatism versus enquiry contest. Your commentary will link all the topics in this section together by assessing how much medicine really changed between 1400 and 1700. And there's a bonus – you will have begun your revision months before you complete your course and take your exam!

Activities

Big Story chart: Over the next twelve pages you will be gathering information to fill in the Big Story chart on the opposite page. You could do this on computer. You will then use the chart to write your own audio commentary on the big fight of 1400–1700. Each topic in the table will be one 'round' in the big fight.

Stage 1: get an overview
Use pages 66–67.

a Pencil information about each topic into column 3 of your Big Story chart.

b On a separate sheet of paper draft first ideas for your commentary for each 'round'. Just a sentence to summarise what happened will be enough at this stage. This is your set of starter ideas to build on.

Remember:

    Round 1 is Knowledge of the human body
    Round 2 is The growth of science
    Round 3 is Physicians and their training
    Round 4 is Hospitals
    Round 5 is Everyday treatments
    Round 6 is Ideas about causes of disease.

Stage 2: fill in the detail
Now work through the tasks on pages 68–79. Some of them will get you working in groups or listening to other groups present, but all the time it is your responsibility to fill in your Big Story chart.

Stage 3: decide on the winners of each round
Complete the final column giving points to each boxer: conservatism or enquiry. Use the table to help you.

If there are …	then conservatism gets …	and enquiry gets …
no discoveries at all	3	0
traditional ideas and methods that still dominate medicine even if one or two new ideas begin to be accepted	2	1
important discoveries that begin to change this aspect of medicine	1	2
really important discoveries that completely change this aspect of medicine	0	3

Stage 4: write your commentary

a Now you are ready to write your commentary. It should say in sports-commentator style: who is winning this round (is it a close run thing or an easy win?); which punches (evidence) have the biggest impact?

b Record your commentary as a podcast. You can also listen to it for revision.

The Big Story of medicine – the Renaissance and Scientific Revolution

	Medicine c.1350, at the end of the Middle Ages	Medicine c.1750	Who won this round: conservatism or enquiry? Which were the strongest punches?
Round 1 Knowledge of the human body (pages 68–71)	Doctors knew about Greek and Roman discoveries but did not learn any more. Dissection was carried out to illustrate what Galen had said, not make new discoveries.		
Round 2 Growth of science (pages 72–73)	There was no understanding of modern scientific methods, of asking questions and testing hypotheses through experiment and observation. Physicians simply learned the writings of Galen and others and were not expected to question traditional ideas.		
Round 3 Physicians (pages 74–75)	a Physicians trained at universities by reading the books by Hippocrates and Galen and some Arab medical writers. b Mothers and family members treated most illnesses.		
Round 4 Hospitals (page 76)	a Hospitals run by monks and nuns provided warmth, food and prayer for the poor. b There were hundreds of small hospitals, but they did not admit people with infectious diseases in case the disease spread among residents.		
Round 5 Everyday treatments (pages 78–79)	a Remedies made up from herbs, minerals and animal parts. b Prayers, charms and rhymes. c Bleeding, purging and other methods to restore the proper balance of the humours, following the methods of Galen. d Rest, exercise and diet.		
Round 6 Ideas about the causes of disease (pages 74–79)	a Many believed that illnesses were sent by God. b Doctors said that many illnesses had natural causes. They followed Hippocrates' theory that illness was caused when the body's humours were out of balance.		

Medical Moments in Time: London, 1665

Activities

Big Story chart: This drawing helps you to develop a quick overview of how medicine was changing and whether conservatism was still beating enquiry in 1665.

1   Divide the six topics among the class. What evidence can you find to start your chart? Who is winning each round?

2   What evidence helps to explain why people were no healthier nor living longer than in the Middle Ages?

Plague struck in 1665. The Mayor of London ordered watchmen to guard houses to make sure the sick and their families stayed shut up.

House owners were ordered to sweep the streets outside their homes.

Taverns and theatres were closed to stop plague spreading.

It's not plague. Your humours are out of balance, that's all. You just need bleeding.

Pity old Henry VIII closed the monasteries and their hospitals. They'd be useful if the plague hits us hard.

What did people discover about anatomy and how the body works?

Pages 68–71 tell you about the two most important discoveries about the human body. They make it look as if medicine is changing completely, as if enquiry has won. But is it that simple? Were these punches really knocking out conservatism or just the start of a much longer contest?

Vesalius – breakthroughs in anatomy

Andreas Vesalius (1514–1564)

- Father a doctor, studied medicine in Paris and Padua, Italy.
- Professor of Surgery in Padua.
- Wrote *The Fabric of the Human Body* (1543), a detailed and fully illustrated description of human anatomy.

Anatomy – the story so far

1 Doctors believed Galen had given a fully correct description of anatomy.

2 Dissection was carried out to show Galen was right, not to check or challenge him, even though Galen had said it was important to learn by dissecting human bodies. He sometimes had to use animals because human bodies were not available.

Vesalius' achievements – Galen could be wrong!

The Fabric of the Human Body was the first highly illustrated book on human anatomy.

Vesalius respected Galen's work but proved that Galen was sometimes wrong by showing that:

- the human jaw bone is made from one bone, not two as Galen said
- the breastbone has three parts, not seven as Galen said
- blood does not flow into the heart through invisible holes in the septum – such holes do not exist.

He showed that doctors could learn more about anatomy and had to carry out human (not animal) dissection to learn more.

Activities

1 Work in groups. Each group tackle one of the developments:
- Vesalius and anatomy (pages 68–69)
- Harvey and blood (pages 70–73)
- The growth of science (pages 72–73).
Report your findings to the rest of the class and then complete the row of your chart about knowledge of the human body.

2 **'Role of the individual' chart:** Convert your findings about Vesalius and Harvey into 'role of the individual' charts for revision.

Source 1

▲ The title page of Vesalius' *The Fabric of the Human Body* tells us about his attitudes to dissection.

Vesalius is shown in the centre, dissecting the body himself. In the Middle Ages, professors sat and read Galen aloud while demonstrators did the dissection. Galen and other Greek doctors are shown at the same level as Vesalius, not higher up as if superior.

Students crowd round the body so they can see what Vesalius is doing rather than simply listening to Galen being read out.

How did he do it?

Vesalius made great use of the new invention of printing. He chose the best printer and supervised the engraving of the illustrations and the printing himself. Printing meant that everything came out the same with no mistakes – which was not the case in books copied by hand. Without printing, his work would not have had such an impact. Thousands of copies were printed quickly and used all over Europe.

TECHNOLOGY

Vesalius was inventive and determined. Once he stole the body of a criminal from the gallows to dissect and he worked at Padua where dissection was encouraged. He insisted on making sure every detail of his book was printed correctly.

INDIVIDUAL GENIUS

In Italy many artists were already interested in dissection to improve their own work. Vesalius used them to illustrate his book.

ART

Vesalius respected Galen but believed that it was vital to ask questions and challenge traditional ideas by carrying out as many human dissections as possible.

ATTITUDES – ENQUIRY

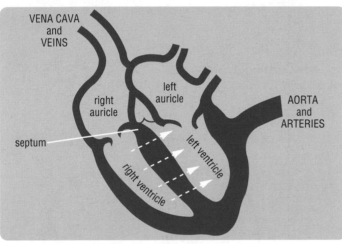

Labels: VENA CAVA and VEINS, right auricle, left auricle, septum, AORTA and ARTERIES, left ventricle, right ventricle

▲ Diagram showing Galen's idea about how blood reached the heart. Vesalius' dissection proved this was not true.

Stepping stones to the future

But …

WARNING

DON'T EXAGGERATE

- **Many doctors refused to accept that Galen could be wrong.** Some said that Vesalius' work only showed that the body had changed since Galen's time. The heavy criticism led Vesalius to leave Padua and work for the Emperor Charles V.

- **Nobody was healthier as a result of Vesalius' work.** His work was only the start. Many more discoveries were needed before people would live longer, healthier lives.

1 Vesalius' insistence on enquiry began to change attitudes and encourage others to follow his example.

3 Accurate knowledge of anatomy was vital for the building up of medical knowledge and paving the way for better treatments later.

2 Doctors realised there was more to be learned – Galen had not discovered everything or got everything right.

4 His book spread knowledge AND his attitude, showing others the way forward.

Improved medicine and health

Harvey – discovering the circulation of the blood

William Harvey (1578–1657)

- Studied medicine in Cambridge and Padua, worked as a doctor in London.
- Published his book *An Anatomical Account of the Motion of the Heart and Blood*, in 1628, which described how the blood circulates round the body.
- Became doctor to King Charles I.

Blood – the story so far

Galen had said:

1 new blood was constantly manufactured in the liver to replace blood burned up in the body just like wood is burnt by a fire

2 blood passed from one side of the heart to the other through invisible holes in the septum. This had been challenged by Ibn al-Nafis (1210–88) and Vesalius but neither could provide an alternative explanation.

Two other doctors had made discoveries that paved the way for Harvey:

- Realdo Columbo (1516–59) said that blood moved along the veins and arteries
- Fabricius (1533–1619), Harvey's tutor at Padua, proved there are valves in the veins.

Despite these pieces of knowledge, nobody could explain how blood moved around the body!

Harvey's achievements

Harvey proved that the heart acts as a pump, pumping blood around the body. He did this by:

- dissecting live cold-blooded animals whose hearts beat slowly so he could see the movement of each muscle in the heart
- dissecting human bodies to build up detailed knowledge of the heart
- proving that the body has a one-way system for the blood – he tried to pump liquid past the valves in the veins but could not do so
- calculating that the amount of blood going into the arteries each hour was three times the weight of a man. This showed that the same blood is being pumped round the body by the heart.

Source 1

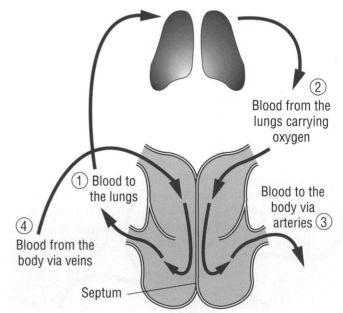

▲ A water pump being used to fight a fire in the 1600s. Pumps like this had valves to direct the flow of water.

▲ A simplified version of the circulation of the blood. Blood leaves the heart (1), then passes through the lungs (2) and back to the heart and then around the body along arteries (3). Then blood comes back to the heart along veins (4) before starting its circulation around the body again.

(1) Blood to the lungs

(2) Blood from the lungs carrying oxygen

(3) Blood to the body via arteries

(4) Blood from the body via veins

Septum

How did he do it?

Mechanical water pumps in London may have given Harvey the idea that the heart is pumping blood.

TECHNOLOGY

Harvey's discovery was the result of careful dissection, observation of detail and experiment.

ATTITUDES

ENQUIRY

Harvey was exceptionally thorough in his work, spending many hours repeating experiments and going over every detail.

INDIVIDUAL GENIUS

Harvey had read the work of earlier doctors and was able to use it to build up his theory.

COMMUNICATIONS

Source 2

◄ Harvey could not explain everything about the circulation of the blood. He did not know how blood moves from the arteries to the veins but later in the 1600s Professor Marcello Malphigi used one of the first effective microscopes to discover the capillaries, which carry blood from arteries to veins. The development of microscopes was a vital technological development helping to transform medical knowledge.

But…

WARNING

DON'T EXAGGERATE

- **There was still much more to discover about the blood.** Doctors could not make blood transfusions until they discovered blood groups in 1901.

- **Harvey's discovery was only gradually accepted.** Some doctors ignored his theory. Others said that he was wrong because he was contradicting Galen. It was nearly fifty years before the teachers at the University of Paris taught Harvey's ideas rather than Galen's.

- **Harvey's discovery did not make anyone better.** The writer John Aubrey noted 'All his profession agree Dr Harvey to be an excellent anatomist, but I never heard any that admired his treatment of the sick.' Harvey himself said that after he published his discovery fewer patients came to see him. Many thought his idea mad.

Stepping stones to the future

1 Harvey's discovery laid the groundwork for future investigation of the blood and physiology (the workings of the body) – see Source 2.

2 Many aspects of medicine depend on understanding the blood system. Surgery, for example, could not develop until after Harvey's discovery.

3 Harvey proved that Vesalius was right about the importance of dissection. He wrote 'I prefer to learn and teach anatomy not from books but from dissections.'

Improved medicine and health

The growth of science

Science – the story so far

1 In the Middle Ages, physicians simply learned the writings of Galen and others and were not expected to question traditional ideas. It was believed that ancient writers had discovered all there was to know about medicine and other sciences.

2 The Renaissance began to change this thinking, as people realised that Greek and Roman thinkers had believed that it was important to keep asking questions and looking for new discoveries.

3 In the 1500s, Vesalius showed that Galen could be wrong about important details of anatomy and that there really were new discoveries to be made.

4 The development of the printing press helped new ideas spread far more rapidly than ever before because books could be printed faster and less expensively.

Activities

1 Read the description of scientific method below.
   a Why was it likely to lead to new discoveries?
   b Why was this so different from past methods?
2 How did the Royal Society help to produce new discoveries?
3 How did each of these factors help the development of science:
   a government
   b technology
   c attitudes: enquiry.
4 **Big Story chart:** Use this page to complete the row of your chart on page 65 about 'Growth of science'.

What was this new science?

Don't worry, this isn't a bit out of a GCSE Physics book – in fact this is remarkably like how we do History!

Was Galen right about how the blood moves round the body? I have a different idea.

This dissection will prove whether my hypothesis is correct or whether Galen was right.

Stage 1
Read what has been written before, e.g. about the human body.

Stage 2
Think about that which you have read and ask questions about it. Don't automatically believe what you read. Take nothing for granted until you have proved it to be true.

Stage 3
Create a hypothesis (a suggested answer) for your question and then test this hypothesis by experiment or by detailed observation. Now you have proved that your hypothesis is right or wrong.

Stage 4
Write up your findings and tell other people about them.

The Royal Society

The first meetings of a group of people interested in discussing new scientific ideas took place in London in 1645. They continued until they were given a royal charter in 1662 and became known as the Royal Society. They met weekly to discuss new ideas in physics, botany, astronomy, medicine and other sciences. Members also demonstrated experiments because the Society had its own laboratory and equipment such as microscopes. It also published books and articles to spread new ideas and discoveries.

▶ King Charles II (1660–85) attended meetings of the Royal Society to watch experiments. He had a laboratory and an observatory built in one of his palaces. After the Civil War, people were suspicious of private meetings, so Charles's support for the Society protected the members from suspicions that they might be plotting a revolution.

◀ In 1665, Richard Lower, of the Royal Society, made the first experimental blood transfusion. He transfused blood from a dog to another dog and later from a sheep to a man, a 'crackbrained' student called Arthur Coga. It was said that people hoped this would make Coga cleverer!

Stepping stones to the future

1. The new experimental approach to science changed the way scientists and doctors thought. Now they were prepared to challenge old ideas by looking for new discoveries that would make a difference to people's lives.

2. Breakthroughs like Harvey's discovery of the circulation of the blood encouraged more scientists to conduct their own experiments.

3. Books by scientists and doctors and their discussions at meetings stimulated more ideas and thinking.

4. Support for the ideas of Galen faded during the late 1600s and 1700s.

Improved medicine and health

But ...

WARNING

DON'T EXAGGERATE

- This change of attitude was only the beginning. Many more discoveries were needed before people's health would be much better. Medical treatments in the late 1600s still included ingredients such as frogspawn and 'cold deadman's skull'.

- It took time to end opposition to experimental science from supporters of Galen.

Physicians and their training

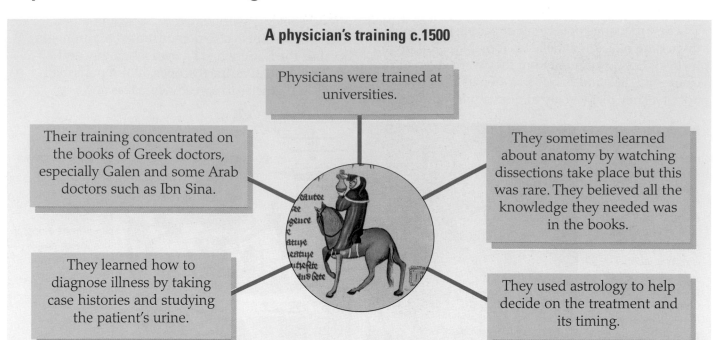

A physician's training c.1500

Physicians were trained at universities.

Their training concentrated on the books of Greek doctors, especially Galen and some Arab doctors such as Ibn Sina.

They sometimes learned about anatomy by watching dissections take place but this was rare. They believed all the knowledge they needed was in the books.

They learned how to diagnose illness by taking case histories and studying the patient's urine.

They used astrology to help decide on the treatment and its timing.

Renaissance   Vesalius   Harvey   Scientific Revolution

A physician's training in the late 1700s

Diagnosis by studying urine and the study of astrology were rarely used.

There was little training at universities in England. Students travelled to universities in Holland, France or Italy, or to Edinburgh in Scotland. By the 1780s, Edinburgh had over 200 medical students each year.

Training at Edinburgh involved some practical training in hospitals, examining patients. Students also took part in dissections, although there was always a shortage of bodies.

In 1768, William Hunter set up his own medical school in his home in London, training physicians specialising in anatomy and obstetrics – care of women in childbirth. Hunter's students studied six days a week for over three months. Other physicians also ran their own courses for medical students and were beginning to use hospital wards for training.

William Hunter (1718–1783)

Hunter trained at Edinburgh University and became a doctor in London. He and his younger brother, John, were important leaders in improving training of doctors in the late 1700s. Both men emphasised the importance of careful observation of patients' symptoms and of experimenting to test treatments, not just accepting what they read in books.

Men versus women

Women were not allowed to attend university so could not become physicians. They continued to work as midwives, but even this came under threat. The first handbooks for midwives were written by men who had little practical experience. The first English handbook by a woman, *The Midwives Book* by Mrs Jane Sharp, was not written until 1671.

Women also found their role in midwifery being downgraded because of a secret discovery. About 1620, Peter Chamberlen invented the obstetrical forceps, used to free a baby from the womb during a difficult birth without hurting or killing baby or mother. The Chamberlens, refugees from France, passed the design secretly from father to son until the death of the last of the family in 1728 revealed their secret. When male physicians learned of the forceps, they said that only men should use them because only they had the necessary anatomical knowledge learned from studying at university. Male midwives were taking over. William Hunter (above) was one of the leading male midwives of the late 1700s.

Source 1

Even in the 1660s, a century after Vesalius had shown how important human dissection was, trainee physicians still sometimes had to make do with dissecting animals. When Samuel Pepys (who wrote a famous diary in the 1660s) feared he was going blind, he took advice from London's leading expert on eye problems, Dr Daubeny Turberville. Pepys tried green lenses in spectacles, eye-drops, pills and even bleeding and purges. On 3 July 1668, Pepys wrote that he had been with Turberville and several other doctors to:

'dissect several eyes of sheep and oxen, to my great information; but strange that Turberville should be so great a man and yet to this day has seen no eyes dissected or but just once ...'.

Activites

1 Which medieval methods of diagnosing illness were little used by the 1700s?
2 Why was dissection only a small part of medical training:
   a around 1500
   b in the 1700s?
3 a How were physicians trained around 1500?
   b Where could you go to train to be a doctor in the late 1700s?
   c In what ways was training becoming more professional?
4 What does Source 1 tell you about the pace of change in training of physicians?
5 **Big Story chart:** Use this page to complete the row of your chart about physicians.

Were hospitals changing and providing better medical help?

Before the Renaissance

Hospitals in the Middle Ages did not provide much medical help. They were usually run by monks and nuns and were more like care-homes for the elderly, providing warmth, food and sometimes herbal remedies for people who could no longer look after themselves. The most important work of the monks and nuns was to pray for the souls of the patients. By the 1400s, there were hundreds of these small hospitals, often only with room for six people. They did not admit anyone with an infectious disease in case the disease spread among the residents.

The effects of the Renaissance and the Scientific Revolution

Hospitals

Many medieval hospitals were part of monasteries, so when Henry VIII closed the monasteries in the 1530s, many hospitals closed too. However, some were taken over by town councils, especially the almshouses that looked after the elderly poor. In London, the city council and charity helped to keep St Bartholomew's Hospital open. By the 1660s it had twelve wards and up to 300 patients. During the early 1700s, many new hospitals were opened, paid for by local people, charities and town councils. Eleven new hospitals were founded in London and 46 in the rest of Britain.

Patients

In 1750, nearly all hospitals still looked after the poor. Anyone with any money paid for a doctor or nurse to look after them at home. Many hospitals still did not admit people with infectious diseases, but this was beginning to change in a handful of hospitals in Edinburgh and London.

Treatments

Patients were kept clean and warm and were fed regularly. If they became sick they were given herbal remedies or bled. Simple surgery was carried out, such as setting fractured limbs, and sometimes desperate surgery was used, such as amputating a limb, if there was no other possible remedy. All treatments were free, but patients were still expected to pray for their recovery.

Doctors and nurses

In the 1660s, St Bartholomew's Hospital in London had three physicians and three surgeons, fifteen nursing sisters and a larger number of nursing helpers. The physicians had been trained at university, but training carried on in the hospital, practising on the poor. Nursing sisters treated patients with herbal remedies, but the nursing helpers did heavy, manual work – washing, cleaning and preparing food – so did not have any medical training.

Stepping stones to the future

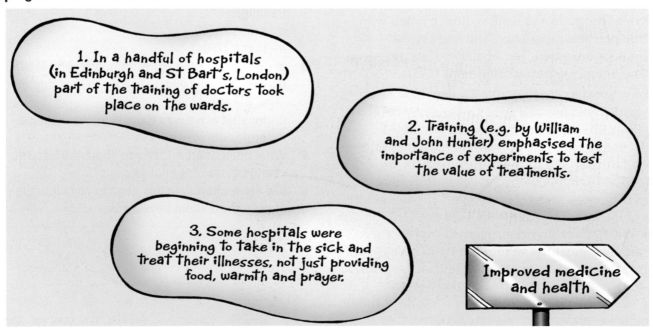

1. In a handful of hospitals (in Edinburgh and St Bart's, London) part of the training of doctors took place on the wards.

2. Training (e.g. by William and John Hunter) emphasised the importance of experiments to test the value of treatments.

3. Some hospitals were beginning to take in the sick and treat their illnesses, not just providing food, warmth and prayer.

Improved medicine and health

Activities

1 Why did the number of hospitals:
   a fall in the 1500s?
   b increase in the 1700s?
2 Had the quality of medical care in hospitals improved since the Middle Ages?
3 Why did so many people get help from local women and quacks rather than physicians?
4 **Big Story chart**: Complete the row of your chart about hospitals.

Who else could you go to for medical help?

▲ Women still played a major part in everyday medicine. The first person to treat nearly all sicknesses was the wife or mother of the sick person.

Source 1

MARGARET COLFE.
HAVING BEEN ABOVE FORTY YEARS A WILLING NURSE, MIDWIFE, SURGEON AND, IN PART, PHYSICIAN TO ALL BOTH RICH AND POOR, WITHOUT EXPECTING REWARD.
(LEWISHAM, 1643)

PRUDENCE POTTER.
HER LIFE WAS SPENT IN THE INDUSTRIOUS AND SUCCESSFUL PRACTICE OF PHYSIC, SURGERY AND MIDWIFERY.
(DEVON, 1689)

DOROTHY BURTON.
HAS EXCELLENT SKILL IN SURGERY, SORE EYES, ACHES ETC AND HAS DONE MANY FAMOUS GOOD CURES UPON POOR FOLKS THAT WERE OTHERWISE DESTITUTE OF HELP.
(1629)

▲ Some memorials put up to women healers

▲ An apothecary sold and mixed medicines that had been prescribed by physicians. They were not supposed to treat the sick or prescribe medicines themselves, but many did so, especially to help the poor by only charging a very small fee. There were many apothecaries in London and several in each town.

◄ Wealthy ladies often provided care for local families. Lady Grace Mildmay (1552–1620) began as a child, being set to read William Turner's book *A New Herbal* by her governess and later read books by Galen and Ibn Sina. She kept records of her patients and the treatments she used.

Source 2

◄ There had always been quacks – healers with no training. Arriving in a town or village with a fanfare of drum and trumpet, they were often accompanied by a capering clown and chattering monkey to draw the crowds. Some pretended to be from faraway places, such as Turkey, to add a sense of mystery and excitement. Many were simply out to make as much money as possible by selling their charms, potions or bottles of medicine. Some did very well indeed. Joanna Stephens (died 1774) claimed to have a remedy that would dissolve bladder stones without needing painful surgery. Parliament paid £5000 to buy the recipe from her!

Were everyday treatments changing?

Bleeding and purging

Source 1

◀ Bleeding was still one of the most common medical treatments and was recommended as a method of preventing illness, too. Physicians continued to believe that many illnesses were caused when the humours in the patient's body were out of balance. Therefore they used bleeding and purging to correct the balance, even though they must have weakened the patients considerably.

Herbal remedies

Many home remedies were handed down through generations from mother to daughter. Girls learned how to mix up remedies, using ingredients such as honey, which we now know kills some bacteria. More people were writing down home remedies because more people could now read and write. Mary Doggett noted a remedy for scurvy which used a mixture of horseradish roots, white wine, water and a quart of orange juice or 12 thinly cut oranges. We know that scurvy, which leads to internal bleeding and death, is the result of not eating enough fruit and vegetables, so long practice had produced an excellent remedy, even if Mary did not know why it worked.

New ingredients from abroad

European travels to America and Asia led to the arrival of new ingredients for medicines. Rhubarb from Asia was used to purge the bowels. Ipecacuanha from Brazil was prescribed for dysentery and used to make people vomit. The bark of the cinchona tree was imported from South America because of its effectiveness in treating fevers. In Europe, it became known as quinine and helped people with malaria.

Tobacco was greeted as a cure-all when it arrived from America, being recommended for toothache, poisoned wounds, and as protection from plague. A schoolboy at Eton College said that he had never been flogged so much as during the Plague of 1665, when he was beaten for not smoking often enough!

The bezoar stone – testing a magical cure

In 1566, a visitor to King Charles of France gave the king a bezoar stone which came from the stomach of goat-like animals. The visitor insisted that it would cure all poisons but when King Charles asked Ambroise Pare, his surgeon, Pare said that it could not possibly cure all poisons because a hot poison needed a cold antidote and vice-versa. Pare then suggested a test on a live patient! A cook who had been sentenced to death for theft was offered the chance to live if he took poison and then the bezoar stone. If the bezoar stone worked he would be free! The cook accepted the chance, took poison and then the stone. He died in agony several hours later. It was another triumph for experiment and enquiry, though not so good for the cook.

Source 2

▲ The printing revolution meant that more people had books in their homes containing advice on herbal remedies. One of the most popular was Nicholas Culpeper's *Complete Herbal* which recommended simple homegrown herbal remedies.

Source 3

From James Woodforde's diary (Woodforde was a parson in Norfolk and Somerset):
27 May 1779 'My maid Nanny taken very ill with dizziness and a desire to vomit but could not. Her straining to vomit brought on the hiccups which continued very violent. I gave her a dose of rhubarb before going to bed.'
1 March 1778 'Ben brought me a letter saying that Juliana is in a decline on account of lately having had measles and catching cold after, which has affected her lungs. She has been bled seven times.'
17 May 1778 'Ben brought letters which gave the disagreeable news of Juliana's death.'
11 March 1791 'The stye on my eye was still swelled and inflamed very much. As it is commonly said that rubbing the eyelid with the tail of a black cat would do it much good, and having a black cat, I made a trial of it. Very soon after dinner I found my eyelid much abated of swelling and almost free of pain. Any other cat's tail may have the above effect in all probability but I did my eyelid with my own black tom cat's tail.'
16 March 1791 'My eyelid rather better. Just before dinner I washed it well with cold water and the evening appeared much better for it.'

Source 5

Two suggestions from the 1660s on how to help plague sufferers:
'To draw the poison from the plague sore, take the feathers from the tail of a chicken and apply the chicken to the sore. The chick will gasp and labour for life. When the poison is drawn by the chicken, the patient will recover.'

'Wrap in woollen clothes, make the sick person sweat, which if he do, keep warm until the sores begin to rise. Then apply to the sores live pigeons cut in half or else a plaster made of yolk of an egg, honey, herb of grace and wheat flour.'

Source 4

▲ Between 1660 and 1682 over 92,000 people visited the King's court, believing that if Charles II touched them they would be cured from scrofula, a skin disease known as the King's Evil.

Source 6

From *The New London Dispensary*, published in 1682:
'To cure malaria, take the hair and nails of the patient, cut them small and either give them to birds in a roasted egg or put them in a hole in an oak tree or a plane tree. Stop up the hole with a peg of the same tree.'

Why was medicine so slow to change during the Renaissance?

So far this section has mostly been investigating the changes and continuities in medicine. To finish we'll concentrate, with the help of a concept map, on **why** medicine was slow to change. On this page, we're going to show you how to build up a concept map.

The students on the opposite page are building a concept map. Concept maps help you develop good explanations. They will:
- help you identify the factors that explain why medicine changed or stayed the same
- show how the factors worked together
- show which factors were the most important (that's what the crowns are for!).

Activities

We have built up this concept map for you. It explains why medicine was slow to develop. It's almost finished. All you have to do is copy it and finish it off.

1 The factors standing up and linked to the question with red string were important in hindering medical developments.
The pink cards A–D provide evidence of this. On your own version of the map write or place the cards in the correct places on the red string.

2 The green string links the factors that worked together to prevent progress.
The green cards explain these links. On your own version of the map write or place cards E–F in the correct places on the green string.

3 The crown shows which factor we think was most important in hindering medical progress. Do you agree? Why?

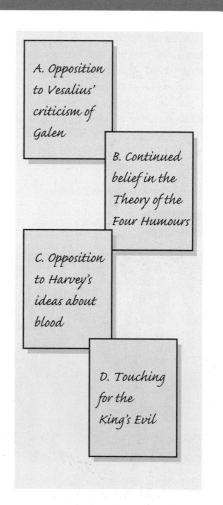

A. Opposition to Vesalius' criticism of Galen

B. Continued belief in the Theory of the Four Humours

C. Opposition to Harvey's ideas about blood

D. Touching for the King's Evil

E. The Church still supported many traditional ideas.

F. Kings still believed their task was making decisions about war and religion, not improving living standards and health.

Analysing factors

Some questions in the exam ask you to explain why something happened and to analyse the factors involved. This type of question usually carries a lot of marks.

You have already been introduced to the key factors, which help explain the continuities in medicine during the Renaissance period, on pages 80–81. These pages will help you use the concept map you produce to tackle questions that ask you to analyse factors.

Look at the question below. Look at the advice on decoding questions on page 36.

The content focus for this question is on **medical treatments**.

Stick to the date boundaries of the question. You must focus on the period 1500–1750. Explaining how discoveries made during the Renaissance helped medicine progress during the nineteenth and twentieth centuries are not relevant.

> Why did the discoveries of the Renaissance period have so little impact on medical treatments in Britain between 1500 and 1750?
>
> [12 marks]

The question asks **why** major discoveries had little impact on treatments. A list of factors is not enough. You need to explain how each factor held back medicine. The advice below on how to write effective explanations will help you.

12 marks are available. You will need to give a range of reasons why, despite important discoveries, medical treatments did not improve.

How to write effective explanations

Step 1: Identify a range of factors

that help explain why medical treatments were slow to change during the Renaissance period. Use the concept map you produced on page 80 to help you.

Step 2: Select two or three factors to write about

Do not try to cover everything!

Remember that in the exam you would have approximately 15 minutes to answer this type of question. Choose two or three factors that were obstacles to improving treatments at the time.

Step 3: Use connectives to tie in what you know to the question

Do not 'say' that a factor played a role; **prove it!**

Explain how each factor held back progress.

You can do this by using connectives such as 'this meant that ...', 'this led to' and 'this resulted in ...' to tie the factors you identify to the question.

Give specific examples of how medical treatments were slow to change as a result of this factor.

One reason why the great discoveries of the Renaissance had so little impact on medical treatments was the conservative attitudes of many people living at the time.

The student identifies a factor – conservative attitudes

Most people at the time continued to follow the ideas of Galen. The Christian Church supported Galen's ideas and said that they should not be questioned. The Church controlled universities and medical training.

The student explains how this factor was important

This resulted in doctors being discouraged from researching and developing new ideas and treatments. People living at the time did not want to challenge Galen's ideas. This meant that people continued to use treatments based on Galen's ideas.

The student ties this factor to the question

For example, many treatments such as bleeding continued to be based on the idea of balancing the four humours.

The student gives a specific example to support their argument

Another important reason was that the discoveries that were made tended to be about the structure of the body or how the body worked.

    Vesalius ...

    Harvey ...

    Their work was important but it did not explain the causes of disease.

    This meant that ... For example ...

Step 4 Structure your conclusion so that it does analyse the factors

Your conclusion is very important. It should be short and focus on the question. It is not a detailed summary of everything you have already written.

Many people had conservative attitudes and still followed Galen's ideas instead of looking for new treatments and explanations for disease.

Start by showing that a range of factors played a role.

Important new discoveries were made by individuals such as Harvey, but they did not lead to new ideas about the causes of disease. This is the key reason why treatments did not improve.

Make it clear which factor you think played the most important role.

Support your argument with your key reason why you have come to this overall judgement.

Overall the discoveries did not change treatments because no one had discovered what really caused disease.

In 1750, people were not living longer and were no healthier than they were 1000 years earlier, but changes in medicine were taking place that were the launch pad for future improvements. This section rapidly sums up those changes, then takes you on a quick tour of the medical breakthroughs that made huge improvements in health and life expectancy. Which of these changes do you think were most important?

5.1 What progress had been made by the 1750s?

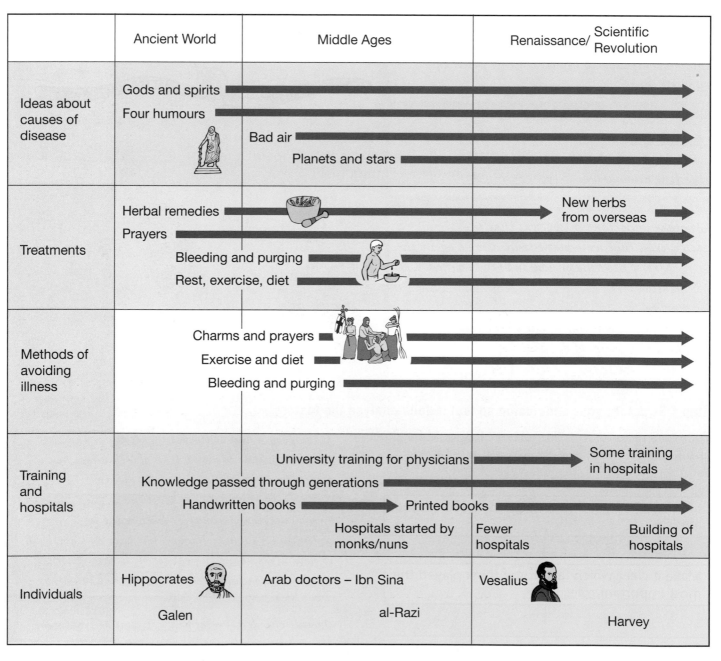

	Ancient World	Middle Ages	Renaissance/ Scientific Revolution
Ideas about causes of disease	Gods and spirits		
	Four humours		
		Bad air	
		Planets and stars	
Treatments	Herbal remedies		New herbs from overseas
	Prayers		
	Bleeding and purging		
	Rest, exercise, diet		
Methods of avoiding illness		Charms and prayers	
		Exercise and diet	
		Bleeding and purging	
Training and hospitals		University training for physicians	Some training in hospitals
	Knowledge passed through generations		
	Handwritten books	Printed books	
		Hospitals started by monks/nuns	Fewer hospitals / Building of hospitals
Individuals	Hippocrates / Galen	Arab doctors – Ibn Sina / al-Razi	Vesalius / Harvey

Activities

1 Life expectancy had not increased since the Middle Ages. Which of the themes in the table opposite is most significant in explaining why life expectancy had not increased?
2 Why were doctors optimistic of further progress in medicine in the late 1700s? Use the illustration below to help you.
3 **Living graph:** Look at the living graphs you began on page 8. Use the details on these pages to make sure they are complete to 1750.

The trouble is they still don't know what causes disease.

Pasteur

Healthier Longer Lives

Beginning of challenges to old ideas. Vesalius showed that Galen could be wrong about anatomy.

Development of scientific method – asking questions and testing hypotheses by observation and experiment. Harvey used this method to discover circulation of the blood.

Doctors increasingly trained to use scientific method, for example William and John Hunter. Beginning of more professional training of doctors in hospital wards.

1500s Renaissance   1600s Scientific Revolution   1700s

5.2 When and why did life expectancy improve after 1750?

Now travel back in time, first to 1848, then to 1935 to find out how medicine changed and how quickly it changed. Which vital discoveries can you see in the pictures on this page and the next?

Activities

1 What evidence can you find in this 1848 picture of continuities in:
   a ideas about the causes of disease
   b treatments
   c training of doctors and nurses?
2 What changes can you see in any aspect of medicine?
3 What adjectives would you use to describe the degree of change between 1665 (see page 66) and 1848?
4 In 1848, the average life expectancy was still only around 40 for men and a few years lower for women. Why do you think it was still so low?

Medical Moments in Time: London, 1848

Hush, Victoria, it's only a graze. I'll bandage it with dropwort and comfrey.

Put honey on it. Mother said honey heals cuts and scrapes.

But will he survive being on the hospital ward?

Some nurses do more harm than good. They get no medical training.

And that is how you amputate a leg. I will discuss this in my lecture tomorrow.

Vaccination saves many children from smallpox. Dr Jenner was the greatest hero in medicine. I do hope science and experiments give us vaccinations against other diseases.

Roll up! Roll Up! Buy the great 'Cure-all tonic'. Two spoonfuls will save you from cholera.

1 What evidence can you find in this 1935 picture of continuities in:
   a ideas about the causes of disease
   b treatments
   c training of doctors and nurses?
2 What changes can you see in any aspect of medicine?
3 What adjectives would you use to describe the degree of change between 1848 and 1935?
4 In 1935, the average life expectancy was just over 50 for men and a few years higher for women. Why do you think life expectancy had improved since 1848?
5 Create your own version of 'Medical Moments in Time' for today. Include:
   a details that show changes since 1935
   b reasons why life expectancy in many parts of Britain has risen to nearly 80
   c any problems that continue to threaten people's health.

Medical Moments in Time: London, 1935

Governments had passed laws saying that
• every town and county had to have a medical officer responsible for safeguarding the health of the people
• everyone received fresh water and had good sewers. All new houses had to have their own toilets.
After the First World War (1914–1918), many slum houses were demolished and new housing was built.

Now then, mothers. This class helps you keep your children healthy. Remember the law says that you must get your children vaccinated. Let's start with keeping your babies clean.

I wish I didn't have to charge for visits and medicines. Many people can't afford to pay so never see a doctor.

But we haven't finished paying him for last time.

Jill's got measles. I'd better call in the doctor.

We have to. The girl down the road got measles and now she's deaf in one ear.

From the early 1900s children could receive free school meals and had medical inspections to check their health.

Don't play out in the cold in bare feet. No wonder they hurt.

Mother used hot turnip mash to treat chilblains. No need for anything else.

What were the key breakthroughs in medicine after 1750?

On pages 86–89 you discovered some of the vital changes in medicine that have led to us living much longer, healthier lives today. This timeline continues the summary timeline you used on page 84.

1 Summarise in your own words the key changes in each of the themes shown in the table.

2 Which of these changes or discoveries do you think was most important – and why? Think about possible links between changes in these themes.

3 **Living graph:** look at the living graphs you began on page 8. Pencil in how you think each graph develops after 1800. You will then check these ideas in later chapters.

	1750	1825
Ideas about causes of disease	Bad air	Germ theory; Spontaneous generation
Treatments	Herbal remedies; Bleeding and purging; Quack remedies	'Cure-alls' – patient medicines
Methods of avoiding illness	Immunisation against smallpox; Vaccination against smallpox; Bleeding and purging; Exercise and diet	
Training and hospitals	Increased training of doctors in hospitals	
Individuals		Jenner; Pasteur; Lister; Nightingale

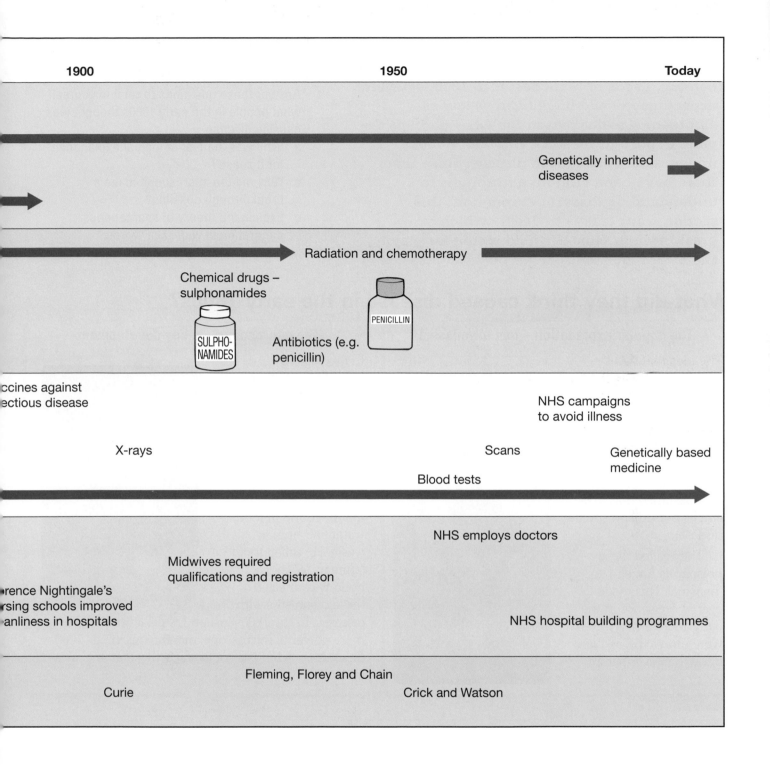

Section 6: Understanding disease – which medical breakthrough deserves the gold medal?

If you had been born into a poor family in London, Leeds or Manchester in 1800, your life expectancy would have been as low as eighteen. A major reason for this – perhaps the most important reason – was that nobody understood what caused disease. Since then, there have been vital breakthroughs in understanding disease. Throughout this section, your task is to decide which breakthrough wins the gold medal for playing the most important part in defeating disease.

Activity

1 Answer these questions to remind yourself what people in the early 1800s thought was causing disease.
   a Why was 'bad air' a logical explanation for disease?
   b Why did the microscope make a breakthrough possible?
   c Explain the theory of spontaneous generation in your own words.

What did they think caused disease in the early 1800s?

The popular explanation – bad air/miasma

The idea that bad air causes diseases had been around for centuries. People could see rotting food and flesh and even faeces in the streets. They knew that this dirt gave off terrible smells and they assumed that these smells caused and spread disease.

They called these poisonous fumes 'miasma'. This made even more sense in the early 1800s when towns were more crowded and filthy than ever before.

Towns are filthier today than ever and the air smells really bad. So it's logical there's more disease than ever before.

The microscope – a key development

In the 1600s a Dutchman, Anthony van Leeuwenhoek, made a microscope that magnified things by 300 times. He wrote descriptions of what he saw, including tiny living organisms that he found in food, water and human waste. He called them 'animacules' but nobody connected these organisms with diseases. In the 1800s Joseph Lister developed a much more powerful microscope, magnifying things 1000 times. Now scientists could study these 'animacules' in detail.

The latest theory – spontaneous generation

Scientists used the new microscopes to study the micro-organisms (which we call bacteria or germs) on rotting food and tried to work out where these organisms were coming from. They decided that the organisms were spontaneously (automatically) generated (created) by the process of decay in, for example, meat and then the organisms spread disease. This was the theory of spontaneous generation.

As this meat decays the organisms appear. So they must be generated by the process of decay.

Activities

2 Work in pairs on one of these discoveries. You have **one minute** to explain to the rest of the class why it was so important. Include briefly:

  a what the discovery was and who made it

  b what it led to.

3 Can you see evidence of the impact of any of the factors on page 11?

The key breakthroughs in the fight against disease

1. The development of vaccinations

Who did what?
In 1798, Edward Jenner proved that vaccination prevented people catching smallpox, one of the great killer diseases. Jenner's work was based on observation and scientific experiment. However, he did not understand what caused smallpox or exactly how vaccination worked.

Why was it important?
This discovery saved many thousands of lives in Britain and millions world-wide. Eventually, vaccination led to smallpox being wiped out world-wide.

2. Germ theory

Who did what?
Louis Pasteur published his 'germ theory' in 1861. He had carried out experiments to prove that bacteria (also called microbes or germs) make milk and beer go bad and that bacteria cause diseases in animals. His theory was that germs also cause human diseases. In 1864, his experiments convinced other scientists that this theory was correct.

Why was it important?
Bacteria (microbes) are the true cause of diseases, so Pasteur's theory put an end to all other ideas, such as bad air and spontaneous generation. Now scientists could build on this theory to find out which individual bacteria cause individual diseases.

3. The identification of bacteria that cause individual diseases

Who did what?
In the 1870s, Robert Koch and his research made the first discovery of a bacterium that causes an individual human disease – tuberculosis.

Why was it important?
Koch's methods were copied by other scientists, who discovered the bacteria that cause other diseases. Once they had identified the bacteria they could develop vaccines to prevent people getting diseases. Tuberculosis, for example, killed many thousands of people each year.

4. The discovery of DNA

Who did what?
In 1953, Francis Crick and James Watson discovered the structure of human DNA and how it is passed on from parents to children. In the 1990s, the Human Genome Project, a world-wide project, began working out exactly how each part of human DNA affects the human body.

Why was it important?
These discoveries have led to treatments for diseases which have genetic causes rather than being caused by bacteria. These include some cancers. Until the discovery of DNA, these illnesses were untreatable. Further discoveries using DNA will be made in the future.

Which breakthrough deserves the gold medal?

Activities

Now you know a little about the four major breakthroughs in the story of fighting disease. You can see them again opposite awaiting the award of the gold medal for Most Significant Breakthrough. Your task is to decide which breakthrough deserves the gold medal.

1 What initial ideas do you have about which breakthrough was most significant after reading page 97?

2 **Significance table:** Use the case studies on pages 96–105 to build up your knowledge of each breakthrough. Complete the table below with evidence of the significance of each breakthrough.

3 After completing your research, make your decision, then:

   a summarise your findings on your own version of the gold medal

   b on the reverse of your copy of the medal, summarise the key factors which helped in this breakthrough.

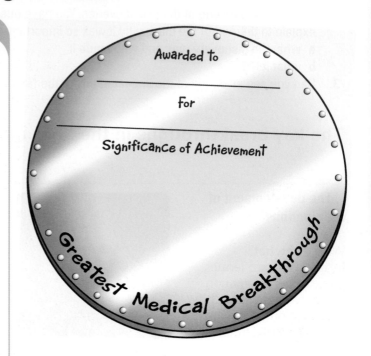

Awarded to

_____

For

_____

Significance of Achievement

Greatest Medical Breakthrough

Criteria for judging significance – award up to 3 marks for each criterion	Vaccination (Jenner)	Germ theory (Pasteur)	Identifying bacteria (Koch)	DNA (Crick and Watson)
Changing ideas a Which problem or gap in understanding did this breakthrough solve? b How important was this breakthrough in changing thinking about disease?				
Stimulating other discoveries Did this discovery lead to other important developments in fighting diseases?				
Wider consequences Did this discovery lead to improvements in other areas of medicine?				
Overall significance Total marks				

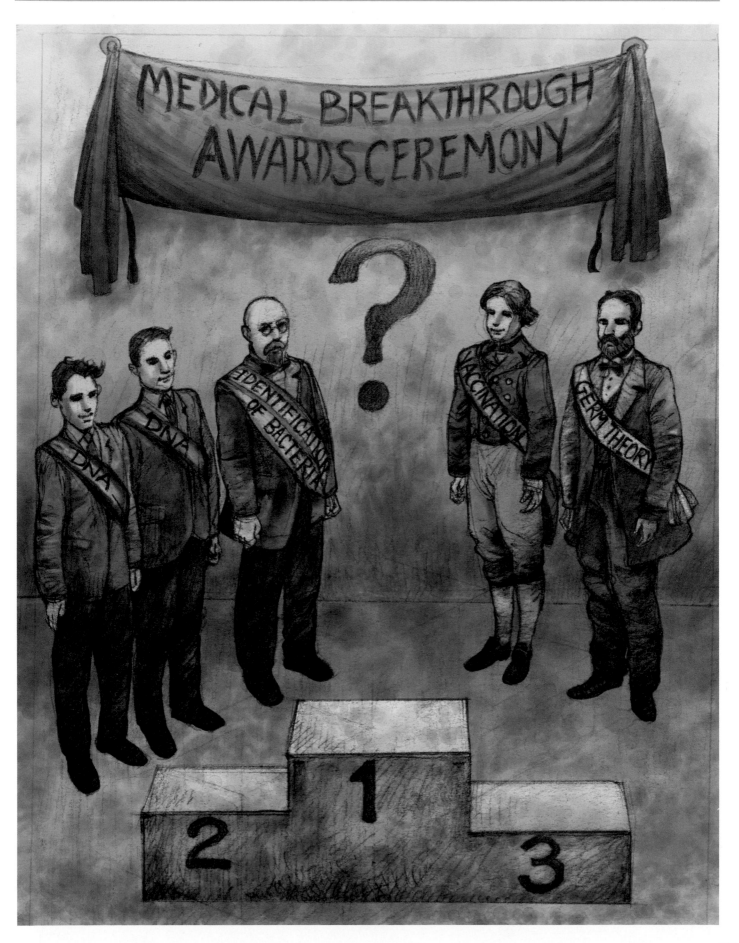

Breakthrough 1: Vaccination – the work of Edward Jenner

Source 1

An extract from a letter written by Thomas Jefferson, President of the USA, to Dr Edward Jenner, a Gloucestershire doctor, in 1808:

'Sir, I avail myself of rendering you a portion of the tribute of gratitude due to you from the whole human family. Medicine has never before produced any single improvement of such utility. Harvey's discovery of the circulation of the blood was a beautiful addition to our knowledge, but on a review of the practice of medicine before and since, I do not see any great amelioration which has been derived from that discovery. You have erased from the calendar of human afflictions one of its greatest. Yours is the comfortable reflection that mankind can never forget that you have lived. Future nations will know by history only that the loathsome small-pox has existed and by you has been extirpated.'

Smallpox – the story before Jenner and vaccination

1 Smallpox killed more children than any other disease in the 1700s. Survivors were often severely disfigured by scars from the scabs that formed on the skin.

2 Lady Mary Wortley Montagu had watched inoculation carried out in Turkey. This involved spreading pus from a smallpox pustule into a cut in the skin of a healthy person. If the person was lucky they got a mild dose of smallpox and did not catch it again because their body had developed antibodies against smallpox – although they did not know this. During a smallpox epidemic in England, she had her daughter inoculated in front of important doctors and the method rapidly became popular.

3 Inoculation became big business. Robert and Daniel Sutton became very wealthy by carrying out many thousands of inoculations, charging up to £20 per patient.

4 However, there were problems with inoculation:

   a The person inoculated could get a strong dose of smallpox and die.

   b The person inoculated could pass smallpox onto someone else.

   c Most people could not afford inoculation so were not protected.

Activities

1 Why did President Jefferson believe that Jenner's discovery was so important?

2 Why had inoculation **not** solved the problem of smallpox?

3 a How did Jenner prove that vaccination prevented smallpox?

   b What had he learned from John Hunter that was so important?

Edward Jenner (1749–1823)

- Aged 13 apprenticed to a surgeon for six years. Aged 21 studied with John Hunter in London, the greatest surgeon of the time. Hunter taught his students to observe carefully and make their own experiments to increase their medical knowledge, instead of just relying on knowledge in books.

- 1772 began work aged 23 in Berkeley, Gloucestershire as a country doctor, but kept in touch with Hunter about medical developments.

- 1798 published his book *An enquiry into the causes and effects of Variola Vaccinae, known by the name of cowpox*. This showed that vaccination could save people from catching smallpox.

Jenner's discovery

A handful of doctors had realised that milkmaids who caught the mild disease of cowpox never got smallpox. Some had even deliberately infected themselves and others with cowpox. However, they had not made this method widely known nor tested the idea scientifically. Jenner had long known this theory and kept it in mind, thinking about how to test and prove it. In the 1790s, he carried out experiments to test the theory, observing and recording all the details carefully (see Source 2). In 1798, he published his book describing vaccination and presenting his evidence, describing 23 different cases to prove the theory. He called this method 'vaccination' because the Latin word for cow is *vacca*. The discovery saved many thousands of lives in Britain and millions world-wide.

Source 2

Extracts from Dr Jenner's casebook, published in 1798:

Case 16

'Sarah Nelmes, a dairy maid, was infected with cowpox from her master's cows in May 1796. A large sore and the usual symptoms were produced.'

Case 17 James Phipps

'I selected a healthy boy about 8 years old. The matter was taken from the cowpox sore on Sarah Nelmes' hand and inserted on 14 May 1796 into the boy by two cuts each half an inch long. On the seventh day he complained of uneasiness, on the ninth he became a little chilly, lost his appetite and had a slight headache and spent the night with some degree of restlessness but on the following day he was perfectly well.

In order to ascertain that the boy was secure from the contagion of smallpox he was inoculated with smallpox matter but no disease followed. Several months later he was again inoculated with smallpox matter but again no disease followed.'

How did Jenner develop and spread the use of vaccination?

Attitudes – Enquiry:
Jenner, following Hunter's advice, tested the connection between cowpox and smallpox in experiments, collecting evidence carefully as proof that catching cowpox really did protect people against smallpox.

Government:
In 1802 and 1807, Parliament gave Jenner £30,000 to develop his work on vaccination. Fifty years later, in 1852, vaccination was made compulsory in Britain, helping to cause a huge drop in smallpox cases.

Individuals:
Jenner had the insight to realise that the link between cowpox and smallpox was important and the determination to carry on and publish his research despite opposition and criticism.

Communications:
In 1798, Jenner published his own account of his discovery, spreading the details of his method worldwide.

Activities

1 **Significance table:** Complete your table from page 94 for vaccination, using these questions to help you:
   a Did vaccination lead to methods of preventing any other diseases than smallpox?
   b Why did vaccination against smallpox not lead directly to other discoveries?
   c What do you think was the most important consequence of the development of vaccination?
2 Look at Source 1. What does it tell you about:
   a people's attitudes to vaccination
   b the government's attitude to making vaccination compulsory?
3 Look at the reasons for opposition. Which reasons do you think explain why ordinary people did not have their children vaccinated?
4 What answers can you suggest to the questions around Source 2?
5 Who or what is the 'curse of humankind'? and what is the artist's attitude to vaccination?

The impact of vaccination – stepping stones to the future

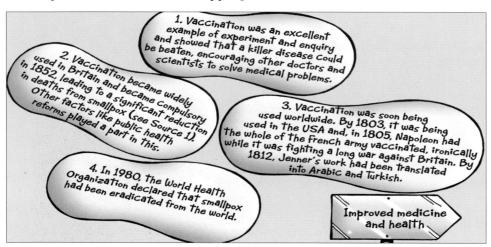

But ...

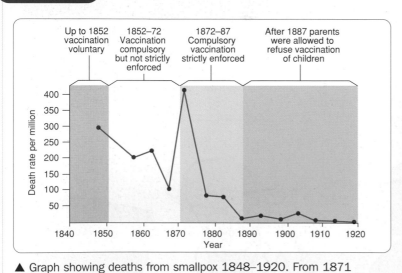

▲ Graph showing deaths from smallpox 1848–1920. From 1871 people were fined for not having their children vaccinated.

1 Jenner's use of vaccination only dealt with one disease. There were many more infectious diseases, such as cholera and typhoid, which were killing thousands in epidemics.

2 Pasteur did not publish his germ theory until 1859, so Jenner did not know that bacteria cause disease. This meant that he did not know exactly how vaccination worked. Therefore, it was not possible to learn from this discovery how to prevent the spread of other diseases.

3 Many people opposed vaccination. An anti-vaccine league was formed in 1866.

4 Governments could not decide whether they wished to force people to vaccinate their children. Source 1 shows the changes in laws about vaccination being compulsory.

Why was there opposition to vaccination?

1 It's against God's laws to give people an animal disease.

2 Smallpox is a punishment for sin. The only cure is prayer and living a godly life.

3 It will cost us inoculators our jobs and profits.

4 The Royal Society says this idea is too revolutionary. They refused to publish Jenner's book.

5 I've never heard of Jenner – why should we believe a country doctor?

6 These vaccinators are clumsy. They do it in a rush and it doesn't always work.

7 I've got enough to worry about finding work and food. I don't have time to have my children vaccinated.

8 The government shouldn't interfere. It's got no right to fine people who don't get their children vaccinated.

What work did these three men do?

What are they talking about?

Why is 'milk of human kindness' written on here?

Who is the man in the black coat?

What is the angel doing?

Source 2

What are they holding and what is written on them? Why is it written on them?

Who are the people in the background and on the ground?

The roll of paper says 'Bill to …' – what is this?

Explain what he's saying in your own words.

▲ 'The Curse of Humankind', drawn by Isaac Cruikshank in 1808.

Breakthroughs 2 and 3: Germ theory and the hunt for microbes – the work of Pasteur and Koch

Activity

This page deals with two breakthroughs because they were closely connected. Although Pasteur and Koch were great rivals, their work was closely linked because first one man made a discovery, then the other built on that discovery to make another.

Significance table: Complete your table from page 94 for these two breakthroughs, using these questions to help you:

a   Why was Pasteur's germ theory such a special event in medical history? (Stage 1)

b   What did Koch discover that Pasteur had not? (Stage 2)

c   Why was it possible to develop vaccines against a range of diseases in the 1880s when Jenner's work had not led to the development of other vaccines? (Stage 3)

You will find more information for your table on pages 102–103.

Louis Pasteur (1822–1895)

Born in France, Pasteur was a university scientist, not a doctor. He loved to demonstrate his experiments in public, especially if he could show that he was right and someone else was wrong. He was also a hugely determined man. He suffered a stroke in 1868 and was paralysed down the left side of his body, but kept working and went on to make some of his greatest discoveries.

◀ Pasteur in his laboratory. Although he is alone, he actually worked with a team of research scientists. Which vital piece of equipment is shown?

Stage 1: Pasteur's germ theory

Pasteur developed his theory while working for industries in France. His experiments suggested that beer, wine and milk were going sour because of microbes (which we also call bacteria or germs) in the air. From this he suggested that microbes were also the causes of diseases. He published his germ theory in 1861 and three years later carried out a series of experiments that convinced scientists that his germ theory was correct.

So, for the first time in history, scientists and doctors knew the true cause of disease – in general. But they did not know exactly which microbes were causing which diseases. In 1865, the death of Pasteur's young daughter and an outbreak of cholera led him to investigate human diseases. He took samples of air from a cholera ward but under his microscope he could only see a confused mass of bacteria. He could not discover which one was causing cholera.

It's OK. He knows we're here but he can't tell which of us is causing cholera.

Robert Koch (1843–1910)

Born in Germany, Koch was a doctor who became interested in Pasteur's work and began to study bacteria himself. He was just as brilliant as Pasteur at detailed laboratory work with a team of assistants. They saw each other as rivals after the war between France and Germany in 1870–1871. Both men wanted to be successful to glorify their countries.

▲ A cartoon from the 1870s showing Koch slaying the bacterium that causes tuberculosis.

You've got me! I give in. I'm the one that causes anthrax.

Stage 2: Robert Koch – microbe hunter!

Koch set out to find the specific microbe or bacterium that was causing an individual disease. He succeeded when he investigated anthrax, a disease common in animals that could also infect people. This was the first time anyone had identified the specific microbe that causes an individual disease.

Next, Koch investigated tuberculosis and in 1882 found a way of staining the microbe causing the disease so that it stood out under a microscope from other microbes. This breakthrough was important because now other scientists could use this method. They quickly found the microbes causing these diseases:

1882 Typhoid

1883 Cholera

1886 Pneumonia

1887 Meningitis

1894 Plague

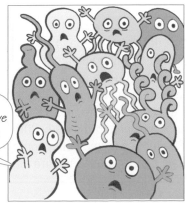

There's nowhere to hide any more. You've got us. We surrender.

Stage 3: Pasteur and the development of vaccines

Jenner's use of vaccination
Pasteur's germ theory
Koch's work identifying microbes causing individual diseases

↓

Pasteur develops the first new vaccines since Jenner's vaccine against smallpox

Koch's work identifying microbes didn't save people's lives by itself. What were needed were more vaccines to give people weak doses of diseases to build up their immunity. Pasteur knew all about Jenner's work and that Jenner had not known exactly why vaccination worked. However, now that Pasteur knew that microbes caused diseases he carried out experiments to find more vaccines. He developed vaccines to prevent anthrax and chicken cholera in animals. Next, he investigated rabies, testing his vaccine on dogs and then, in 1885, on Joseph Meister, a boy who had been bitten by a rabid dog. Pasteur gave Joseph 13 injections over a two-week period. Joseph survived.

Other scientists developed vaccines to prevent other diseases. Their successes included:

1896 Typhoid

1906 Tuberculosis

1913 Diphtheria

1927 Tetanus

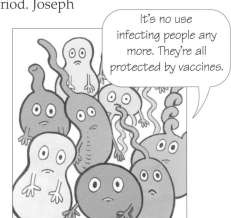

It's no use infecting people any more. They're all protected by vaccines.

Why were germ theory and the identification of microbes so important?

Activities

1. Work in pairs. Your teacher will allocate you one of the topics on this page. When your topic is called you have 45 seconds to explain how your topic is linked to either germ theory or Koch's identification of bacteria – or both.

2. **Significance table:** Now complete your table for these two breakthroughs.

Germ theory

Pasteur convinced other scientists that diseases are caused by microbes (also called bacteria or germs).

Identifying bacteria

Koch was the first scientist to identify specific microbes that caused individual diseases.

Antibiotic medicines

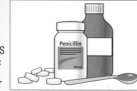

Antibiotics are cures that use one kind of microbe to kill other microbes that are causing illness. The first antibiotic medicine was penicillin, which was first widely used in the 1940s (see page 120).

Vaccines

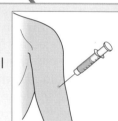

Once scientists had identified the microbes causing individual diseases, they could create vaccines using weakened microbes. These vaccines prevented people catching the disease. The development of vaccines began with an anti-rabies vaccine in 1885 and continued for many years. A vaccine against polio, for example, was developed in the 1950s (see page 117).

Magic bullets

'Magic bullets' are chemical drugs that destroy bacteria in the body without harming human tissue. Once bacteria had been identified scientists began looking for chemicals that would destroy them. The first 'magic bullet' (Salvarsan 606) was developed in the early 20th century. In the 1930s Prontosil, a magic bullet containing sulphonamides, was used to cure blood poisoning.

Public health

During the early nineteenth century, there was a lot of controversy about whether governments should force local councils to improve public health facilities by providing cleaner water, sewerage systems, etc. Part of the reason for the controversy was the uncertainty about what really caused disease. Pasteur's germ theory clearly linked disease to microbes bred by dirt and living in water supplies, so this gave campaigners a scientific argument to demand change. The result was the 1875 Public Health Act that forced councils to improve public health (see page 161).

Antiseptic surgery

Many surgeons had carried out operations in dirty coats, with instruments that had been used before and not cleaned, and on old tables. Nobody linked these conditions to the high death-rate after surgery. However, once Pasteur's germ theory was known surgeons, led by Joseph Lister, realised that they needed to get rid of microbes from operating theatres. This led to many more patients surviving operations because they no longer caught infections during operations.

Cleaner hospitals

Until the late 1800s, people preferred to stay at home if they were ill (and even if they needed an operation) rather than go to hospital. Many hospitals were dirty. Florence Nightingale began the movement to clean up hospitals before Pasteur published his germ theory, but the campaign won a lot of support after its publication because people now believed there was a clear link between dirt and disease (see pages 130–131).

Training of doctors and nurses

Now that people understood the cause of disease, training needed to change to include Pasteur's work and to examine its effects on all aspects of medical care.

More investment in science

Pasteur had shown how important science could be in improving health and saving lives. Governments began to invest more money in training scientists and purchasing top quality equipment.

Higher life expectancy

In the hundred years after Pasteur's germ theory, average life expectancy increased from about 45 to 70 – the first significant, long-term increase in life expectancy in history.

Breakthrough 4: DNA – the work of Crick and Watson

In the same week this page was written, two medical stories hit the headlines. One was about finding a way to help people paralysed in accidents to walk again. The other was about giving the newly-blind back their sight. Both possibilities still have a long way to go before they become fact, but they are both the result of one discovery – the discovery of the structure of DNA.

DNA stands for deoxyribonucleic acid, but you do not need to remember that – just talk and write about DNA. And you don't need to understand how DNA works or learn a list of scientific terms. We are interested in:

- Causes: How the structure of DNA was discovered.
- Significance: Why these discoveries are so important.

Turning point 1 – Discovering the structure of DNA

DNA wasn't 'discovered' in one brilliant experiment. It took a series of discoveries over a long period. In the 1800s, scientists knew DNA existed and that it somehow controlled what we are like. However, they did not know how it did this.

The first step came in 1953 when two scientists in Cambridge, Francis Crick and James Watson, discovered the structure of DNA illustrated on the right. They proved that this DNA structure was present in every human cell and showed how it passed on information from parents to children. This was the launch pad for further discoveries.

Turning point 2 – Mapping the human genome

The complete set of genes in a living creature is called a genome. In 1986, the Human Genome Project began to identify the exact purpose of each of the genes in the human body, compiling a complete map of human DNA. The task was completed in 2001, fifteen years later.

This research was so complicated it needed teams of scientists in eighteen countries to take part, including the USA, Britain, Japan, France and Canada. Each team worked on a different part of human DNA. This work could not have been done before computers. The information carried in human DNA would fill 80,000 books the size of this one, but the electronic equivalent can be passed around the world instantly via the internet.

What is DNA?

- Inside every cell of your body are several identical strings of DNA.
- A tiny part of your DNA looks like this:

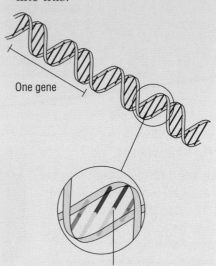

One gene

The structure of DNA is a double helix – a pair of interlocking spirals. They are joined by 'bases', set in pairs, which are like the rungs of a ladder.

- Think of DNA as a long list of instructions like a computer program that operate every cell of your body. There are more than 3000 million letters of code in your body's program.
- These instructions are grouped together into sets of instructions called genes.
- Each gene has a different function. Some decide your eye colour, some how much hair you have, some whether you will develop a disease or disability.
- Everybody's DNA carries slightly different instructions – which is why human beings are all different.

Why was the structure of DNA discovered in 1953?

Activities

1 Draw a diagram with four boxes like the ones below.
2 Read the information in the diagram and decide on a suitable 'factor' heading for each box. Use the factors on page 11 to help you.
3 Write your own summary in each box of your diagram, explaining how each factor helped to make this discovery.

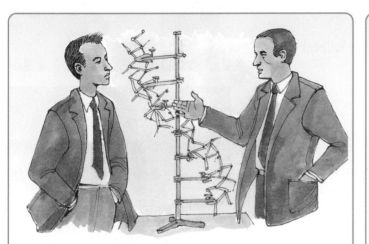

Francis Crick and James Watson were great scientists, and very adventurous in their ideas. They tried out ideas and methods other scientists did not try.

Crick and Watson did not work alone. They had help from a team of scientists with a wide range of skills and knowledge. Maurice Wilkins was an expert in X-ray photography. Rosalind Franklin developed a technique to photograph a single strand of DNA and was the first person to take X-ray photographs of DNA.

Why was the structure of DNA discovered in 1953?

Crick and Watson had the latest and best equipment, using new technologies such as X-ray photography and improved microscopes. They also built on new knowledge in other types of science, such as genetics and biochemistry.

Their research was very expensive because of the cost of complex equipment and the number of highly skilled people involved. Most of the money came from the government, but industries also made a contribution.

Why is DNA so important?

What has the discovery of DNA got to do with Superman?

In 1995, the actor Christopher Reeve, known world-wide as Superman, was paralysed after a riding accident. For the rest of his life (he died of a heart attack in 2004 at the age of 52) he was confined to a wheelchair. From his wheelchair, he campaigned for scientists to have the right to develop research to help people who are paralysed. In particular, he campaigned to support the use of stem-cell research (see opposite) which is one of the scientific developments that has followed on from the discovery of DNA.

To understand the importance of DNA in medicine, it's helpful to compare this discovery with Pasteur's germ theory.

Comparing germ theory and DNA as breakthroughs

In the hundred years after Pasteur's germ theory, average life expectancy increased from about 45 to 70 – the first significant, long-term increase in life expectancy in history. Germ theory affected medicine in all kinds of ways (see pages 102–103), but only helped doctors and scientists to deal with illnesses caused by bacteria. Many illnesses have genetic causes, i.e. they are inherited in the sufferer's genes. These include:

- some forms of cancer
- diabetes
- Down's syndrome
- cystic fibrosis
- Parkinson's disease
- Alzheimer's disease.

Other problems, such as paralysis or some cases of blindness, are caused, for example, by accidents.

Work on DNA holds out the hope that scientists can find ways of helping sufferers from these and many more genetic illnesses and help people paralysed in accidents.

That is why the discovery of DNA may turn out to be an even more important breakthrough than Pasteur's germ theory.

▲ The actor and activist Christopher Reeve campaigned for the use of stem-cell research.

Activities

1 **Significance table:** Complete your table from page 94 for DNA.
2 During the week that you cover this topic look at a news site such as http://news.bbc.co.uk.
   a Which medical developments linked to DNA are being reported and what benefits might they lead to?
   b Are any moral or ethical issues mentioned in relation to the developments? If so, what are they and how important are they?
   c Do these debates about using new medical methods remind you of any past breakthroughs? What are the similarities and differences?

How could research on DNA affect health and medicine?

There are lots of 'mays' and 'mights' here. This is because we are still at the beginning of the DNA revolution, even if there have been headlines about 'breakthroughs' for the past several years. We do not know where these discoveries will lead. Remember – when Pasteur developed his germ theory, scientists did not know exactly what it would lead to. It took many years for the full impact to be clear. We cannot say for sure what these DNA discoveries will lead to – even in five years' time, let alone a hundred!

However, here are some of the possibilities:

Gene therapy – using genes from healthy people to cure the sick

Research has shown that some diseases and disabilities, such as cystic fibrosis, Huntington's chorea, sickle-cell anaemia and muscular dystrophy are caused by a single abnormal gene passed from parents to child. Gene therapy would take normal genes from a donor and put them into the DNA of someone suffering from one of these illnesses.

One approach to this is to use 'stem cells' from embryos. In 2009, the possibility of trialling the use of such cells became headline news. Trials investigated whether one type of cell could reverse a common form of blindness. Another cell could be used to re-grow damaged nerves and restore movement to people paralysed in accidents. However, there is a major ethical debate about this stem-cell research because the process of taking the cells from the embryos usually kills the embryos.

Customised drugs – creating drugs to cure one person's particular health problem

Drug treatments of the future could be designed to deal with a particular gene in a particular person. These 'custom drugs' would be less haphazard than at present where the same drug is given to millions of different people regardless of their genetic make-up.

Understanding DNA could lead to …

Genetic engineering – choosing the nature of a child

Genetic modification of plants is already happening. For example, a gene from drought-resistant wheat can be added to the DNA of high-yielding wheat to make a new variety of wheat that produces lots of grain, even in dry conditions. In theory, the same techniques could be used to produce more perfect human beings – with parents being able to 'design' their children: not only their gender, but also their appearance, and intellectual ability.

Genetic screening or testing – identifying the illnesses people could suffer from and preventing them

If doctors know the exact gene responsible for medical conditions, they can test or screen patients as part of preventive medicine. For example, they can spot who is likely to get cancer and help them to avoid activities that might trigger the cancer to start. This is already done to check unborn babies for possible conditions such as Down's syndrome. This, however, raises one important ethical question – if an embryo is found to be carrying a gene that's linked to a major disability, is that justification for the embryo to be aborted?

This Exam Buster contains important advice on questions that ask you to evaluate the importance of an individual, event or discovery. It models how to approach a question that requires you to evaluate the importance of Pasteur's germ theory for preventing disease. However, you can use this advice to analyse the importance of any discovery and we have suggested some further practice questions on page 109.

Look at the question below:

---

*7 How important for the prevention of disease in Britain was the discovery of the germ theory? Explain your answer. **[16 marks]**

(Total for spelling, punctuation and grammar = 3 marks)

(Total for Question 7 = 19 marks)

Tip 1: Decode the question and stick to the content focus of the question.

It is very important that you decode the question carefully so that your answer is focused on the question. Use the advice on decoding questions on page 36 to help you. Note that the content focus of the question is on the impact the discovery had on the **prevention of disease**.

Tip 2: Prove the event was important.

Note the question type. You are not being asked to describe how Pasteur produced the germ theory, you are being asked to evaluate how important this discovery was. The main focus must be on:

- how the discovery changed the way that people in Britain tried to prevent disease
- how the discovery led to other breakthroughs
- any limitations of the discovery, for example how the germ theory needed to be built on by other people to make a practical difference.

Proving a discovery or individual was important – the keys to success

There are two things that you need to do in order to prove that an event was important.

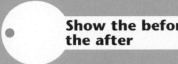

Show the before as well as the after

Show how, before Pasteur's germ theory, our understanding of the causes of disease was limited and this made it difficult to prevent disease.

> BEFORE Pasteur's germ theory people believed that ...
>
> Louis Pasteur published his 'germ theory' in 1861. His theory was that ...
>
> Pasteur's experiments convinced other scientists that this theory was correct. The germ theory was a crucial turning point. It <u>meant that</u> for the first time in history scientists and doctors knew the true cause of disease.

Show what it led to

Show how a better understanding of the cause of disease led to real breakthroughs in the battle to prevent disease. Give specific examples to prove your case.

> Pasteur's germ theory was important because once scientists knew what caused disease they could develop vaccines to prevent people getting diseases. For example ...
>
> The germ theory also led to cleaner hospitals because ...
>
> Once Pasteur's germ theory was known surgeons, led by Joseph Lister, realised that they needed to get rid of microbes from operating theatres. This led to ...
>
> Public health was also improved as Pasteur's theory gave campaigners evidence to support their demand for change. A number of important changes took place including ...

Activity

Work in groups. Use the advice provided to answer the practice questions.

Take one question each and produce a draft answer. Then check each other's work carefully.

- Does the answer focus on the question? Remember some questions may ask you to focus on a specific area of medicine.
- Is there a sense of before and after (in order to show how the individual or event **changed** medicine)?
- Does the answer show what the discovery led to?
- Does the answer evaluate the limitations of the discovery?

Provide feedback to each other and improve each draft answer.

Practice questions

- How important for the understanding and prevention of disease in England was the discovery of DNA in 1953?
- How important for the prevention of disease in England was the discovery of a smallpox vaccination in 1796?
- How important for the treatment of disease in England was the discovery of penicillin in 1928?

To do well in your GCSE History exam you need to be able to use visual and written sources effectively. The first question on the paper will usually be an inference question based on two sources, like the one below.

What do Sources A and B show about changes in people's understanding of the causes of disease in England?

Explain your answer, using Sources A and B and your own knowledge.

[8 marks]

Source A

This chart from the Middle Ages is called a Zodiac Man. It gave details about when each part of the body was affected by the planets and the stars. If the stars told the surgeon not to bleed the patient in that area, then he would not do so for fear of causing death.

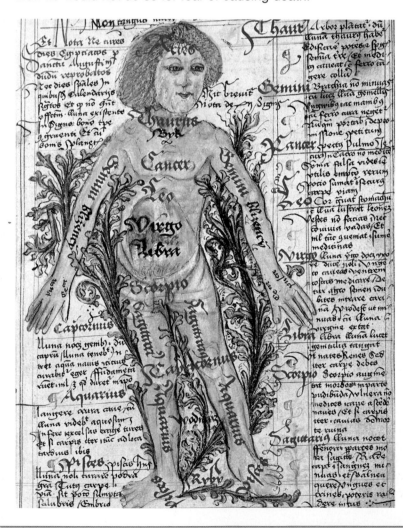

Source B

From Pasteur's lecture at the University of Paris, 1864.

'What difference is there between my two flasks? They contain the same liquid, they both contain air, both are open. Why does one decay and the other remain pure? The difference is that in the first one the germs can fall into the flask. In the second flask it is impossible. The dusts in the air and their germs fall on its curved neck.'

Developing your inference skills

To get high marks, you must do more than simply summarise what each source says.

- You need to use the sources and your own knowledge to explain how ideas about the causes of disease changed between the Middle Ages and the nineteenth century.
- You need to support your explanation with details from **both sources**.
- You must also include additional information from your **own knowledge of both periods.**

Step 1

Identify the clues in both sources that can help you answer the question.

Start with what each source tells you …

> Source A tells us that in the Middle Ages they believed that the planets and the stars affected the body.
>
> Source B tells us that by the second half of the nineteenth century Pasteur was able to prove that germs caused decay. It also tells us that they carried out experiments.

Step 2

Use your knowledge of the topic to go beyond the obvious clues and explain what each source shows us about peoples' understanding of disease in that particular time period. You also need to **add extra information from your own knowledge** of the period. Place the sources in their historical context. For example, explain that Source B reflects how, at the time of Pasteur's discovery, people were thinking scientifically and carrying out experiments.

> Source A tells us that in the Middle Ages they believed that the planets and the stars affected the body. This reflects how people at that time were superstitious. During the Middle Ages people were not thinking scientifically about the causes of disease. They developed theories about the cause of diseases based on superstition and religion. For example, many people at the time thought that disease was a punishment from God.
>
> Source B tells us that in 1864 Pasteur was carrying out experiments to show that germs caused decay. This …

Remember …

Stick to the focus of the question

- There is no need to evaluate how trustworthy the source or the limitations of the source. If you stray from the question you will waste valuable time and pick up no extra marks.
- Stick to the content focus of the question. It is on how peoples' understanding of disease changed. You do not need to explain how the Germ Theory was discovered or provide a detailed description of medicine in the Middle Ages.

Activity

Finish the answer that has been started for you. Make sure you place the source in its historical context. **Use your own knowledge** of the period to explain how ideas about the causes of disease changed as a result of Pasteur's discovery.

You already know that medicine has changed dramatically since 1750. Vaccinations, antibiotics and X-rays are just some of the things that our ancestors would have thought of as miracles. This section begins by taking you back to the treatments your great, great-grandparents used and then sets you off on a factor hunt to decide which factors played the biggest part in transforming treatments and prevention.

7.1 Were home remedies changing?

Source 1

A disagreement between doctor and patient described in F.B. Smith, *The People's Health*, 1971 (Holloway's ointments were 'cure-all' medicines – see opposite):

'The man who came to see Dr Strachan of Clackmannan, Scotland in 1861 was one of many poor patients who were suffering from leg ulcers. We now know that this, with typhus, is a classic indication of poor diet and hygiene. The doctor recorded that his patient "had been at many doctors, and had tried all the Holloway's ointments and other infallible remedies".

The doctor examined him and "with great difficulty ... got him a larger allowance from the poor's funds, and some of his friends assisted him ... As soon as the man's system got into good condition the ulcers began to heal and ... the poor man was restored and fitted for his work."

When the man next met Dr Strachan he informed the doctor that he was getting on very well. "Well doctor, I tell you what it was that cured my legs, and it will be useful to other folk. It was just moose wels [spiders' webs]. Jenny Donald advised me to try them, and they cured my legs at once."

Activities

1 a How did the doctor and patient disagree about the reason for his recovery?
   b What does this tell you about ordinary people's attitudes to treatments in the 1860s?
2 Why might doctors be surprised to discover that remedies such as spiders' webs were still being used? (Think about the discoveries in Section 6.)
3 Why do you think spiders' webs and the remedies in Source 2 were still being used?

Domestic medicine

Many illnesses were treated at home, as they had been for centuries. Home care still mainly involved providing comfort, food and warmth – so long as the family could afford them. Home carers also used treatments such as herbal remedies (which had been passed from generation to generation because they did help the sick) that they had learned from their ancestors or which had been published in early medical books.

One new development was the introduction of thermometers, which helped home carers make simple diagnoses.

Source 2

Some traditional home remedies used in the nineteenth century:

a For influenza, either mix ginger into a drink of tea or mix half a pound of treacle with half a pint of vinegar and three teaspoonfuls of laudanum. Take three times a day.

b To cure tuberculosis, breathe into a freshly-made hole in the turf or try the breath of stallions and cows.

c To cure smallpox, apply cool boiled turnips to the feet or make a drink out of ground ivy.

Patent medicines in the 1800s

If home remedies did not work, people could visit quack doctors or shops where they could buy 'patent' medicines, often known as 'cure–alls'. Patent medicines were big business. Between 1850 and 1900, sales of patent medicines increased by 400 per cent, largely thanks to massive advertising campaigns by the manufacturer. One of the best known was James Morison (1770–1840) who started manufacturing his Vegetable Universal Medicines in 1825. They were made of lard, wax, turpentine, soap and ginger. They had no ingredient that would cure infections or illnesses, but Morison claimed that the pills could cure everything from fever, scarlatina, tuberculosis, smallpox and measles to the effects of old age. By 1834, Morison was selling over one million boxes of pills a year throughout Europe and the British Empire. Another highly successful manufacturer of patent medicines was Thomas Holloway, as you can see below:

Patent medicines did not come under any government control until the 1880s, so false claims about their effectiveness could be made without any fear of prosecution.

Thomas Holloway's pills contained ginger, soap and aloes, a very powerful purgative, until a court case against him in the 1860s.

There was also no control over the manufacturing standards or the ingredients in the medicines – some of which werepositively dangerous.

Afterwards they contained milder ingredients – lard, wax and turpentine – but they still claimed to cure all illnesses.

Deaths and illnesses resulting from overdoses and addiction were common when some patent medicines were taken regularly.

In the 1880s, governments introduced laws controlling the marketing of patent medicines. By 1900, most of the harmful ingredients had been removed.

Holloway became a multi-millionaire, using some of his money to pay for the setting up of Royal Holloway College, part of the University of London.

Activities

4 Why were Morison and Holloway so successful in selling huge quantities of their 'cure-all' pills?

5 What does their success tell you about the effectiveness of reatments from trained doctors in the mid-1800s?

7.2 What have been the key changes in treating and preventing disease?

Activities

1   On your own copy of this timeline, pencil in when you think the following began to be used:
    a   vaccination against smallpox
    b   vaccination against polio
    c   antibiotic medicines
    d   X-rays
    e   radiotherapy.
2   Now check your answers with the information on pages 90–91 and 116–123 and add to your timeline at least three more new methods of treating or preventing illness.

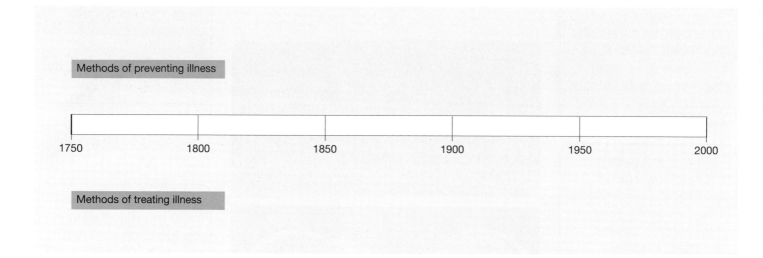

Methods of preventing illness

| 1750 | 1800 | 1850 | 1900 | 1950 | 2000 |

Methods of treating illness

Why did these changes happen?

Now you have a good knowledge of the changes that have taken place – but why have they happened? You are going to investigate the impact of the factors on then right. Before you begin, it's worth thinking about which factors you expect to be most important.

Activities

3   Work with a partner. Which two factors do you think played the biggest part in the changes on your timeline?
4   Why have you chosen these two factors?

The factor hunt

Activities

The factor hunt takes place over pages 116–123. Your task is to collect evidence of the impact of each of the factors opposite. Work with a partner. This will help you particularly with columns 2 and 3.

5 For each of the four topics on pages 116–123:

   a Fill in column 1. Begin each entry with a short heading. Then identify the factors that helped this topic develop and write brief details of the effect of the factor.

   b In column 2, assess the importance of the factor in that topic. Use this code:

      ** = very important role

      * = helpful role

      Make sure you add a sentence explaining the reason for your choice.

6 When you have investigated all the topics and completed columns 1 and 2, fill in column 3, assessing the overall impact of each factor. You could use this scoring system:

   3 = factor vital to most or all topics

   2 = important to most topics

   1 = important to one or two topics

You will find more help on completing the table on pages 124–125.

Factor chart

Factor	1 Evidence of factor helping a development	2 Importance of factor helping a development	3 Assessment – How important was this factor overall?
War			
Government			
Individuals			

Development 1: Vaccinations

A. Jenner and smallpox

You have already studied Jenner's work, but including smallpox vaccination here helps you recap some key features of that discovery and identifies some key factors.

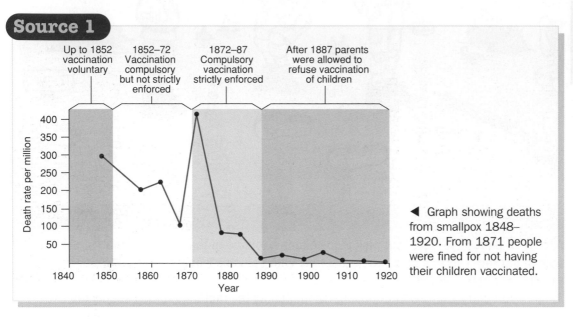

Source 1

Up to 1852 vaccination voluntary

1852–72 Vaccination compulsory but not strictly enforced

1872–87 Compulsory vaccination strictly enforced

After 1887 parents were allowed to refuse vaccination of children

◀ Graph showing deaths from smallpox 1848–1920. From 1871 people were fined for not having their children vaccinated.

Look back to page 101. Which factors helped Jenner's work?
Look at Source 1. Which factor helped reduce smallpox, especially after 1872?

You should be able to find four factors at work on the rest of this page.

B. Pasteur, Koch and the development of vaccines

Pasteur's germ theory was a critical moment in medicine. It led to Koch and his research team discovering the specific microbes that cause individual diseases. Pasteur and his team then developed vaccines for individual diseases. Both men used high-technology equipment such as the latest microscopes. Without them, they could not have seen the microbes. They also received funding from their governments to pay for their work. Other scientists followed, producing vaccines that cut deaths from the diseases below.

Source 2

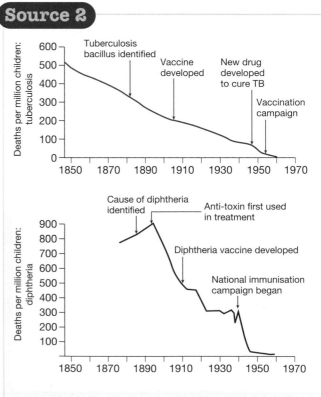

Tuberculosis bacillus identified

Vaccine developed

New drug developed to cure TB

Vaccination campaign

Cause of diphtheria identified

Anti-toxin first used in treatment

Diphtheria vaccine developed

National immunisation campaign began

▲ Graphs showing the decline in deaths of children from TB and diphtheria, two major killers of young children in the 1800s. After 1948, vaccinations were free under the NHS.

C. Polio

Can you imagine hearing that a Premier League footballer had died of a disease like polio? That is what happened in the major polio outbreaks of the 1950s when Jeff Hall, a Birmingham City footballer, died of polio. Although many diseases had been beaten in the early 1900s, the microbe causing Poliomyelitis wasn't identified until 1946 and it wasn't until 1954 that American research scientist Jonas Salk developed a vaccine that protected people from the disease.

> What evidence can you find on this page of the impact of technology, communications, government and individuals?

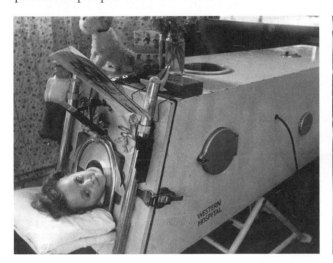

▲ Iron lungs kept polio victims breathing.

▲ Developing a vaccine was only the beginning of saving people. Mass production was needed to create enough vaccines to use throughout Britain and the world. Pharmaceutical companies invested heavily in new technology to make vaccines available. This picture shows the Eli Lilly factory in the USA where one line of workers boxed up 360,000 doses of polio vaccine in a day.

D. Measles and flu

Measles and Influenza were major killers in the 1800s, even though today we often think of them as common and not dangerous diseases. In the 1950s, measles was still common and seen as a serious illness, leading to many weeks off school and maybe a spell in hospital. Children could die from the disease and it sometimes led to other problems. For example, my mother had measles when she was three, back in 1928, and lost the hearing in one ear as a result. Fortunately, the vaccine developed in 1964 did a great deal to wipe out the disease, aided by the availability of free vaccines under the NHS and widespread advertising campaigns. However, the near-wiping out of measles has led to people underestimating its effects and recently there has been a rapid increase in the number of measles cases in Britain because people have stopped using the vaccine for fear – now disproved by research – that it led to other medical problems.

Influenza is another disease that can rapidly cause death, especially in the elderly and those already sick. That is why governments have invested heavily in providing free flu jabs for many groups of people, including the elderly and key workers, for example those in hospitals.

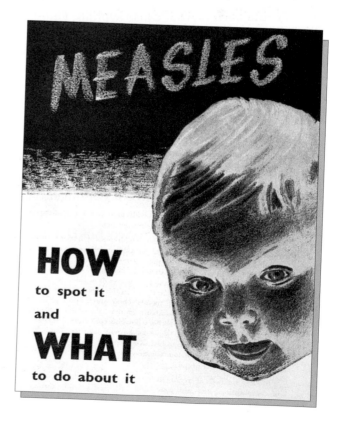

MEASLES

HOW to spot it and WHAT to do about it

Development 2: Treatments and cures – aspirin, magic bullets and alternative medicine

A. The late 1800s – the growth of the pharmaceutical industry

By 1900, the 'cure-all' pills of Holloway and Morison were being replaced by effective treatments made by large pharmaceutical companies. These included Boots, Welcome and Beechams, which all became world-wide businesses in the twentieth century. Their success was built on making good use of the latest developments in science and technology. A good example is the development of aspirin as a painkiller and remedy for fevers. The bark of the willow tree had been used as a medicine for many centuries, by the Ancient Egyptians and Greeks and in North America. It was identified as a useful medicine in England in the 1760s and the growth of science meant that scientists were able to identify the exact chemical having the beneficial effect. When it was manufactured in 1890 by a company called Bayer AG, it was called Aspirin.

Many other drugs were manufactured because the pharmaceutical companies were:

- investing in research and development (including employing scientists) to look for better remedies
- using improved scientific techniques and equipment to identify the precise chemicals that work as medicines
- using industrial technology to make huge quantities of each remedy and using commercial skills to market them world-wide
- using experiments and experience to find the exact dosages needed by patients.

B. The early 1900s – 'magic bullets' (sulphonamides)

'Magic bullets' was the name given to the first chemical drugs that fought and killed bacteria inside the body. In 1909, Paul Ehrlich (who had been part of Koch's research team) developed the first chemical cure for a disease. This was Salvarsan 606, which he called a 'magic bullet' because it homed in on and destroyed the harmful bacteria that cause syphilis. Unfortunately, while Salvarsan 606 killed the microbes, it could also kill the patient. Ehrlich had proved the theory of chemicals killing bacteria could work – but they needed cures that did not kill the patients, too.

It wasn't until the 1930s that Gerhard Domagk developed Prontosil, the second chemical 'magic bullet'. Domagk was trying out a chemical mix called Prontosil on mice and discovered that it was killing the microbes causing blood poisoning. He didn't try it on people until his daughter pricked her finger on an infected needle and developed blood poisoning.

Normally she would have died, but Domagk risked giving her Prontosil. She was the first human cured by a chemical cure. Scientists then discovered that the important chemical in these cures was sulphonamide and drug companies then developed more sulphonamide cures for diseases such as pneumonia.

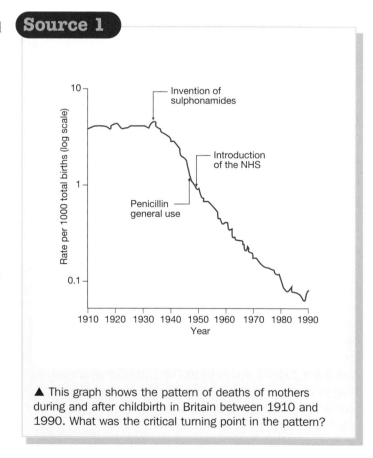

Source 1

▲ This graph shows the pattern of deaths of mothers during and after childbirth in Britain between 1910 and 1990. What was the critical turning point in the pattern?

C. The 1940s – antibiotics

The next great discovery was penicillin, the first antibiotic that killed staphylococcus germs, which caused major infections and in the past often killed the victims. Antibiotics are cures that use beneficial bacteria to kill the harmful bacteria causing a disease. You will find out a lot more about how this incredible breakthrough happened on the next page, but even after penicillin was first used to cure infections there was still a great deal to do. How did this new miracle treatment come to be widely used?

- Investment in the discovery and development of other antibiotics by pharmaceutical companies.

- The growth of scientific techniques and equipment, which were used in the development of antibiotics.

- The development of the government-funded NHS provided antibiotics free to many people. Without the NHS, many could not have afforded antibiotics and would have continued being ill and could have died.

- Reporting and communication of research by scientists and doctors so they could all learn from each other.

D. The later 1900s – alternative therapies

Millions of people spend a huge amount of money on alternative therapies such as those below, although there is little or no scientific proof that they are effective. Alternative remedies became much more widely used towards the end of the twentieth century, sometimes reviving treatments which had been used for centuries, then gone out of fashion. Why have alternative remedies become more fashionable?

- Science has shown that many herbal treatments contain chemicals that have medical benefits.

- Commercial companies have used effective advertising to sell their products.

- Some people have grown suspicious of scientific remedies, preferring methods they regard as more natural.

Information

Antibiotic
A drug made from bacteria that kill other bacteria and so cure an infection or illness.

Source 2

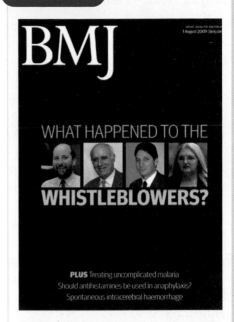

▲ Medical journals such as this report the latest research to doctors, building up their knowledge of the most effective treatments and methods of preventing illness.

Three kinds of alternative therapies

Acupuncture	**Homeopathy**	**Herbal remedies**
Acupuncture has been used in China for 4000 years. It involves inserting fine needles at pressure points on the body to release blocked energy. It has been used as an anaesthetic in operations.	Homeopathy was founded in the 1700s by a German doctor, Samuel Hahnemann. It involves the patient taking a very weak amount of a substance which, in a healthy person, would produce symptoms similar to those the patient has. It is said to encourage the body to heal itself.	Many health shops sell 'herbal remedies' made from plants and animal substances that have been used in medicine for centuries. Examples include honey (which has been used against infection since Ancient Egypt) and valerian, a herb which helps people to sleep.

Development 3: Penicillin and antibiotic medicines

Stage 1: A false start

There are many examples in medicine of false starts and penicillin is one of them. In 1872, a doctor called Joseph Lister noticed that the mould of a bacteria called penicillin killed other bacteria. Years later, in 1884, he used this mould to treat a nurse who had an infected wound. But Lister did not use it again. A miracle cure lay waiting for someone else to rediscover it.

Stage 2: 1928 – Fleming's discovery of penicillin – another false start?

During World War One (1914–1918) a scientist called Alexander Fleming was sent to France to study soldiers' wounds infected with streptococci and staphylococci bacteria. These wounds were not healed by chemical antiseptics and many soldiers died from them. Back home, Fleming worked on finding a way of dealing with these bacteria.

Ten years later, in 1928, Fleming found what he'd been seeking. He was working at St Mary's Hospital, London. Going on holiday, he left a pile of Petri dishes containing bacteria on his laboratory bench. On his return, he sorted out the dishes and noticed mould on one of them. Around the mould, as you can see in the picture, the staphylococci bacteria had disappeared.

Fleming carried out experiments with the penicillin mould on living cells. He discovered that, if it was diluted, it killed bacteria without harming the cells. He made a list of the germs it killed and used it to treat another scientist's eye infection. However, it did not seem to work on deeper infections and, in any case, it was taking ages to create enough penicillin to use.

In 1929, Fleming wrote about penicillin in a medical journal but nobody thought his article was important. He had not used penicillin on animals to heal infections, so had no evidence of it being useful.

Why is this page so important?

Penicillin was the first antibiotic medicine. Since then, other antibiotics have been developed which kill particular bacteria. Antibiotics have saved an estimated 200 million lives in less than 70 years – you may well be one of those people, although we are so used to taking antibiotics we longer think of them as the miracles they are.

▲ Alexander Fleming

Antibiotic

A drug made from bacteria that kill other bacteria and so cure an infection or illness.

Source 1

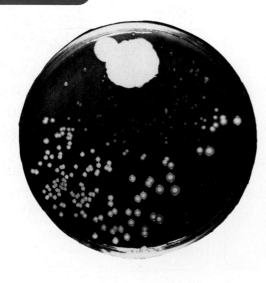

◀ Fleming's original dish. The mould is at the top. The bacteria originally around it have been killed, but the bacteria further away have survived. The mould had probably been grown by another scientist in the room above Fleming's and spores had floated out of the window, then downwards and in through Fleming's window before landing on the one place they could have an effect and then be noticed.

Stage 3: 1938 – Florey and Chain's research and trials

In 1938, Florey and Chain were researching how germs could be killed and read Fleming's article on penicillin. They realised that it could be very effective and tried to get funding from the government. They got £25. With a war about to start and no proof that penicillin could help people, the government had other things to spend its money on. Florey therefore asked for money from America, and got enough to pay for five years' research.

They discovered that penicillin helped mice recover from infections, but to treat one person they needed 3000 times as much penicillin! Even large drug companies could not afford to fund this quantity of work. So Florey and Chain began growing penicillin in whatever they could, using hundreds of hospital bedpans even though bedpans were now in demand to make Spitfires!

By 1941, there was enough penicillin to test it on one person. The volunteer was Albert Alexander, a policeman who had developed septicaemia – a bacterial infection that attacks the whole body – from a tiny cut. Alexander was dying. Chemical drugs had not killed the infection. Florey and Chain requested permission to try their new 'purified' penicillin and injections began. The penicillin worked and Albert began to recover. However, they ran out of penicillin after five days even though Florey and Chain were even extracting unused penicillin from the man's urine and reusing it in a desperate attempt to keep treating him. The poor policeman became ill again and died. Penicillin had shown that it worked and that it wasn't harmful to the patient – but how could they make enough of it?

▲ Left: Howard Florey, Australian doctor and Head of Pathology at Oxford University. Right: Ernst Chain, a Jewish German who escaped persecution in Nazi Germany to become a scientist at Oxford.

Stage 4: 1941 – Wartime need for penicillin

Florey and Chain needed help to mass produce penicillin, but English factories were busy helping the war effort and couldn't be used. So Florey went to America – at just the right time. In 1941, America was attacked by the Japanese at Pearl Harbour and entered the war. The American government realised the potential of penicillin for treating wounded soldiers and made interest free loans to US companies to buy the expensive equipment needed for making penicillin. Soon British firms were also mass producing penicillin, enough to treat the allied wounded on D-Day in 1944 – over 2.3 million doses.

Source 2

An account of the first use of penicillin in the British army in 1943, written by Lt Colonel Pulvertaft:

'We had an enormous number of wounded with infections, terrible burn cases among the crews of armoured cars. The usual medicines had absolutely no effect. The last thing I tried was penicillin. The first man was a young man called Newton. He had been in bed for six months with fractures of both legs. His sheets were soaked with pus. Normally he would have died in a short time. I gave three injections of penicillin a day and studied the effects under a microscope. The thing seemed like a miracle. In ten days' time the leg was cured and in a month's time the young fellow was back on his feet. I had enough penicillin for ten cases. Nine were complete cures.'

Source 3

▲ Tanks used to produce penicillin. The quantity needed is difficult to comprehend: 2000 litres were needed to treat one case of infection. In June 1943, 425 million units of penicillin were being produced – enough for 170 cases.

Development 4: Prevention: From X-rays to scanners – the growth of technology

This section has focused on treatments – methods of curing people who have already become ill. However, over the twentieth century and into the twenty-first century, medicine has increasingly developed ways of preventing illness – sometimes by catching illnesses in their very early stages so that action can be taken before an illness has become serious. This page looks at some of the technology that is helping to prevent illnesses developing.

A. X-rays

In 1895, a German scientist, Wilhelm Rontgen, was carrying out experiments when he realised that rays of light in a covered tube were lighting up a far wall. They could pass through black paper, wood and flesh. He did not know what they were so he called them X-rays. Within months of Rontgen publishing his discovery, the first X-ray machines were being used in hospitals to identify diseases and broken bones.

World War One had a major impact on the frequency of use of X-rays. Surgeons needed to locate bullets and shrapnel lodged deep within wounded men and X-rays provided the answer. Governments ordered the making of many more X-ray machines and they were installed in all major hospitals on the Western Front. Nowadays, X-ray technology is an everyday part of medicine as a result of governments investing in equipment, especially since the beginning of the NHS.

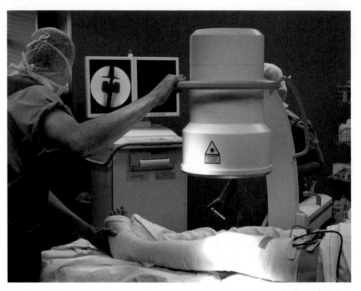

▲ The development of X-rays is the basis for many other methods of prevention, such as the examples on this page.

B. Marie Curie and radiation therapy

Radiation therapy (or radiotherapy as it is also called) developed closely from Rontgen's discovery of X-rays through the work of the Polish scientist Marie Curie, together with her French husband, Pierre. In the process of researching the use of X-rays they noticed that the skin on their hands was being burned by the material they were handling. They investigated this further and this led to the discovery of radium, which has been used ever since to diagnose cancers, and in radiotherapy to treat cancers, often reducing the need for surgery. Their research was the beginning of the modern treatment of cancers. As the research continued, it became so complex that they built up a team of research scientists to share ideas.

Nowadays, radiotherapy and chemotherapy have become accepted parts of cancer treatment, which save increasing numbers of lives. Improved knowledge of techniques, doses and other aspects of treatment are spread through medical journals, conferences, the internet and other forms of communication.

▲ Marie Curie (1867–1934), photographed with her daughter, Irene, in 1920. Marie Curie is the only woman to have won two Nobel Prizes, for her work on X-rays and on radium. She died of leukaemia contracted from the radioactive material she handled as part of her work.

C. Scanning to diagnose early stages of illness

X-ray technology is also used to detect the early appearance of cancers and other illnesses. This has happened as a result of improvements in technology, enabling more complex machinery to be developed, and large amounts of government funding which has paid for equipment to be available in every region of the country.

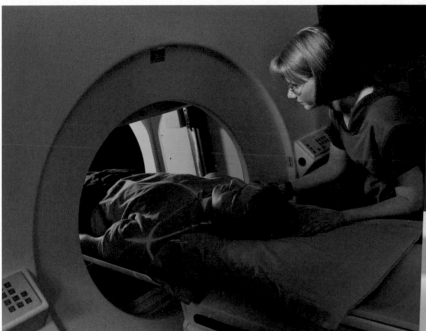

◀ A patient undergoes an MRI scan.

▲ Screening for a variety of cancers and other illnesses has become routine because of the wide availability of the scanners to carry out mammograms and other examinations.

D. Technology in the home

In the 1800s, the new piece of 'miracle' equipment was the thermometer, used to take temperatures and track the progress of an illness. Today, many more pieces of equipment are available, often purchased from pharmacies, for use in the home. These include machines for monitoring blood pressure, blood sugar levels (for diabetics), heart monitors and cholesterol monitors.

▲ Blood pressure being monitored at home.

Analysing the importance of factors

Medicine has often been helped or hindered by factors such as government or war. Your new task is to identify and analyse the importance of the factors that improved methods of preventing and treating disease after 1750. Then use your findings to answer this question:

> Why have ways of preventing and treating illness improved since 1750? **[12 marks]**

A good answer identifies the factors that played a part but in an exam you do not have time to explain how every factor played a role. You only have about 15 minutes for the question. Columns 2 and 3 in your table are really important because they help you identify three or four key factors to write about.

The advice on writing effective explanations (page 82) helps you tackle this question. The key is to prove that a factor was important. In column 2 of your table you must analyse the importance of a factor. This means doing far more than saying that a factor played a 'helpful' or 'very important' role. You must prove it! Follow this advice to fill in your table and write a good exam answer.

Step 1: Filling in your factor table

Activities

1 Look at how the student has filled in the factors table for 'government'. Read the examiner's comments carefully. They will help you fill in the table for other factors.
2 Do you agree with the rating in column 3? If you do not, give your own rating. Make sure you give a reason for coming to this decision.

Step 2: Using your table to answer the question

If you have filled in your table well, you should have no problem answering the exam question.

- Use your table to select the three or four most important factors to write about in your answer to the exam question.

- Start a new paragraph each time you move on to analyse the importance of a new factor. Use the advice box below to help you structure each paragraph.

- In your last paragraph, you should aim to reach an overall judgement. Which factor played the most important role overall in improving ways of preventing and treating illness? Use column 3 to help you give your key reason for coming to this conclusion.

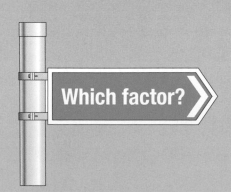

Which factor?

Factor	1 Evidence of factor helping a development	2 Importance of factor in helping a development	3 Assessment – How important was this factor overall?
Government	*Vaccinations* · Jenner – grant for clinic from government · 1850s – Government made smallpox vaccinations compulsery · 1960s – paid for free vaccines against measles · Today – pays for flu jabs *Penicillin* American government – large loans to companies to buy equipment to mass produce penicillin. *X-rays* Governments ordered the making of many more X-ray machines for use in World War One	** very important because – compulsory smallpox vaccinations led to a dramatic drop in deaths from the disease – without government funding only rich could could afford vaccinations * helpful because although penicillin had been developed only large amounts of funding could make mass production possible * helpful because government funding resulted in X-rays being used on a wider scale	2 important to most developments – especially the prevention of the spread of disease through funding vaccination programmes

Give a range of examples

The student gives a range of examples to show that government action played a role in developing new methods of preventing and treating illness.

Use connectives to prove your point

The student has analysed the importance of the role played by government action in each development. They reach a judgement and use connectives such as 'this led to', 'without' and 'this resulted in' to prove that government action played an important role.

Reach an overall judgement

The student reaches an overall judgement about the importance of the role played by government action in developing methods of preventing and treating illness.

Writing an effective paragraph

In each paragraph, make sure that you:

- clearly **signpost** at the start of the paragraph which factor you are focusing on

- **select** three or four examples that **show how** the factor played an important role in the development of new ways of preventing and treating illness. Use columns 1 and 2. Remember to **use connectives** to tie what you know to the question and prove that the factor played an important role.

WHAT YOU KNOW — WHAT THE QUESTION ASKS

One reason why methods of preventing and treating illness improved after 1750 was because of government action.

The government played a very important role in the development of vaccinations. Jenner was given a grant by the British government to ...
This helped to ...
In the 1850s, the government ...
This led to ...
Funding from the American government played an important role in the development of penicillin.
It meant that ...
In addition, during the First World War government funding ...

125

Section 8: How have hospitals and medical training changed since 1750?

Developing inference skills to spot key changes in medicine

To do well in your GCSE History exam, you need to be able to use visual and written sources effectively. The first question on the paper will usually be an inference question based on two sources. For questions like the one below, you will need to **combine clues in the sources with your own knowledge** to explain changes that have taken place. We have begun to annotate the sources and add our own knowledge of each period. On your copy of these sources, add your own annotations and notes, then draft an answer. Use the advice on pages 110–11 to help you.

After you have finished the work on hospitals and training on page 133, return to your draft and review your answer. By this point you should be able to add your own knowledge of how the work of nurses has changed since 1750.

1 What do Sources A and B show about changes in the work done by nurses in England?

Explain your answer, using Sources A and B and your own knowledge. **[8 marks]**

Source A

The best medieval hospital, the Hotel Dieu in Paris. ▼

Crucifix – reflects how the nuns who looked after the patients spent a lot of time praying for the sick. In the Middle Ages people believed that God sent sickness to punish them for their sins so they joined in the prayers, hoping that God would realise they were sorry for their sins.

Nursing care was provided by nuns – they had a good knowledge of herbal remedies.

Source B

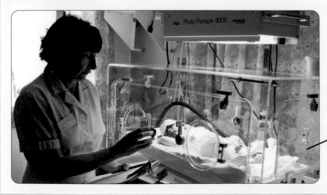

◄ A photograph of a nurse caring for a newly born baby in a modern hospital maternity ward.

New technology – reflects how nurses are now well trained and use modern technology to monitor a patient's health.
The work of nurses has changed because they can now record important details such as temperature, heartbeat …

Did Florence Nightingale revolutionise nursing and hospitals single-handed?

People in the Middle Ages thought of hospitals as places to go to die rather than be cured. This was still the belief in the early 1800s but by the late 1900s this attitude had changed completely. One woman often gets the credit for this transformation – Florence Nightingale. Your task is to decide whether she really did change nursing and hospitals single-handed.

Activities

1 Using Sources 1 and 2 make a list of the reforms that were needed to improve hospitals and nursing.
2 Which developments that you already know about do you think helped to improve hospitals and nursing?

What were hospitals and nurses like in the early 1800s – before Nightingale?

Source 1

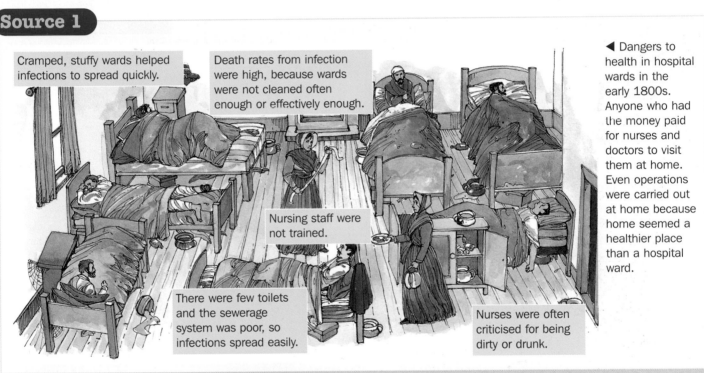

Cramped, stuffy wards helped infections to spread quickly.

Death rates from infection were high, because wards were not cleaned often enough or effectively enough.

Nursing staff were not trained.

There were few toilets and the sewerage system was poor, so infections spread easily.

Nurses were often criticised for being dirty or drunk.

◄ Dangers to health in hospital wards in the early 1800s. Anyone who had the money paid for nurses and doctors to visit them at home. Even operations were carried out at home because home seemed a healthier place than a hospital ward.

Source 2

An extract from *Martin Chuzzlewit*, a novel by Charles Dickens, published in 1844. In this extract, the nurse, Betsy Prig, is handing her patient over to the care of another nurse, Sarah Gamp. Dickens wrote in his introduction to this novel that 'Mrs Betsy Prig is an accurate description of a hospital nurse.'

'"How are we?" asked Mrs Gamp.

Mrs Prig said, "He's as cross as two sticks. He wouldn't have washed if he'd had his own way."

"She put soap in my mouth," said the unfortunate patient, feebly.

"Couldn't you keep it shut then?" said Mrs Prig.

Mrs Prig seized the patient by the chin and began to scrape his unhappy head with the hair brush. The brush was the hardest possible instrument and his eyelids were red with the pain. Then Mrs Gamp and Mrs Prig put on his coat.

"I don't think it's quite right" said the poor invalid. "There's a bottle in my pocket. Why have you made me sit on a bottle?"

"Oh" cried Mrs Gamp, "he's got my gin bottle. I put it in his coat when it hung behind the door."'

The work of Florence Nightingale (1820–1910) – how much credit does she really deserve?

Activities

1. In what ways did Florence Nightingale change conditions in the Crimea?
2. What kinds of training did she provide for nurses at her schools?
3. Which major breakthrough in medical knowledge had little impact on her work?
4. Begin completing the table below with evidence explaining why hospitals and nurses were revolutionised between 1750 and today. Then continue collecting evidence using pages 130–133.

	Impact on nursing	Impact on hospitals
The impact of Florence Nightingale		
The impact of other factors		

▲ Florence Nightingale in 1845. She became the first woman to receive the Order of Merit for her tireless efforts during the Crimean War.

Florence horrified her wealthy family by wanting to be a nurse. After many arguments she had her way, training in Germany before returning to Britain to work as a nurse, and eventually becoming Superintendent of Nurses in a London hospital. When the Crimean War broke out in 1854, she heard reports of the terrible conditions in the Crimea and so she talked to the Minister for War, Sidney Herbert, a family friend. He arranged for her to take 38 nurses to the Crimea.

In the Crimea

Arriving at the army hospital at Scutari, Florence was appalled by the dirty conditions. She concentrated on cleaning the hospital and patients. She wrote back to the British government:

▲ The Crimea, scene of the war between Britain and France on one side and Russia on the other.

25 November 1854

'It appears that in these [army] hospitals the washing of linen and of the men are considered a minor detail. No washing has been performed for the men or the beds – except by ourselves. When we came here, there was no soap or basins or towels in the wards. The consequences of all this are fever, cholera, gangrene, lice … Two or three hundred arm-slings, stump-pillows and other medical appliances are being weekly manufactured and given out by us. No arrangement seems to have been made to do this before.'

10 December 1854

'What we have achieved:

* a great deal more cleaning of wards – mops, scrubbing brushes given out by ourselves
* the supervision and stirring up of the whole organisation generally
* repair of the wards for 800 wounded.'

The death-rate in the hospital fell from 40 per cent of the wounded to 2 per cent. Florence and her nurses worked at the hospital rather than visiting the front-line of fighting.

Source 1

▲ A painting from 1855, showing Florence Nightingale in Scutari Hospital. Newspapers began to call her 'the lady with the lamp' because it was claimed that she walked the wards at night making sure wounded soldiers were comfortable.

The impact of Florence Nightingale

Florence returned to Britain a national heroine and this helped her raise money to set up her first nursing school. She was not a hands-on nurse but a great organiser, convinced that her life's work was to improve conditions in hospitals and training of nurses for the good of the patients. Those skills and beliefs were visible in the Crimea where she concentrated on improving hygiene and cleanliness. She continued to focus on these aspects of care throughout her life. In 1859, she wrote her book *Notes on Nursing*, and in 1863, *Notes on Hospitals*. Both books were very influential all over the world, providing the basis for training nurses and hospital design.

One surprising thing about her was that she paid little attention to Pasteur's germ theory when it appeared in the decade **after** the Crimean War. She had been brought up in the early 1800s when miasma (bad air) was the main theory about what caused disease. She continued to associate disease with dirt, which is why she concentrated on improving:

- sanitation in hospitals – clean water supplies, good drains and sewers, toilet facilities, total cleanliness
- good ventilation in hospitals to make sure patients got fresh, clean air to breathe
- good supplies, clothing and washing facilities for patients.

As a result, her nursing schools concentrated on training nurses in very practical skills. She did not let doctors teach nurses about germ theory because she felt that such ideas would simply get in the way of the nurses' more important task – keeping patients and wards clean.

The impact of other factors on nursing and hospitals

Although Florence Nightingale's nurses were not taught about some of the major medical breakthroughs, these did affect their careers and the development of hospitals.

The improvements in hospital buildings and sanitation could not have come about without improved engineering techniques and new government laws passed to enforce public health improvements. Changes in surgery increased the numbers of complex operations and so surgeons required better-trained nurses to assist them. And, despite Nightingale's relegation of germ theory, it had a very significant impact on all aspects of medicine, including surgery, and so in turn affected the ways that nurses carried out their work.

What had changed in hospitals and nursing by the 1920s?

Source 1

	1861	1921
Number of patients	About 65,000	228,500
Hospital beds per thousand people	3.2	6.1

▲ The number of patients and hospital beds 1861 and 1921.

Source 2

Problems in 1860	Solutions in 1920
Unhygienic surgery dressings	Aseptic surgery and and dressings
Untrained nurses	Trained nurses
Cramped, stuffy wards	Spacious, light, well-ventilated wards
Poor sanitation and sewerage	Good sanitation, toilets
Lack of cleanliness	Cleanliness

▲ A summary of changes in hospitals between 1860 and 1920.

Source 3

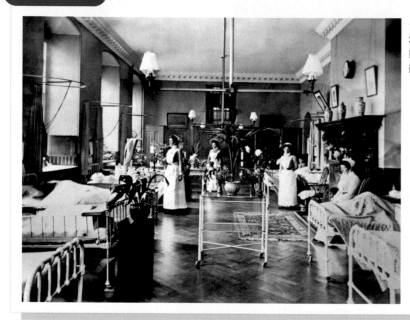

◄ A ward in St Bartholomew's Hospital, London, in 1909.

Activities

Florence Nightingale died in 1910, still working even when she was in her 80s. This activity helps you weigh up the importance of her work and the roles played by other breakthroughs and factors.

1   Using Sources 1–3, list the changes in hospitals and nursing that took place between 1850 and 1920.
2   The cards opposite can be organised into a pattern to explain why hospitals and nursing changed a great deal between 1850 and 1920. Your task is to create that pattern, using what you have learned from pages 128–130. These hints may help:
    a   Begin by thinking about which cards might start and finish the sequence.
    b   Look for links to those start and finish cards.
    c   Build up links – draw in lines on your own copy and annotate the lines, explaining why you have made the links.
3   Which of the developments on the cards do you think were most important in changing:
    a   hospitals
    b   nursing?
    (Think about how many cards are linked to Nightingale herself.)

Florence Nightingale's work in the Crimea.

The discovery that bacteria cause diseases.

Florence Nightingale's books influenced training and the design of hospitals.

Increased public awareness of the need for clean hospitals and qualified nurses.

A wider range of operations and treatments carried out so the demand for good nurses increased.

Developments in surgery such as anaesthetics and antiseptics.

Improvements in engineering and public health.

Better hospitals and better-qualified nurses.

Florence Nightingale set up training schools for nurses. These nurses showed their value, increasing respect for nurses and leading to more women becoming nurses.

Money raised for Nightingale fund.

Activities

The Florence Nightingale Debate

Was Florence Nightingale the heroine who revolutionised hospitals and nursing? Divide into small teams. Each team has to decide whether they support the idea that Nightingale's role was the most important or whether you think other factors were more important.

4   Your first task is to collect your evidence. You need to think about the following:
   a   Which evidence best supports your case? Identify the two best pieces of evidence for this.
   b   What are your opponents likely to say and what evidence will they use? Think how you could argue back against their points.

5   Your second task is to spend **10 minutes** outlining what you will say. Your group will be given **two minutes** to put your case. Your teacher will chair the debate.

131

How have hospitals and nursing changed since Nightingale's death in 1910?

A report in the *Suffolk Times and Mercury*, 16 December 1892:

'An enquiry was held on Tuesday before Mr. Coroner Chaston into the death of Maggie Alderton Wade, aged 1 year and 9 months, the child of Henry Wade, agricultural labourer. The evidence of the mother showed that the child accidentally overturned on herself a boiling cup of soup, sustaining scalds from which she died 40 hours later. No doctor was called in but Mrs Brundish was sent for to charm the fire out of the deceased; she repeated some words and passed her hands over the injured places. In the opinion of the parents some good was done. The witness added that Mrs Brundish's power was generally believed in, in the village. A verdict of accidental death was returned.'

New understandings of disease

Free treatments and visits

This report dates from 30 years **after** Pasteur published his germ theory and after Florence Nightingale had begun work improving hospitals and nursing. Despite these changes, many people still turned first of all to local wisewomen such as Mrs Brundish rather than pay to see a doctor or visit a hospital. There were still no regulations about who could call themselves a nurse or a midwife.

Protecting patients

Activities

The cards on the right can be added to the cards on the previous page to explain changes in nursing and hospitals. Your task is to complete this set of cards to explain changes in nursing and hospitals after the 1920s. Clues 1–7 give you the information you need.

1 Some cards already have headings that identify a reason for changes. Your task is to add at least one example to each card showing the effects of the reason on nursing or hospitals.

2 Some cards are blank. Your task is to give each blank card a heading and then add one example of its effects.

3 Now create a pattern with these cards to show which ones you think have been most important in changing hospitals and nursing. What links can you find between them?

4 Look back to Sources A and B on page 126. Did the key developments that changed nursing and hospitals happen during or after Florence Nightingale's lifetime? What evidence supports your opinion?

Clue 1

New technologies have changed the work done in hospitals and hospitals themselves. Hospitals have needed rebuilding to house X-ray units and modern scanners, together with many more surgical theatres for operations. The use of ultrasound technology has, for example, changed care of pregnant women and their babies as it has become much easier to monitor the development of babies still in the womb.

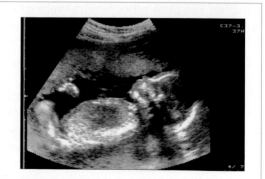

Clue 2

In the late 1800s, hospital care involved either surgery, at one extreme, or much more basic care, based on keeping the sick clean, warm and well-fed. There were few other treatments. However, the development of chemical and antibiotic drugs and the use of technologies such as radiotherapy and chemotherapy have greatly widened the range of treatments in use. This has meant that hospitals have become much larger because they can help many more people and have many more staff.

Clue 3

In 1902, the Midwives Act required everyone calling him or herself a midwife to be registered. It also set qualifications for midwives. At first people ignored this regulation, using unregistered midwives because they were cheaper or because that was what they had always done, but in time this changed, especially after the setting up of the NHS made the services of a trained midwife free of charge.

Clue 4

Much more is understood about disease today than a century ago. The major breakthrough has been the developing understanding of genetic illnesses based on knowledge of human DNA. This increased understanding has meant better treatments and longer life for patients with incurable conditions such as cystic fibrosis, which in turn has meant a need for more facilities in hospitals and more specialised nursing care for patients.

Clue 5

Government spending on hospitals has increased hugely, especially since the founding of the NHS in 1948. This money has been spent on new buildings and equipment, on free treatment and medicines for many patients and on staff wages.

Clue 6

Nurses in the early twenty-first century train for a diploma or degree in nursing and it is intended that in time all nurses will have degrees in nursing. Many continue their training to develop specialist skills in particular branches of nursing such as care of patients who have had breast surgery or cancer patients undergoing radiotherapy or chemotherapy. Some of these specialist nurses have the ability to prescribe a limited range of medicines – something which in the past could only be done by doctors.

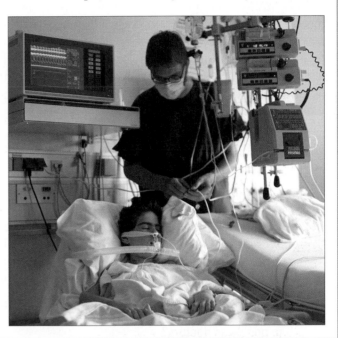

Clue 7

Protecting patients from acquiring illnesses in hospital has become a major aspect of hospitals' work. This was always a problem in hospitals, but became worse in the later 1900s as bacteria developed immunity to some antibiotics and outbreaks of 'superbugs' (such as MRSA) killed patients in some hospitals. Since then, hospitals and governments have taken action to protect patients from such infections. The Care Quality Commission checks aspects of care in hospitals and forces hospitals to make improvements, if necessary. In March 2009, it reported that new regulations and work by hospital staff had helped reduce the cases of MRSA in many hospitals, but that greater efforts were still needed in about 20 hospitals to reduce the number of cases of this infection.

When and how did women win the right to become doctors?

In 2002, 60 per cent of the trainee doctors in Britain were women. This is remarkable, as 150 years earlier there were none. Why did this remarkable change happen?

Until the 1700s, women had been able to qualify as surgeons and midwives as well as playing the main role in everyday medicine as mothers and wisewomen. However, they were never allowed to become physicians as that required university training – and women were not allowed to go to university. In the 1800s, men even succeeded in preventing women qualifying as surgeons and midwives, however good their practical skills. In 1852, a new law required all doctors to belong to one of the Colleges of Surgeons, Physicians or Apothecaries. All were closed to women.

Activities

1 Read Sources 1–3 and the text on this page.
   a How did women's right to work as doctors change between the 1600s and 1850s?
   b Why did many men think women unfit to be doctors in the 1800s?
2 Complete your own version of the timeline opposite by placing boxes A–E in the correct places on the line.
3 a What words would you use to describe the reactions of the male students to women's fight to qualify as doctors?
   b What words would you use to describe women's actions in their fight to qualify as doctors?
4 Why were both Elizabeth Blackwell and Elizabeth Garrett Anderson significant in the history of medicine?
5 Which factors since 1876 have contributed to so many women training as doctors today?
6 **Living graph:** Work as a group to create your own living graph, recording changes in women's role as doctors over time.

Source 1

Some memorials put up to women healers:

'Margaret Colfe. Having been above forty years a willing nurse, midwife, surgeon and, in part, physician to all both rich and poor, without expecting reward.' (Lewisham, 1643)

'Prudence Potter. Her life was spent in the industrious and successful practice of physic, surgery and midwifery.' (Devon, 1689)

'Dorothy Burton. Has excellent skill in surgery, sore eyes, aches etc and has done many famous good cures upon poor folks that were otherwise destitute of help.' (1629)

Elizabeth Blackwell (1821–1910)

Born in Bristol, she had to go to the USA to qualify as a doctor. She qualified in 1849 and later set up the New York Infirmary for Poor Women and Children, staffed completely by women. She also travelled back to Britain to encourage other women wanting to become doctors, including Elizabeth Garrett.

Elizabeth Garrett Anderson (1836–1917)

Anderson was the first woman to qualify as a doctor in Britain. You can follow her story through the activity opposite.

Source 2

Thomas Huxley, a leading scientist, in 1851:

'In every excellent characteristic, whether mental or physical, the average woman is inferior to the average man.'

Source 3

Dr H. Bennett, writing in the medical journal *The Lancet* in 1870:

'I believe most thoroughly that women as a body are sexually, constitutionally and mentally unfit for the hard incessant toil, and for the heavy responsibilities of surgical practice. There is a branch of our profession – midwifery – to which they may be admitted in a subordinate position.'

1859 Elizabeth Blackwell was registered as a doctor by the British Medical Association after qualifying as a doctor in the USA.

Early 1860s Elizabeth Garrett trained as a nurse and attended lectures for trainee doctors at the Middlesex Hospital.

1870 Elizabeth Garrett studied privately with professors of medicine and then passed her medical exams to become a doctor – in Paris and in French! She also qualified as a midwife with the Society of Apothecaries. The two qualifications together allowed her to practise as a doctor.

1874 Six women, led by Sophia Jex-Blake, persuaded Edinburgh University to let them attend lectures from 1870, although there were lengthy protests from male students who also tried to stop them taking exams, hurling mud and shouting insults at them. In 1874, the women completed the medical course at Edinburgh.

1876 Parliament opened all medical qualifications to women as part of a law giving women the same rights to university education as men.

1860
1862
1864
1866
1868
1870
1872
1874
1876
1878
1880

Warning – boxes A–E are in the wrong places on the timeline. You need to put them in the correct order – see Activity 2.

Box A

The Colleges of Surgeons and Physicians refused to allow women members in order to try to stop Garrett working as a doctor. The College of Apothecaries also changed its rules, banning students from getting private tuition. This meant all medical students had to go to university – but they did not take women as students.

Box B

Male students at the Middlesex Hospital protested that Elizabeth Garrett should not be allowed to attend lectures.

Box C

For five years after 1876, the Royal College of Surgeons refused to allow anyone to take exams in midwifery as a way of getting around the law and preventing women from learning alongside men.

Box D

Edinburgh University gave the women certificates but said it could only give medical degrees to men. The women had to complete their degrees in Dublin or Switzerland.

Box E

In 1860 the British Medical Association changed its rules saying that only people who qualified at a British university could become registered doctors.

Source 4

An extract from Sophia Jex-Blake, *Medical Education of Women*, 1878, describing the women's arrival to take their anatomy examination:

'On the afternoon of Friday 18 November 1870, we women walked to the Surgeon's Hall. As soon as we came to the Surgeon's Hall … we saw a dense mob filling up the road in front … and was sufficient to stop the traffic for an hour. Not a single policeman was visible through the crowd. We walked up to the gates which remained open until we came within a yard of them, when they were slammed in our faces by a number of young men.'

135

Developing inference skills to spot key changes in medicine

How has the training of doctors changed?

This is another opportunity to practise answers for the first question on the examination paper which will usually be an inference question based on two sources, like the one below.

Look at the question below. On your own copy of these sources, add your own annotations. Look back to pages 110 and 126 for ideas. Then draft an answer. After you have finished the work on the training of doctors on pages 138–139, return to your draft and review your answer.

1 What do Sources A and B show about changes in the way doctors in England found out about a patient's health?

Explain your answer, using Sources A and B and your own knowledge. **[8 marks]**

Source A

A urine chart used by doctors in the Middle Ages to help them diagnose a patient's illness. ▼

Source B

A check sheet showing the kinds of tests a doctor in the late twentieth century could use to help diagnose a patient's illness. ▼

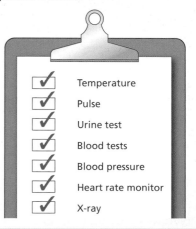

✔	Temperature
✔	Pulse
✔	Urine test
✔	Blood tests
✔	Blood pressure
✔	Heart rate monitor
✔	X-ray

Activity

On pages 138–139 you are going to investigate when the training of doctors changed the most. Think back over the work you have already covered.

How did the training of doctors change as a result of the Renaissance and Scientific Revolution and how great a change was that?

Getting better in 1800?

This drawing from 1801 makes you very glad you were not born two hundred years earlier. It is a drawing by James Gillray called 'Metallic Tractors'. Gillray was making fun of a treatment invented by Elisha Perkins, an American physician. Perkins called his instruments 'Perkins Tractors' – they consisted of two rods made of different metals which he passed over the body. He claimed they drew out disease using natural electricity in the body. Perkins' son, Benjamin, moved to London to promote his father's invention, charging a large fee of over £5 and claiming that he cured over five thousand people in England using his 'tractors'.

Activity

What reasons can you suggest for why people risked going to see a quack like Perkins in 1800 rather than get treatment from a physician?

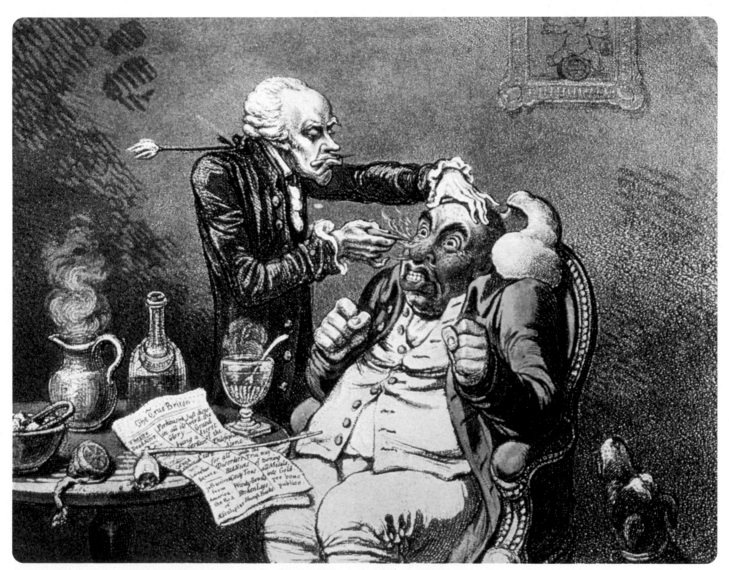

▲ Gillray has drawn the medical man as a sinister figure, using one tractor to direct electricity into the man's nose to cure his red lumps. Perkins was actually pleased by the cartoon and thought it would be useful in attracting business!

How has the training of doctors changed?

Today, very few people would go to see a quack like the man on the last page because the training and knowledge of doctors has changed greatly since 1800. If you think back over Sections 6 and 7 you should be able to list many of the major changes that have taken place. Try that to begin with before you work on this page in detail.

Activities

1 Make your own copy of this table and complete columns 1 and 2, using the information on this page.

2 Fill in column 3 suggesting the reasons for these changes. Use the factors listed on page 11 as a guide.

3 Compare the information in columns 1 and 2 of your table. Do you think the most important changes happened before or after 1930? Give two reasons to support your choice.

4 Which development or developments do you think have been most important in:
   a increasing confidence in doctors
   b increasing the frequency with which people visit their doctor?
   Explain the reason for your choices.

	1 Changes between 1860 and 1930	2 Changes between 1930 and 2009	3 Reasons for changes
Training			
Understanding of causes of illness			
Equipment for diagnosing illness			
Ability to treat less well-off			
Treatments			
Method of payment			

He relies on payments from patients for his income – payments for visits and for medicines which he mixes.

He believes that illness is caused by spontaneous generation – microbes that are caused by decay spread by bad air. News is just arriving that a French scientist has a new theory but as yet there is no proof.

His training is decided by the teachers at the university he attended and by the professors he went to for private tuition. The government plays no part in regulating the education of doctors.

Dr Smith 1860

He has little equipment to help him – a thermometer and one of the new stethoscopes.

His training at university consisted mainly of lectures and reading books, with some practical training on hospital wards. He is trained in scientific method, to observe symptoms and take case-histories and to think for himself rather than simply relying on what he has read.

He holds a surgery for the poor in a local dispensary, but still charges a small fee for medicines.

He treats patients with medicines made up from herbs and may bleed them. He may also recommend changes in diet and exercise and rest.

Dr Jones
1930

He relies on payments from patients for his income – payments for visits and for medicines which he mixes. He employs a debt collector to collect payments, but up to one-third of patients cannot afford to pay their bills.

He knows that infectious diseases are caused by bacteria but there are many illnesses, including some that babies are born with that cannot be explained in this way.

His training is decided by the teachers at the university he attended and by the Royal Colleges, the medical authorities who can discipline or strike off a doctor who has failed his patients. The government plays no part in regulating the education of doctors.

He has a thermometer, a stethoscope and can carry out blood tests. He can also send patients for X-rays at the local hospital, although this requires a charge.

His training at university consisted of lectures and reading books, with a considerable amount of practical training on hospital wards. He is trained in scientific method, to observe symptoms and take case-histories and to think for himself rather than simply relying on what he has read.

He does some charity work for the poor, but still charges a small fee for medicines.

He can offer vaccinations against some of the most dangerous diseases and there is news of the first sulphonamide drugs that may be able to cure other diseases. However, many common illnesses, including very dangerous ones, can only be treated with changes in diet and exercise and rest.

Dr Brown
2009

She is paid by the government, either directly or through the NHS Trust or GP partnership that she works for.

She knows that infectious diseases are caused by bacteria, but also that many illnesses have genetic causes stemming from the individual DNA of the person. She is aware of how treatment for these genetic diseases is developing and which hospitals can provide treatment.

Her training is decided by the teachers at the university she attended and by the Royal Colleges, the medical authorities who can discipline or strike off a doctor who has failed their patients. The government now plays a part in regulating the education of doctors in order to safeguard patients against poor treatment.

She has a thermometer, a stethoscope and can carry out blood tests. She may also have the facilities for X-ray at her GP surgery or will send people to hospital for X-rays, and a variety of types of scan. Some GPs can carry out minor surgery at their local practice base.

Her training at university consisted of lectures and reading books, with a considerable amount of practical training on hospital wards. She is trained in scientific method, to observe symptoms and take case-histories and to think for herself rather than simply rely on what she has read. She keeps up to date by reading medical journals, as research and treatments are changing quickly.

She provides vaccinations against many diseases and can remind parents who have not had their children vaccinated that they should do so. She has a wide range of antibiotic drugs which are used against common infections which are now easily treated but once could have been fatal. She also does a lot of preventative work, giving anti-flu vaccine and advising people on diet and exercise, how to give up smoking and lose weight.

What did they do about public health in fourteenth-century London?

1 Butchers were put in the pillory for selling 'putrid, rotten, stinking and abominable meat'. The meat was burnt in front of them.

2 1301 – Four women butchers were caught throwing rotten blood and offal into the street.

3 1343 – Butchers were ordered to use a segregated area for butchering animals.

4 Wide streets had two gutters, one at each side. Narrow streets had one gutter in the middle.

5 By the 1370s, there were at least twelve teams of rakers with horses and carts, removing dung from the streets.

6 In 1345, the fine for throwing litter in the street was increased to two shillings. In 1372 anyone who had filth outside their house could be fined four shillings. Anyone throwing water from a window was fined two shillings.

7 There were open sewers carrying refuse to the river.

8 By the 1380s, there were at least thirteen common privies (public toilets) in the city. One on Temple Bridge was built over the Thames.

9 Houseowners living next to streams built latrines over the streams.

10 Houses away from streams sometimes had their own latrines. In 1391, a latrine built in a house cost £4. The mason dug the pit, and used stone, tiles and cement to line it.

11 Butchers carried waste through the streets, loaded it onto boats and threw it into the middle of the river at ebb tide.

12 Wells for fetching water and cesspools for dumping sewage were often close together. Regulations said that cesspools had to be built two and a half feet (76 centimetres) from a neighbour's soil if walled with stone, three and a half feet (106 centimetres) if walled with earth.

13 1364 – Two women were arrested for throwing rubbish in the street.

14 1307 – Thomas Scott was fined for assaulting two citizens who complained when he urinated in a lane instead of using the common privy.

Activities

This illustration shows London in the fourteenth century. Match the descriptions 1–14 with events A–N shown in the picture.

1 List the problems in keeping London clean and healthy.

2 List the methods used to keep London healthy by:
   a governments
   b individual people.

3 Does the evidence suggest that people cared about keeping London healthy?

Why was public health so poor in 1350?

Public health in 1350 was poor. In the early 1800s, it was even worse. Gradually and then more rapidly it improved. This chapter explains this pattern of change but first pages 146–150 investigate why it was so difficult to keep towns clean and healthy before 1800.

What is public health?

Governments organise public health systems to protect their people from disease. This includes providing, for example, fresh water and sewers, hospitals and making laws to force towns and people to try to prevent diseases spreading.

Source 1

Adapted from Ian Mortimer's *The Time Traveller's Guide to Medieval England*, 2008:

Arriving in Exeter

'When you draw closer to the city walls you will see the great gate-house, high circling walls, the statue of the king, the great round towers and – above it all – the immense cathedral, collectively impress you with their sheer strength.

And then you notice the smell. Four hundred yards from the city gate, the muddy road you are following crosses a brook. As you look along the banks you see piles of refuse, broken crockery, animal bones, entrails, human faeces, and rotting meat strewn in and around the bushes. As you watch, two semi-naked men lift another barrel of excrement from the back of a cart and empty it into the water. A small brown pig roots around on the garbage. It is not called Shitbrook for nothing.'

The streets of London

'The streets – even the main ones – have tubs of putrid water positioned here and there, supposedly in case of fire but more often than not full of decaying rubbish. The few streets which do preserve some vestige of road surface are so badly paved that the stones serve more to preserve the puddles than to assist transport. Elsewhere the heavily-trodden mud seems to last all year. Inhabitants will draw your attention to how "evil-smelling" this mud is just after it has rained. And yet these are not the worst of London's problems. The stench and obstruction of the animal dung, vegetable rubbish, fish remains and entrails of beasts present problems of public sanitation on a scale unmatched by any other town. With 40,000 permanent citizens and sometimes as many as 100,000 mouths to feed and bowels to evacuate, it is impossible for a city with no sewage system to cope. You will see rats everywhere. The place is infested with them. Such is the level of detritus, especially in the town ditches, that it is also infested with dogs and pigs.

You know things are really bad when, in 1355, the London authorities issue an order preventing any more excrement from being thrown into the ditch around the Fleet Prison on account of fears for the health of the prisoners.

London does improve, largely due to the efforts of successive mayors and aldermen to clean up the streets. The first step is appointing official swine killers, who are paid 4d for each pig they remove. In 1309, punitive fines are levied on those who leave human or animal excrement in the streets. From 1357 there are rules against leaving dung, crates and empty barrels lying by the doors of houses, and against throwing rubbish into the rivers. In 1371 all slaughtering of large beasts within the city is prohibited. Finally, a law passed in Parliament in 1388 makes anyone who throws "dung, garbage, entrails and other ordure" into ditches, ponds, lakes and rivers liable to pay a fine of £20 to the king. The idea of parliament working to improve public hygiene had begun.

You will also find a communal running water supply – fed through a series of conduits – even though the pressure is sometimes low, as a result of all the siphoning off to private houses. On certain special occasions the conduits are even made to run with wine – for example, on the arrival of the captive king of France in 1357, or to celebrate the coronation of Henry IV in 1399.'

Source 2

In 1332 Edward III wrote to the city of York:
'The King detests the abominable smell abounding in the city, more than in any other city of the realm, from dung and manure and other filth and dirt, which fills and obstructs the streets. Wishing to protect the health of the inhabitants and those coming to the parliament to be held in the city, orders the city to cause all the streets and lanes to be cleansed and to be kept clean.'

Activities

1 After reading this page, revise your lists of:
   a public health problems
   b methods of keeping London clean.
2 Why wasn't London kept clean and healthy in the 1300s? Choose the three reasons you think were most important.

Solutions
A small number of rakers employed to clean streets.
Building public latrines and regulations about where to build private latrines.
Laws to punish throwing waste.
A small number of officials tried to enforce laws.

Problems
People dropping waste and litter – and worse!
Open sewers.
Butchers throwing out waste.
Animals in streets.
Streets were often muddy with open drains along the middle.
Contents of cesspits emptied into streams and rivers used for washing and drinking water.

Why didn't their efforts work?

It is not my task as King to safeguard people's health. People expect me to lead my army and defend them – against the French, not against disease. I collect taxes to pay for wars, not to clean the streets or build sewers.

▲ King Edward III

We do not have enough officials to punish all the people who break the laws. Londoners will not pay the taxes we need to employ more officials.

▲ Lord Mayor of London

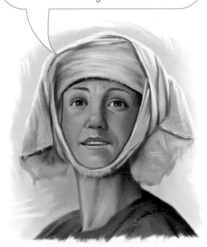

Why should I worry about dirt? God sends the diseases we suffer from. What's illness got to do with dirty streets?

▲ Londoner in 1300s

Had public health improved by 1700?

Activities

1 Look at the Lord Mayor's orders in 1665 below. Which two orders were most likely to help stop the spread of plague?

2 Look at the table column headed 'But …'. What were people's attitudes to the problem of plague? (Identify the attitudes of at least two groups of people.)

3 Read the opposite page. For each topic, explain whether London was healthier in 1700 than it had been in 1350.

4 Suggest two reasons why the problems of public health had not been solved. (You can follow up your suggestions on the next page.)

The Mayor of London's orders, 1665

1 Victims and their families were shut up in their homes and watchmen stood guard to stop anyone going in or out.

2 Bodies were examined by 'women searchers' to check that plague was the cause. Their findings were confirmed by surgeons.

3 Bedding had to be hung in the smoke of fires before being used again. Fires were lit in the streets to cleanse the air of poisons.

4 Householders were ordered to sweep the street outside their door.

5 Pigs, dogs, cats and other animals were banned inside the city.

6 Plays, bear-baitings and games were banned to prevent the assembly of large crowds.

But …

a Parliament refused to turn the orders into laws because members of the House of Lords refused to be shut in their houses.

b People ignored the rules. Over 20 watchmen were murdered by people escaping from houses that had been shut up.

c The King and his council left London. They discussed what to do about plague three times in seven months and two of those discussions were about the King's safety.

d Nine men were put in charge of dealing with the plague in London. Six of them left London as soon as they could.

How did they deal with the plague in 1665?

Plague never completely disappeared after the Black Death of 1348. Leicester, for example, suffered ten outbreaks between the 1550s and 1640s. A third of the people of York died from plague in 1604. Then, in 1665, came another epidemic that killed around 100,000 people in London, a quarter of the city's population and many thousands more all over Britain.

The Mayor of London published detailed orders aimed at preventing the spread of plague. The table below lists some of these orders – and the reasons why they were difficult to enforce.

Source 1

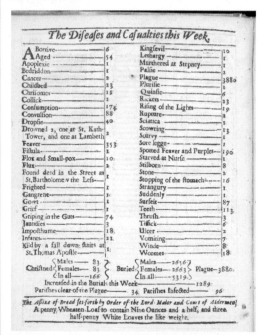

▲ A mortality bill for 1665, listing the numbers and causes of deaths in each parish. The bills showed that highest numbers of deaths were in the poorest, dirtiest, most overcrowded parishes. This led some people to link dirt and disease, a sign of a more scientific approach based on observation of the evidence.

What did they do about public health in London in the late 1600s?

The streets – clean or dirty?

1350 Paving was poor and streets were often muddy and full of dirt with open drains running down the centre or side. Horses and animals brought for slaughter added a great deal of dirt. Rakers were employed to keep the streets clean but there were never enough of them.

1700 The animals still filled the streets with dirt because they needed to be walked to London to be slaughtered to feed the people. Pigs, cattle, sheep and turkeys all arrived in large numbers. There were still plenty of horses as carriages had become popular.

Streets were cobbled or paved but this was still haphazard, with more mud than paving, and there were few pavements. Many streets sloped down to a central drain, but this was often blocked with rubbish and animal droppings. Many homes now burned coal in fires which added to the dirt. Rakers were still employed to keep the streets clean, but there were still never enough of them. Householders were told by law to sweep the areas outside their homes every day.

Water supplies

1350 Water for drinking and washing was carried from rivers, collected in barrels or from the conduits (public standpipes) in the streets or bought from water-carriers, men who carried water around the streets.

1700 Most people still got their water from the conduits, from barrels or from water-carriers. People with larger gardens could dig wells to collect water but there was often a danger of the well being too close to the family cesspit which could leak into the water supply.

There was now a network of wooden pipes under much of the city, although children had fun making holes in them to create fountains! Wealthier families obtained water from a reservoir after paying an annual fee, but this was often for only two or three days a week so they stored water in tanks in the cellars of houses. This water rapidly became stagnant and couldn't be used for drinking.

Public toilets

1350 There were public toilets, but not nearly enough for the size of the population. This meant that people used street corners, the river, anywhere quiet. The famous Mayor, Richard Whittington, gave money in the 1420s to build a public toilet with 128 seats, but over time the city government failed to keep it in good repair.

1700 There were still some public toilets, but most Londoners used toilets in taverns or the houses of friends or the quiet corners or doorways that became accepted as 'pissing places'. A writer called Anthony Wood who lived in Oxford commented that, when King Charles II and his courtiers visited Oxford, 'They were neat and colourful in their clothing yet they were very nasty and beastly, leaving their excrements in every corner, in chimneys, studies, coalhouses, cellars.'

Sewers and waste removal

1350 There were open sewers taking away dirt and human excrement, but people also used the rivers or simply emptied chamber pots into the street.

1700 Night soil men were employed to carry away human excrement from cess pits but this didn't happen every day and sometimes not every week. Cesspits that were full could overflow into the cellars of neighbouring homes or into nearby water tanks. Many people were too poor to afford night soil men, so they still emptied their waste into the rivers or drains or out of the window.

Householders were ordered by law to put out rubbish every Wednesday and Saturday to be collected by the rakers. However, there were too few officials to make sure this happened. The rakers then left the rubbish in open spaces so that country carts would take it out of the city – which meant that it might not be taken away at all.

Why had public health not improved by 1700?

Activities

1 The three factors on the left, science and technology, attitudes and beliefs in society, and government, are the main reasons why public health did not improve much between 1350 and 1700. Which cards provide evidence of the impact of each of these three factors?

2 Which of these factors do you think is most important in explaining why public health had not improved? Explain why you chose this factor.

3 Use Sources 1–3 opposite. Why did public health get even worse in the early 1800s?

4 Each of the five factors above played a part in improving public health after the early 1800s. Suggest how you think each one might have had a positive impact on public health? For example, think about what kinds of chance events might have led to improvement and what contributions might individuals have played.

1. People did not pay taxes every year. Taxes were mostly collected to pay for defence and wars.	2. The monarch's most important work was war and defence and preventing crime.	3. Building in stone and brick was increasing but there were many wooden houses in towns. There was little experience of large engineering projects apart from the rebuilding of parts of London after the Great Fire of 1666.	4. People still believed that disease was caused by a combination of bad air and their humours being out of balance. They were worried about dirt but there was no clear link between dirt and disease.	5. Ordinary people had no say in electing MPs or in which laws were passed by Parliament.	6. People did not have a strong expectation of improvement in living conditions or that the monarch and government should work to improve everyone's lives.

How did the Industrial Revolution change the towns in the early 1800s?

Source 1

◄ *Coalbrookdale at Night*, painted by Philippe Jacques de Loutherbourg in 1801. Coalbrookdale in Shropshire was the home of the iron industry. The great orange light comes from the fires in the furnaces where the iron was made. Artists flocked to paint scenes like this, which had never existed before. They also painted pictures of large textile factories, another new arrival in the landscape. However, for the people working in these industries the scenes were not so picturesque. Ten- or twelve-hour working days were common in hot and dirty conditions, surrounded by dangerous machinery.

Source 2

▲ *Over London by Rail*, an engraving of London housing by Gustave Doré in 1872. Houses in the towns were crammed together in the centre because people had to walk to work until the later 1800s. As towns grew fast between 1750 and 1850 there were no laws forcing local councils to provide sewers, fresh water or toilets in homes. Water came from pipes in the streets.

Source 3

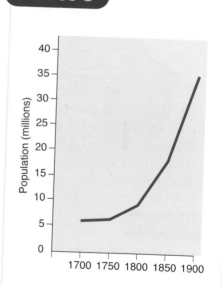

▲ The growth of the population of England and Wales 1700–1900.

147

How bad was public health in the early 1800s?

The Industrial Revolution was a time of huge change, transforming people's lives, mostly for the better. But its immediate effects were terrible, with people living and working in worse conditions than they had in the Middle Ages. So how bad was life in the early 1800s?

My name is Edwin Chadwick. In 1842, I completed my 'Report on the Sanitary Conditions of the Labouring Population'. My conclusion is that the public health conditions of working people are worse than they have ever been. I have based my conclusion on statistics like these in Source 1. What can you learn from Sources 1–6 to support my conclusion?

Source 1

Gentry or Professionals		Tradesmen		Labourers or artisans	
35	52	22	41	15	38
Liverpool	Rutland	Liverpool	Rutland	Liverpool	Rutland

▲ This shows the differences in average age at death among different groups of people in 1840. Chadwick collected these statistics for his report. Liverpool was chosen as an example of a large, rapidly growing town. Rutland was chosen as a country area.

Source 2

A traveller's description of Leeds, reported in *The Morning Chronicle*, 1848 (scavengers were employed to take away refuse and empty the privies):
'The east and north-east districts of Leeds are, perhaps, the worst, a perfect wilderness of foulness.

Conceive acre on acre of little streets, run up without attention to plan or health, acre on acre of closely-built and thickly-peopled ground, without a paving stone on the surface, or an inch of sewer beneath, deep trodden-churned sloughs of mud forming the only thoroughfares, privies often ruinous, all most horribly foul. Conceive streets and courts and yards which a scavenger never appears to have entered since King John's time and which gives the idea of a town built on a slimy bog. Conceive such a surface drenched with the liquid slops which each family flings out daily and nightly. Pigs seem to be the natural inhabitants, more common in some parts of Leeds than dogs and cats.'

Source 3

Death rates in cholera epidemics in Britain:

1831–2	26,101 deaths
1848–9	53,293 deaths
1853–4	20,079 deaths
1865	14,378 deaths

Source 4

▲ A cartoon called 'A Court For King Cholera'. It is a drawing of London published in 1852.

The street is overcrowded – how could this affect health?

The children look very dirty and are playing with the rubbish – what can you infer from this?

Activity

What can you infer (work out) from Source 4 about dangers to health in this part of London? Use the clues we have included and then list other evidence in this picture.

Source 5

▲ A cartoon published in 1831. It is commentating on where the Southwark Water Company in London got its water from.

Source 6

THE WATER THAT JOHN DRINKS.

THIS is the water that JOHN drinks.

This is the Thames with its cento of stink,
That supplies the water that JOHN drinks.

These are the fish that float in the ink-
-y stream of the Thames with its cento of stink,
That supplies the water that JOHN drinks.

These are vested int'rests, that fill to the brink,
The network of sewers from cesspool and sink,
That feed the fish that float in the ink-
-y stream of the Thames, with its cento of stink,
That supplies the water that JOHN drinks.

This is the price that we pay to wink
At the vested int'rests that fill to the brink,
The network of sewers from cesspool and sink,
That feed the fish that float in the ink-
-y stream of the Thames with its cento of stink,
That supplies the water that JOHN drinks.

▲ 'The Water that John drinks', a cartoon from *Punch* magazine, October 1849.

Activities

1 List the details in Sources 1–6 that show that public health conditions were very poor.
2 Which evidence do you think is the strongest argument against going back in time to live in the first half of the 1800s?

Why wasn't anything done to protect people's health in the early 1800s?

What is an iceberg doing in a history book? It's here to warn you of a hidden danger beneath the surface of this enquiry. It's easy to assume the only danger to health was the selfishness of the rich who refused to pay for improvements. But what are the other reasons on the iceberg, hidden below the surface?

Source 1

From 'Report on the Condition of the Town of Leeds' by James Smith, 1844:

'A proposal was made for the complete sewerage of the streets. I was present for nearly six hours of this debate. The chief theme of the speakers in opposition related to saving the pockets of the ratepayers and had very little regard to the sanitary results.'

Source 2

Extracts from a letter in *The Times* newspaper, 1 August 1854:

'We prefer to take our chance with cholera than be bullied into health … '

'There is nothing a man hates so much as being cleaned against his will, having his floors swept, his walls whitewashed, his pet dung heaps cleared away.'

Vested interests

Activities

Complete your own copy of this iceberg illustration to explain fully why public health was so poor.

1. Read Sources 1 and 2. What exactly were the vested interests that were against improving public health? Add short notes to the bullet points at the top of the iceberg to summarise them.
2. What should go in the rest of the iceberg? Use the clues on the page opposite to write a series of short headings summing up the other reasons. Use the factor list (page 146) to help you.
3. Now think about which reasons were most important. Review the reasons on your own iceberg drawing. How would you redraw it to show which reasons were most important?
4. What was most needed to improve public health? Make three suggestions before you turn over and find out what happened.

Clue A

Pasteur's germ theory was not published and accepted by scientists and doctors until the 1860s. Pasteur's discovery of the value of boiling milk (pasteurisation) did not become common until the 1880s because many people believed that boiling killed the goodness.

Clue B

Towns had grown very fast. Landlords made profits from renting out houses so wanted them built quickly.

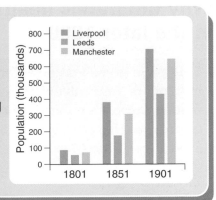

Clue C

Railways were not built to take people in and out of town centres in large numbers until the 1850s and later. Workers therefore had to live close to their places of work.

Clue D

There was a strong belief that people should help themselves to live better, healthier and more comfortable lives. People objected to local and national governments 'interfering' in their lives. The protests against compulsory smallpox vaccinations, which you read about in Section 6, are a good example.

Clue E

Governments were still not expected to play a major part in improving the living and working conditions of the people. There were no pensions or help for the sick and unemployed from governments. The first income tax was collected in 1798 and stayed low in the 1800s.

Clue F

Doctors were not paid by the government so had to charge fees to their patients. Therefore the poor could not afford to go to a doctor.

Clue G

Fresh food was difficult to get in many towns because it had to be brought in by horse and cart and was expensive. Food was often adulterated – mixed with other things (chalk in bread, sand in sugar, sawdust in flour) – by shopkeepers to increase its weight and so make more money from sales.

Clue H

Working conditions were at least as bad as home conditions. Workers in mines, workshops and factories had long hours and only very short breaks. Their toilet and washing facilities were very poor, with many people sharing one privy and only a pipe to wash at. Many people also fell ill from the work itself, swallowing coal and textile dust, which caused lung diseases.

Why did public health eventually improve in the later 1800s?

This page gives you an interpretation of why public health improved. Your task is to test this interpretation and then reach your own conclusions about why public health improved. Use pages 154–163 to help you. Pay special attention to the Meet the examiner on pages 156–159 as this will help to structure your investigation.

My name is Edwin Chadwick. I can tell you exactly why public health improved. It was all my doing! Let me explain how I did it.

1 My great report

In 1842 I wrote my 'Report on the Sanitary Conditions of the Labouring Population'. Here's what my report shows:

1. The poor live in dirty, overcrowded conditions.

2. This causes a huge amount of illness.

3. Many people are too sick to work and so become poorer still.

4. Therefore other people have to pay higher taxes to help the poor.

My solution was simple:

We can cut taxes and save money in the long run by:

1. improving drainage and sewers

2. removing refuse from streets and houses

3. providing clean water supplies

4. appointing medical officers in each area to check these reforms.

2 The Public Health Act 1848

Of course there was opposition. Many local tax-payers did not want to pay for improvements even though it meant lower taxes in the long run. The government was not happy either. It knew that local councils did not want the national government interfering in local matters. However, my ideas won, helped by another outbreak of cholera in 1848. The government, pushed by me, introduced the Public Health Act. It said:

1. A national Board of Health was to be set up.
2. In towns where the death-rate was very high, the government could force the local council to make public health improvements to water supply and sewerage and appoint a Medical Officer of Health.
3. Local councils were encouraged to collect taxes (called rates) for public health improvements if they had the support of local rate-payers.
4. Councils were allowed to appoint Medical Officers of Health to oversee public health.

3 The Public Health Act 1875

Of course I had wanted the government to do more. I wanted them to force all local councils to make changes. Some towns did make changes. Most did nothing. More outbreaks of cholera in 1853 and 1865 showed I was right. In 1875 the government finally did what I wanted and passed a proper Public Health Act. It said:

Local councils forced to provide clean water, public toilets and proper drains and sewers.	**Councils forced to appoint a Medical Officer of Health.**

More changes followed – a law against polluting rivers, a law to improve the quality of food sold in shops, a law to ensure new houses are built to clean, healthy standards.

4 The result of all my work

By 1900 people were living healthier, longer lives. Life expectancy for men had risen to 46, for women to 50. Towns were cleaner and safer. Yet for all my efforts they didn't give me a knighthood until I was 89, the year before I died. How ungrateful! But I died happy. **All those improvements came about because of my great report and hard work.**

Edwin Chadwick (1800–1890)

Chadwick was a civil servant who worked for the Poor Law Commission in the 1830s and 1840s. In 1848 he became a member of the National Board of Health but it was disbanded in 1854 because it was unpopular. Chadwick retired in 1854 and played no part in advising governments after this. He had made too many enemies. His main weakness was that he did not know how to get other people on his side. He was argumentative, arrogant and rude as well as extremely hard-working.

Right up until his death, Chadwick continued to believe that disease was caused by miasmas, or 'bad air'. He did not accept Pasteur's germ theory.

Activities

1   Summarise Chadwick's explanation in two or three sentences. Include:
    a   why public health improved
    b   the major stages in that improvement.
2   Now look closely at the detail and think carefully about the Public Health Acts.
    a   What were the limitations of the 1848 Public Health Act?
    b   Why was the 1875 Public Health Act a major improvement?
    c   How much involvement did Chadwick have with the 1875 Act?
3   a   What seem to be the weaknesses of Chadwick's argument?
    b   What other factors would you expect to play a part in improving public health?

Analysing and evaluating the importance of an individual

The impression that Chadwick gave of public health on page 148 was very accurate. The public health conditions of working people were probably worse than they had ever been before. But does Chadwick deserve most of the credit for improving these conditions?

> How important was the role played by Edwin Chadwick in improving public health services in towns in the nineteenth century?
>
> **[16 marks]**

You need to be careful with this type of question. Like an iceberg, there is more to it than meets the eye! Many students think that a question such as this requires them to write *only* about the importance of Chadwick's work. This would be very dangerous. Look at the question closely. You need to evaluate the importance of Chadwick's work. You need to look at the positive impact of his work *and* you need to consider the limitations of what he did. You also need to **weigh Chadwick's contribution to improving public health services against the contribution made by other individuals and other factors**. Were other factors more important? Follow the steps opposite to negotiate this iceberg question safely and successfully!

Step 1: Deal with the part of the question that is above the surface (evidence that supports the statement)

Paragraph 1 – Explain the importance of Chadwick's role

- Use the information on pages 154 and 158 to help you.
- Remember the importance of connectives to tie your answer together. Do more than simply describe what Chadwick did. Link what he did to changes that took place.

Step 2: Deal with the part of the question that lurks beneath the surface (evidence that challenges the statement)

Paragraph 2 – Explain the limitations of what Chadwick did

- Chadwick's argumentative and arrogant character meant that he found it difficult to get people on his side. Could Chadwick have achieved more? What were the limitations of what he did?
- Use the information on page 158 to help you.

Paragraph 3 – Evaluate the role played by other individuals

Other individuals played important roles in improving public health. Make sure you explain their importance. For example:
- William Farr (see page 158)
- John Snow (see page 159)
- Joseph Bazalgette (see page 163).

Paragraph 4 – Evaluate the role played by other factors

Other factors also played a very important role.
- The cards opposite provide you with other factors that played an important role in improving medicine. But which ones had a real influence on improving public health during the nineteenth century?
- As you study pages 158–163 find out which of these factors played a key role and explain their contribution.

Paragraph 5 – Conclusion

- Time to reach an overall judgement. Do you agree with the statement? Did Chadwick play the main role or were other factors more important?

Using card sorts to evaluate factors

It is important to **establish a clear line of argument** before you begin your answer to this type of question in the exam. As you can see from the cards below there are lots of factors that could have played a role in improving public health. You need to decide which factors were the most important **before you begin your answer**.

Activities

1 Make your own set of the cards below. As you read pages 158–163 you will find evidence that **some** of the factors played an important role in improving public health. Make notes explaining how these factors contributed on the back of the relevant factor card.

2 When you finish making notes organise the cards into a shape that shows how important you think each factor is. You can use one of the shapes below or use your own design. Remember that some factors did not contribute at all.

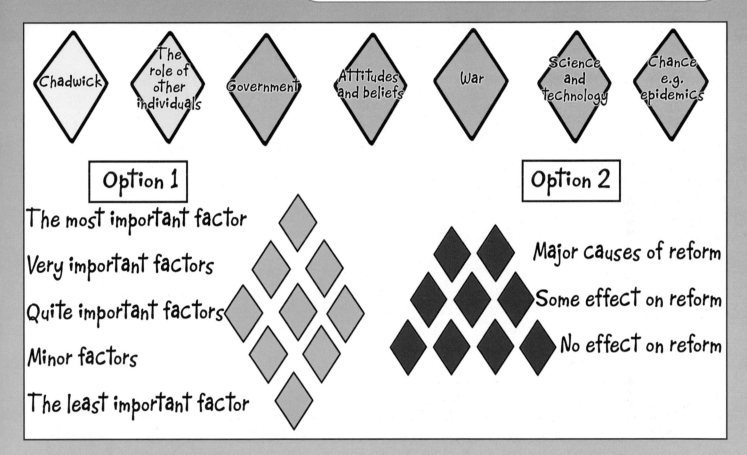

smarter revision

Why are card sorts useful?

- **They help you to select what to include in your answer.** After evaluating the roles played by Chadwick and other individuals you will probably only have time to write about the role played by two or three other factors. The card sort makes sure you include relevant and important factors.

- **They help you develop a clear line of argument.** It is a lot easier to write a good answer that is focused on the question if you have a clear line of argument in your head before you start to write. Successful students spend time thinking about their approach to the question before they start to write.

What was the most important factor in the improvement of public health?

How important a part did Chadwick really play?

Chadwick's positive impact

Hard-work produced a mass of evidence supporting public health reform.

1842 Report influenced the government and persuaded people that reform was needed.

His report's recommendations were the basis for the 1848 Public Health Act.

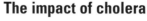

Chadwick's negative impact

1842 Report did not lead to immediate reform. The Public Health Act came in 1848.

The 1848 Act did not force councils to reform public health.

His personality antagonised people and did not win support for his cause.

His influence faded in the 1850s.

What role did William Farr play?

Chadwick was not the only civil servant who built up evidence of the links between poverty, dirt and ill-health. After 1837 all births, deaths and marriages had to be registered and William Farr used this information to build an accurate picture of where the death rate was highest and what people died of. This proved the link between high death-rate and unhealthy living conditions. His statistics shamed some towns into improving local public health conditions. Therefore Farr's evidence also put pressure on local and national government to make changes.

The impact of cholera

The timing of the 1848 Public Health Act was the result of the latest epidemic of cholera. As cholera spread across Europe in 1847 fear grew in Britain of many thousands of deaths to come. Therefore the government finally followed Chadwick's recommendations and passed the Public Health Act in the hope that this would reduce the impact of cholera. However, the 1848 Act was not compulsory. Only 103 towns set up local Boards of Health. Many more did not, and the National Board of Health, set up to oversee reforms, was abolished after only six years in 1854.

The work of John Snow

Snow was a pioneer in surgery as well as in public health, improving medical methods and using detailed evidence to challenge old theories. In 1849 he published a book saying that cholera spread through water, not in 'bad air', but his suggestion was mocked by many doctors. In 1854 another cholera outbreak gave him the chance to prove his theory that people caught cholera from water they used for washing and drinking.

Cholera killed over 500 people around Broad Street, near Snow's surgery, in just ten days. This led Snow to map out the deaths in detail and write a report detailing his evidence: 'On the Mode of Communication of Cholera'.

Snow's evidence was so strong that the handle of the Broad Street water pump was taken away, stopping people getting water from the pump. There were no more deaths. It was later discovered that a cesspool, only a metre away from the pump, was leaking into the drinking water.

Snow had proved that clean water was essential for preventing the spread of cholera but even this did not lead to a new Public Health Act enforcing change. Many scientists still clung to the 'bad air' theory (Pasteur had not yet published his germ theory).

▲ John Snow was born in Yorkshire in 1813, the son of a farm labourer. Aged 14 he was apprenticed to a surgeon and eventually became a fully-qualified doctor.

Source 1

From Snow's 'On the Mode of Communication of Cholera', 1854:

'On proceeding to the spot, I found that nearly all of the deaths had taken place within a short distance of the Broad Street water pump. There were only ten deaths in houses situated decidedly nearer to another street pump. In five of these cases, the families of the deceased persons informed me that they always used the pump in Broad Street as they preferred the water to that of the pump that was nearer.

There is a brewery in Broad Street. Perceiving that no brewer's men were registered as having died of cholera, I called on Mr Huggins, the owner. He informed that there were about 70 workmen employed in the brewery and that only two of them had been indisposed by cholera and then not seriously. The men are allowed to drink beer, and Mr Huggins believed that they do not drink water at all and never obtained water from the Broad Street pump.'

Source 2

▲ This cartoon is called 'Death's Dispensary'. It was published in 1860.

Source 3

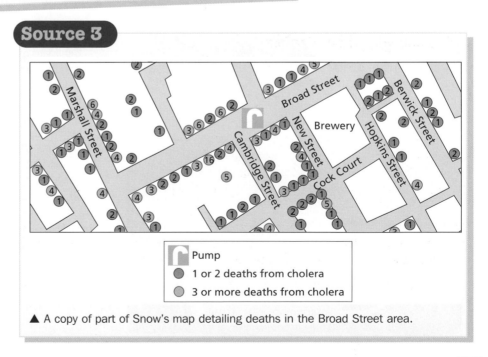

Pump
● 1 or 2 deaths from cholera
● 3 or more deaths from cholera

▲ A copy of part of Snow's map detailing deaths in the Broad Street area.

Activities

1 **a** What is the message in Source 4?
   b Why do you think it was published?
2 Why were there no more public health reforms in the 1850s?
3 Why was another Public Health Act passed in 1875?
4 Add more evidence to your diamond cards (but you'll have to decide which ones to fill in yourselves from information on this page!).

The Great Stink

The summer of 1858 was hot – very hot. There was no rain to fill the rivers and river levels fell, especially the Thames in London. As a result, the smell from the river grew worse and worse; one of the very worst places was at the Houses of Parliament which are right on the river bank. The 'Great Stink' (as it was called) added to the evidence that more public reform was needed. In London itself an effective, modern sewer system was built, but there was no new Public Health Act to enforce improvements throughout the country.

Source 4

◄ This cartoon was published in *The Times* newspaper on 18 June 1858.

FATHER THAMES INTRODUCING HIS OFFSPRING TO THE FAIR CITY OF LONDON.
(A Design for a Fresco in the New Houses of Parliament.)

Why was there no compulsory Public Health reform in the 1850s?

Why should we pay taxes to protect other people's health?

No government interference in my town!

Source 5

A letter in *The Times* newspaper, 1 August 1854:
'The Board of Health has fallen. We prefer to take our chance with cholera than be bullied into health. Everywhere the board's inspectors were bullying, insulting and expensive. They entered houses and factories insisting on changes revolting to the habits or pride of the masters and occupants. There is nothing a man hates so much as being cleaned against his will, having his floors swept, his walls whitewashed, his pet dung heaps cleared away, all at the command of a sort of sanitary bumbailiff. Mr. Chadwick set to work everywhere, washing and splashing, and Master John Bull was scrubbed and rubbed till the tears came to his eyes and his fists clenched themselves with worry and pain.'

So why was conservatism finally defeated?

The impact of Pasteur

In 1861, Pasteur published his germ theory. In 1864, he conducted a series of public experiments that convinced most scientists that diseases were caused by bacteria (germs) (see page 100). This finally provided the clear proof that was needed of the link between dirt and disease and showed that Chadwick, Farr and Snow had all been correct in their arguments.

Faced with this scientific proof, people were more willing to pay taxes to cover the costs of public health reforms – fresh water supplies, good sewers and public toilets – and more local towns began to make these reforms.

Government and political reform

For years governments had been unwilling to make public health reform compulsory. The only voters in general elections were wealthy landowners and the well-off middle classes, the very people who would have to pay more if public health reforms became compulsory. Governments did not want to offend these men (they were all men – no women could vote) and risk losing their votes in an election.

All this changed in 1867 when working men in towns were given the right to vote for the first time. Suddenly the numbers of voters had doubled. It increased again in 1884 when many working men in country areas got the vote. Politics had changed dramatically even though all women and some men still could not vote.

If politicians wanted to win elections they had to promise laws to win the votes of working men, not just the wealthy and middle classes. The 1870s and 1880s saw many new laws passed designed to improve the lives of ordinary people. One of these was the Public Health Act of 1875.

The result: The Great Clean-up

The Public Health Act (1875) made it compulsory for local councils to improve sewers and drainage, provide fresh water supplies and to appoint Medical Officers and sanitary inspectors to inspect public health facilities.

Other laws were passed that:
- improved the standards of housing
- stopped the pollution of rivers (from which people got water)
- shortened working hours in factories for women and children
- made it illegal to add ingredients that made food unhealthy
- made education compulsory.

How did technology make the Great Clean-up possible?

Science and Technology	Individuals	Government

Sewers

Passing a law saying public health reform was compulsory was only the beginning. After that came the hard engineering work, building the new systems. This used engineering knowledge that had not been available a hundred years earlier but there had been great improvements in technology during the Industrial Revolution and the building of the railways (e.g. machinery powered by steam engines, methods of building pipelines and embankments). This knowledge was essential to make the laws effective.

Source 1

▲ Until the 1860s cities had open sewers like this one in London. This photograph, taken in 1900, shows how long it took for local councils to get rid of the many, many miles of open sewers.

Source 2

▲ Public health reform involved huge engineering projects to build sewers and water pipes under city streets. This photograph shows sewers being built.

Joseph Bazalgette (1819–1891)

Bazalgette was the engineer who designed and built London's sewer system after the Great Stink of 1858. He spent his early career in the railway industry, gaining experience of large engineering projects. After 1858 he planned and organised the building of London's sewer system, the same system that is till used today. This system included:

- 83 miles of main sewers, built underground from brick
- 1100 miles of sewers for each street and connecting to the main sewers
- a series of major pumping stations to drive the flow of sewage along the pipes.

The core of the work was completed by 1865 but it was such a huge project it took another ten years to complete. Fortunately Bazalgette looked ahead and forecast the growth of population so made sure the system had a much higher capacity than was needed in the 1860s.

Lavatories

Source 3

▲ An invention that also made a difference was the flushing lavatory. Instead of privies needing to be emptied by hand and spade (and left rotting for days or weeks) the flushing system sent the waste instantly down into the sewer network. Of course at first such lavatories were only available to the rich but it was the beginning of a very important change.

Soap

Source 4

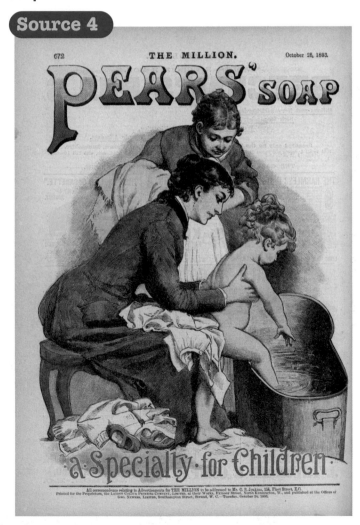

▲ And there was soap! Today a bar of soap is a very ordinary thing but it was much rarer in the mid-1800s, partly because it was taxed and so was too expensive for many people to buy. In 1853 the tax was taken off soap so many more people could afford it, and so washing did more to kill germs even if people did not know it at the time.

Evaluating the usefulness of a source

In the exam you will be asked to evaluate the value of a source for a specific enquiry.

Look at this exam question:

3 Study Source C.

How useful is this cartoon to a historian who is investigating public health problems in Britain in the nineteenth century?

Use Source C and your own knowledge to explain your answer.   **[8 marks]**

Source C

This cartoon by George Pinwell is called 'Death's Dispensary'. It was published in an English magazine in 1866.

Advice

This question requires you to evaluate the extent to which the source would help a historian investigating public health problems in Britain in the nineteenth century. You need to think carefully about how you approach this type of question.

Often students answer utility questions by either commenting on:

* the **relevance** of the information contained in the source, or
* the **reliability** of the source.

You must aim to do **both**! Consider the content **and** the reliability.

Try to be positive

You need to consider the strengths **and** weaknesses of a source.

REMEMBER ... The question is asking you how **useful** the sources are, not how **useless** they are. There will not be any sources that are completely useless. Do not get bogged down telling the examiner what is wrong with the source. Try to begin and end your answer positively.

Activity

Use the planning grid below to help you develop an effective answer.
Remember to support your comments with evidence from the sources.

SOURCE EVALUATION GRID		
	Strengths	**Limitations**
Step 1: Consider the content of the source **a What do we learn?** (Use your inference skills) Explain why the source contains useful information. Explain how the source can be used. **b** What do we not learn? Use your own knowledge to explain what information is missed out. What else would a historian want to know?	*Source C is useful because it helps us understand …* (lack of a clean water supply, many people in the 1800s died from drinking infected water) *It shows us that …* (despite the work of John Snow and the publication of Pasteur's germ theory cholera epidemics existed in the mid 1860s) *The phrase 'gratis to the poor' shows how it was mainly the poor people who were affected.*	*However, Source C has some limitations. It does not provide us with …* [information about the numbers of people who were killed, other public health problems, e.g. lack of sewers]
Step 2: Consider the provenance of the source? What is the **nature** of the source? What type of source is it? What are the **origins** of the source? Who wrote or produced the source? When was it produced? What was the **purpose** of the source? Why was it produced?	*Source C is a …* (cartoon, produced in the 1860s) *The fact that it was published in a magazine shows that …* (the views expressed by the artist were shared by other people)	*However, we need to be careful about totally trusting the impression given in Source C. It was probably produced to…* (raise awareness of the problems caused by unclean water supplies) *The artist may have …* [exaggerated the problem to grab people's attention]
Step 3: Use your own knowledge to place the source in its historical context. How **typical** is the source?	*Source C was produced at the time of …* (another cholera epidemic – mid 1860s – over 14,000 deaths in Britain – the problem the artist highlights was a major one and deaths from cholera were common)	*However …* (the epidemic that hit Britain in the 1860s was not as devastating as previous ones, e.g. over 50,000 deaths in 1848–1849. The cartoon could give the impression that things had not changed – but Snow had shown the cause of cholera and there was greater public awareness)

Step 4: Reach an overall judgement

Students often fail to reach an overall evaluation.
Make sure you do not forget a conclusion that really addresses the question.
Always end with a conclusion in which you reach a judgement.
- How useful is the source (very/quite)?
- What is your key reason for reaching this judgement?

Why did public health improve further in the twentieth century?

We guided you through the story of nineteenth-century public health. Now you have to plan your own investigation using pages 168–177 so that you can answer the question in the title above.

How much had public health really improved?

By 1900, life expectancy was starting to rise. It had reached 46 for men and 50 for women. Towns were becoming cleaner. Public health facilities were beginning to improve. But the key words so far are 'starting to' and 'beginning to'. Many people still suffered major health problems, partly because of dirt but even more because of poverty. The government still gave no help to the sick, unemployed and elderly no matter how poor they were. Those who could not get help from friends and relatives or charities had to give up their homes and go into a workhouse, run by the local council.

Sources 1 and 2 show the kind of statistics that led to demands for more reforms. Source 3 gives a different kind of information – the experience of one family living in poverty. Even more influential were two detailed reports by Charles Booth and Seebohm Rowntree that demonstrated the extent of poverty and highlighted the links between poverty and ill-health.

Source 1

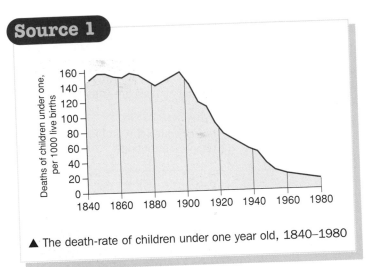

▲ The death-rate of children under one year old, 1840–1980

Source 2

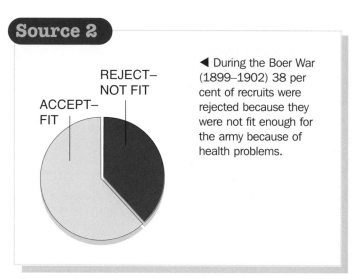

◄ During the Boer War (1899–1902) 38 per cent of recruits were rejected because they were not fit enough for the army because of health problems.

Source 3

From the memoirs of Mrs John Brown (1847–1935) describing a visit in the late 1800s:

'In the bed was a young woman, wan and dazed. She was holding a week-old baby to her empty breast. It was so pitiful I did not know what to say. "I thought there were two children."

   "There was three days ago," the woman said. "Show her, Jem."

   The man opened the bottom drawer of a rickety chest and there lay a little dead child of two. He said, "We be waiting for the parish to come and bury her." The mother said 'We couldn't put her upstairs, alone in the empty room."I stood still, sobbing, but the parents shed no tears nor said a word, except when Jem closed the drawer.
"She were a nice little lass, she were," he said.'

Charles Booth (1840–1916)

Life and Labour of the people in London

Booth was a successful Liverpool businessman and a friend of Octavia Hill and others who were trying to improve living conditions for the poor. He was well aware of the effects of poverty on health among the Liverpool poor, but thought that campaigners were exaggerating when they said that 25 per cent of Londoners lived in poverty. In 1886, Booth set about collecting the detailed, accurate evidence that would prove or disprove that figure. He financed research into poverty in the East End of London, but also spent weeks living in the area himself, renting rooms in a common lodging house. The result was an extremely detailed description of living conditions and poverty, complete with coloured maps identifying the extent of poverty in each street of east London. Booth's research discovered that 35 per cent of people were living in poverty – far more than had been claimed.

Appalled by these results, Booth continued his work, building up evidence of poverty and ill-health in London that was published in 17 volumes. He argued that government had to take responsibility for caring for people in poverty. One of his suggestions was the creation of an old age pension.

Seebohm Rowntree (1871–1954)

Poverty: A Study of Town Life

Rowntree investigated poverty and living conditions in York where his family had been in business for many years. In 1901, he published *Poverty: a Study of Town Life* providing detailed evidence that more than a quarter of the people in York were living in poverty, even through they were in work, and that poverty was having a serious impact on their health. This led him to increase his own workers' wages and to continue his research, charting changes in conditions. In 1941, he published a new report *Progress and Poverty* which showed a 50 per cent reduction in poverty since 1901 and that poverty in the 1930s was mostly the result of unemployment rather than low wages.

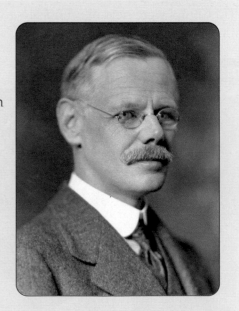

Activities

1 What do Sources 1–3 suggest about how much public health had improved by 1900?
2 Why was the research by Booth and Rowntree important?

What difference did the Liberal government of 1906–1914 make?

In 1906, a new Liberal government was elected with a landslide majority of votes. Many people expected this government to make major reforms to improve everyday life. To do this, the Liberals had to raise taxes to pay for improvements. Here are some of the measures the government took. They may seem unimportant nowadays, but a hundred years ago they were revolutionary.

1902 Compulsory training for midwives.

1906 Meals provided free for school children in need.

1907 All births had to be notified to the local Medical Officer of Health. A health visitor visited each mother to make sure she knew how to protect her baby's health.

1907 Nurses or doctors had to carry out medical checks on children in schools.

1908 Old age pensions were paid to people over 70 who did not have enough money to live on.

1909 Back to back housing was banned. New regulations enforced higher standards of house building.

1911 National Insurance Act providing help for the sick if they fell ill (see page 171).

1912 Clinics were held in schools to give children free medical treatment.

David Lloyd George (1863–1945)

David Lloyd George was one of the most inspirational politicians in British history. He was a brilliant, persuasive speaker, determined to improve the lives of ordinary people and was a friend of Rowntree. He became a Liberal MP in 1890 and was Chancellor of the Exchequer in the Liberal government which introduced the reforms (above). He insisted on raising taxes on the well-off to pay for old age pensions and the National Insurance Act of 1911 (see page 171). He became Prime Minister in 1916 during World War One.

Source 1

▲ Schools for mothers first opened in 1907.
The schools taught:
- the importance of hygiene and the danger of diarrhoea for infants
- how flies spread disease from privies and rubbish in streets
- that breast-feeding was better than bottle-feeding
- that good mothering was a duty to be performed for King and Country!

A big step forward – the 1911 National Insurance Act

One of the greatest changes introduced by Lloyd George and the Liberal government was the National Insurance Act of 1911. The aim was to give workers medical help and sick pay if they could not work through illness. Until then, workers who fell ill had a choice – carry on working or get no pay, which meant they had no chance of affording medical help.

As Source 2 shows, the National Insurance scheme required the worker, his employer and the government to pay into a sickness fund. It was a major step forward but many people were left out of the scheme. It only included people in work, not their families. Most women and all children were excluded. So were the unemployed and elderly and anyone who had a long-lasting illness.

Source 2

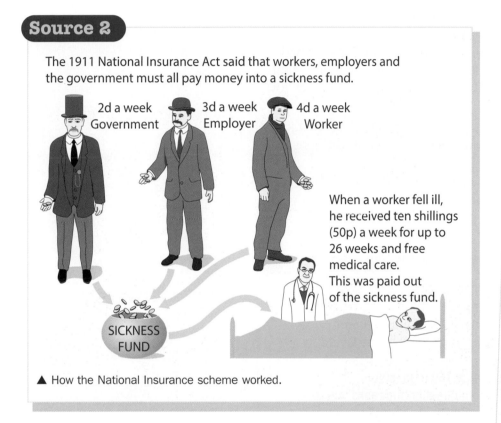

The 1911 National Insurance Act said that workers, employers and the government must all pay money into a sickness fund.

2d a week Government

3d a week Employer

4d a week Worker

When a worker fell ill, he received ten shillings (50p) a week for up to 26 weeks and free medical care. This was paid out of the sickness fund.

SICKNESS FUND

▲ How the National Insurance scheme worked.

Source 3

The Times, 2 January 1905, commenting on plans to provide free school meals for the poorest children: 'We have already reduced personal responsibility by taking away from parents the duty of educating their children. This is now used as an argument for taking away from them the duty of feeding their children. From that it is an easy step to paying for their proper housing. The proposed measure (free school meals) would go far to drain the remaining independence of the parents.'

Activities

1 Why was so much emphasis placed on helping mothers and children by reformers?
2 Why was the 1911 National Insurance Act such an important step forward?
3 a Why was *The Times* opposed to free school meals for the poor (Source 3)?
  b Which past developments were opposed in the same way?
4 What was so different about the laws passed by this government?

How did people react to reforms of the Liberal government of 1906–1914?

The Public Health reforms of the Liberal government were met with opposition from many different areas.

- The Conservative Party thought that the reforms would cost too much. They also did not believe that the government should look after people in this way.

- Some workers did not like the deductions from their wages.

- The Labour Party did not like the fact that workers had to fund their own benefits. They believed that the money should could from more wealthy people paying higher taxes.

- The House of Lords tried to stop the reforms going through. There was a battle between the House of Lords (mainly made up of Conservatives) and the House of Commons (where the Liberals had a majority). Lloyd George, the Chancellor of the Exchequer, argued that as the upper classes inherited a lot of their wealth they should pay for reforms to help those in poverty.

The disagreements that existed over the reforms introduced by the Liberal government in the early twentieth century were reflected in cartoons at the time.

Look at the two cartoons opposite. They give very different impressions of Lloyd George (the Liberal Chancellor of the Exchequer) and his plans to introduce National Insurance.

Activities

1　Why do these two sources disagree so much?
　　Think about the provenance of the source.

2　Which source do you think is the most useful for a historian investigating reactions to the reforms introduced by the Liberal government?
　　Use the source evaluation grid on page 165 to help you.
　　This is excellent practice for the exam question that asks you to evaluate the usefulness of the source.

3　How important do you think were the reforms that took place between 1906 and 1914? Which of these statements do you most agree with? Explain your choice.
　　a　The Public Health reforms of the Liberal government were highly significant, far more important that the reforms that had taken place in the nineteenth century.
　　b　The Public Health reforms of the Liberal government continued to improve people's health.
　　c　The Public Health reforms of the Liberal government did little to improve people's health.

Source 1

THE DAWN OF HOPE.

Mr. LLOYD GEORGE'S National Health Insurance Bill provides for the insurance of the Worker in case of Sickness.

▲ A poster produced by the Liberal government, 1911.

Source 2

THE PITILESS PHILANTHROPIST.

Mr. LLOYD GEORGE. "NOW UNDERSTAND, I'VE BROUGHT YOU OUT TO DO YOU GOOD, AND *GOOD I WILL DO YOU*, WHETHER YOU LIKE IT OR NOT."

▲ A cartoon from *Punch* magazine, November 1911.

Developments in the 1930s

In 1919, after the end of World War One, a new Housing Act became law. Lloyd George had promised 'Homes fit for Heroes' for the returning soldiers and this Act said that local councils had to provide good homes for working people to rent. A quarter of a million new homes were built. In the 1930s, many old, unhealthy slum houses were cleared and another 700,000 new houses were built.

However, in other ways medical care was harder to find. In the 1930s, unemployment rose to over 3 million, leaving all those unemployed outside the National Insurance Scheme. Even people in jobs could not afford to keep up their payments and so could not get free medical help (see Source 4). The system set up in 1911 was failing. The most worrying evidence came from towns where unemployment was high. In some towns the number of deaths among children under the age of one was rising again as you can see in Source 5.

Source 4

From an interview with Kathleen Davys, one of a Birmingham family of thirteen children growing up in the 1920s and 1930s. The local doctor charged sixpence for each visit:

'Headaches, we had vinegar and brown paper; for whooping cough we had camphorated oil rubbed on our chests or goose fat. For mumps we had stockings round our throats and measles we had tea stewed in the teapot by the fire – all different kinds of home cures. They thought they were better than going to the doctor's. Well they couldn't afford the doctor.'

Source 5

Town	1928	1931	1933
Wigan	93	103	110
Liverpool	94	94	98
St Helens	98	88	116
Bath	47	39	52
Brighton	50	54	47
Oxford	38	44	32

▲ The changing death-rate of children aged less than one year in a variety of towns. The numbers show the number of deaths in every 1000 live births.

Activities

1 Which problems remained in the 1930s?
2 Why was the Beveridge Report greeted so enthusiastically?

The impact of World War Two

World War Two had a major impact on people's attitudes. It wasn't just the armed forces who were risking their lives. It was the first war in which all people felt they were 'in it together'. Many people at home died during bombing raids. The feeling grew that everyone should have access to good health care, not just the wealthy. In addition:

- Many children were evacuated from towns to the countryside and to better-off homes. Middle-class families were shocked at the condition of some of the children who were dirty, unhealthy and under-nourished.

- After all the sacrifices of the war, people wanted a better future. Better health care was an important part of this.

- During the war many people did get free health care to keep them fit for the war effort.

The Beveridge Report, 1942

The national coalition government asked a leading civil servant, Sir William Beveridge, to write a report on what should be done to improve people's lives. Beveridge (1879–1963) had played a key part in organising the 1911 National Insurance scheme so had a great deal of experience of the problems and which solutions were needed. He used this great experience in his report which recommended:

- Setting up a National Health Service, free to everyone and paid for from taxes. Doctors, nurses and other medical workers would become government employees instead of charging the sick to create their wages.

- Everyone in work would pay National Insurance out of their wages. This would pay benefits (sick-pay, old-age pensions, unemployment pay, etc.) to everyone whether they were working or not.

The Beveridge Report was greeted with enthusiasm by many people. People queued outside shops to buy their own copy and 600,000 copies were sold.

Source 6

▲ The front page and cartoon from the *Daily Mirror* for 2 December 1942, reporting the publication of the Beveridge Report.

The creation of the National Health Service

Despite the general enthusiasm for Beveridge's report and the idea of creating a National Health Service, there was powerful opposition. The most important opposition came from the doctors themselves, but their opposition ended when Aneurin Bevan, the Minister of Health, agreed that doctors could continue to treat patients privately and charge them fees as well as working for the NHS.

Source 7

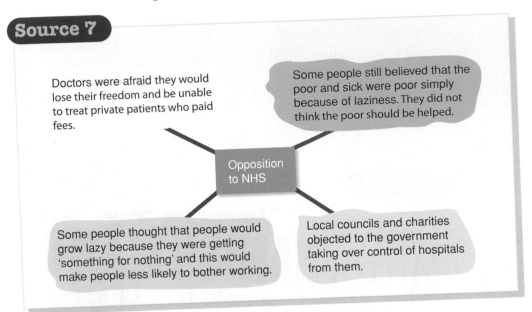

Doctors were afraid they would lose their freedom and be unable to treat private patients who paid fees.

Some people still believed that the poor and sick were poor simply because of laziness. They did not think the poor should be helped.

Opposition to NHS

Some people thought that people would grow lazy because they were getting 'something for nothing' and this would make people less likely to bother working.

Local councils and charities objected to the government taking over control of hospitals from them.

Source 8

Aneurin Bevan, Minister for Health, introducing the National Health Service to Parliament in 1946:

'Medical treatment should be made available to rich and poor alike in accordance with medical need and no other criteria. Worry about money in a time of sickness is a serious hindrance to recovery, apart from its unnecessary cruelty.'

Aneurin 'Nye' Bevan (1897–1960)

Aneurin Bevan was Minister for Health in the Labour government which introduced the NHS. He was the son of a Welsh coal miner and himself started work underground aged 13. His background and work for the miners' union gave him deep experience of the problems of poverty and sickness and inspired him to become MP for Ebbw Vale in 1929. Like Lloyd George, he was an inspiring speaker, an idealist who was determined to make life better for working people. His speeches in favour of the NHS won support while he compromised on details to put an end to opposition from some doctors.

In July 1948, the NHS was introduced. Now everyone could get free treatment. Until 1948, about 8 million people had never seen a doctor because they could not afford to do so. Source 10 shows the range of services provided by the NHS. Many hospitals were rebuilt. Doctors and nurses got new improved equipment. The NHS played an important part in increasing people's life expectancy, particularly helping to reduce the numbers of women dying in or shortly after childbirth.

THE NEW NATIONAL HEALTH SERVICE

Your new national Health Service begins on 5th July. What is it? How do you get it?

It will provide you with all medical;, dental, and nursing care. Everyone – rich or poor, man or woman or child – can use it or any part of it. There are no charges, except for a few special items. There are no insurance qualifications. But it is not a "charity". You are all paying for it, mainly as taxpayers, and it will relieve your money worries in time of illness.

Source 9

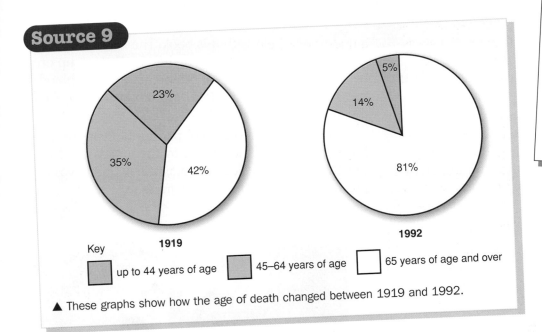

1919

1992

Key

☐ up to 44 years of age   ☐ 45–64 years of age   ☐ 65 years of age and over

▲ These graphs show how the age of death changed between 1919 and 1992.

Source 10

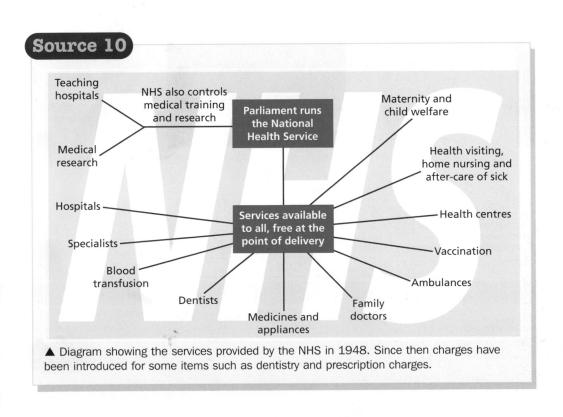

Teaching hospitals

NHS also controls medical training and research

Parliament runs the National Health Service

Maternity and child welfare

Medical research

Hospitals

Services available to all, free at the point of delivery

Specialists

Blood transfusion

Dentists

Medicines and appliances

Family doctors

Health visiting, home nursing and after-care of sick

Health centres

Vaccination

Ambulances

▲ Diagram showing the services provided by the NHS in 1948. Since then charges have been introduced for some items such as dentistry and prescription charges.

The NHS and public health since 1948

Source 11

Alice Law recalling 5 July 1948, the first day of the NHS:
'Mother went and got tested for new glasses. Then she went further down the road to the chiropodist and had her feet done. Then she went back to the doctor's because she'd been having trouble with her ears and the doctor said he would fix her up with a hearing aid.'

Activities

1 Which campaigns of prevention are shown in Sources 12, 13 and 15?
2 Which public health campaigns are taking place as you study this course? Why are they seen as important?
3 How does this approach to prevention contrast with:
   a government attitudes and actions in the 1800s
   b government attitudes and actions between 1900 and 1948?

When the NHS was introduced, the main focus was on treating the sick and providing equipment. So many sick people had not seen doctors before because they could not afford to pay the necessary fees.

However, over the years that priority to care for those who are already sick has been twinned with a second priority – to prevent people getting sick. This can be surprisingly personal. On the morning that I wrote this page I dropped into my GP surgery to ask a question to help with this book. The nurse very kindly answered the question, then looked me up on her computer and said 'We haven't tested your blood pressure recently or checked your bloods' and booked me in for a series of tests!

Prevention is now a major part of the work of the NHS, as this page shows, and by the time you read this there will have been a range of new initiatives to prevent you as well as me becoming ill.

Source 12

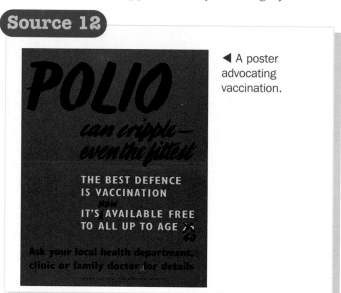

◀ A poster advocating vaccination.

Source 13

◀ An anti-smoking poster.

Source 14

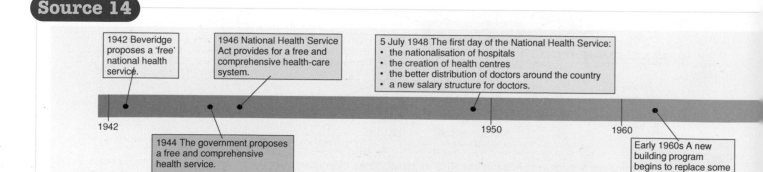

176

Source 15

From the BBC News website, bbc.co.uk/news

January 2008

HEALTH SCREENING PLANS
Patients in England will be offered screening for early signs of heart disease, stroke and kidney disease, Prime Minister Gordon Brown has said. He said he wanted a more 'personalised' NHS with a bigger focus on prevention.

March 2009

UNIVERSAL OVER-40S HEALTH CHECKS
A mass programme of health checks for over-40s in England will be launched this week, with ministers promising it will save 650 lives a year. Every five years, those aged 40 to 74 will be offered blood pressure, weight and cholesterol checks alongside lifestyle advice.

March 2009

A CHEAP FIVE-IN-ONE PILL CAN GUARD AGAINST HEART ATTACKS
    AND STROKE, RESEARCH SUGGESTS
The concept of a polypill for everyone over 55 to cut heart disease by up to 80 per cent was mooted over five years ago, but slow progress has been made since. Now a trial in India shows such a pill has the desired effects and is safe and well-tolerated by those who take it. The polypill used in the latest study combines five active pharmacological ingredients widely available separately – aspirin, a statin to lower cholesterol and three blood pressure-lowering drugs – as well as folic acid.

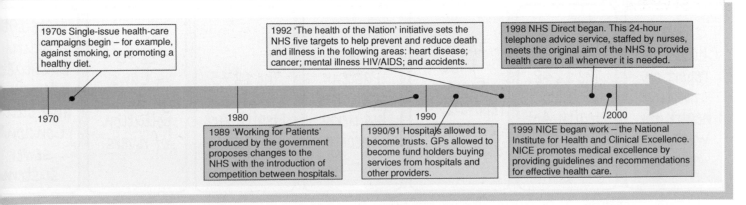

1970s Single-issue health-care campaigns begin – for example, against smoking, or promoting a healthy diet.

1992 'The health of the Nation' initiative sets the NHS five targets to help prevent and reduce death and illness in the following areas: heart disease; cancer; mental illness HIV/AIDS; and accidents.

1998 NHS Direct began. This 24-hour telephone advice service, staffed by nurses, meets the original aim of the NHS to provide health care to all whenever it is needed.

1970   1980   1990   2000

1989 'Working for Patients' produced by the government proposes changes to the NHS with the introduction of competition between hospitals.

1990/91 Hospitals allowed to become trusts. GPs allowed to become fund holders buying services from hospitals and other providers.

1999 NICE began work – the National Institute for Health and Clinical Excellence. NICE promotes medical excellence by providing guidelines and recommendations for effective health care.

Why are some changes more important than others?

Some changes are so important that they can be called '**turning points**' in history. Another kind of change is called a **catalyst** (which speeds up changes that are already taking place). A turning point is more important because it changes the direction of the way that things are going.

For many people the establishment of the NHS is one of the key turning points in the history of medicine. It changed the direction of health care in this country. Was it the key turning point in the development of public health since 1800 or were there other turning points that were more important?

Imagine that you are going on a car journey and you then decided to turn right off the road you had been travelling on and head in a different direction. That would be a turning point in your journey. If you then went down a steep hill, that would act as a catalyst. It would speed up your journey but it would not change the direction in which you were travelling.

Activities

1 Sort the events and developments below into three categories:
   - Turning points
   - Catalysts
   - Events or developments that had little impact

2 Use this information and the advice on 'evaluating progress' questions (see pages 52–53) to plan an answer to the question below.

3 In the exam you will have about 25 minutes for this type of question. Use your plan to produce an answer under timed conditions. Remember to check your work carefully as an additional 3 marks are available for quality of your written communication.

> 'More important changes in public health took place in the nineteenth century than they did in the twentieth century'.
> How far do you agree with this statement?　　　　　　　　　**[16 marks]**
>
> **(Total for spelling, punctuation and grammar = 3 marks)**
> **(Total for Question 6 = 19 marks)**

1842 – Chadwick's report on public health for working people	The 1848 Public Health Act	1854 – John Snow's report links cholera to dirty water	1861 – Pasteur publishes his germ theory	The 1875 Public Health Act	1876 – Laws against the pollution of rivers	Late 19th century Bazalgette designs and builds London's sewer system

Look at the list of public health developments on the cards below. There are eight events or developments from the nineteenth century compared with six from the twentieth century. However, does this mean that the statement in the exam question on page 178 is correct and that more important changes took place in the nineteenth century?

You need to consider how important each change was. Imagine that you are putting each development on a set of scales – some will weigh more than others.

- Develop your own weighing system to evaluate the changes that took place in each century. You could, for example, give turning points a weighting of 3, catalysts 2 and the less important developments a weighting of 1.
- You could also develop a chart like the one below.
- As well as evaluating specific developments you can also **use your knowledge of the big picture**. How much had public health been improved by the end of the nineteenth century? Had most of the major problems really been solved? If so, why was life expectancy still quite low?

Development	Weighting	Explanation

1880s – use of flushing lavatories becomes more widespread

1908 – Old-age pensions introduced

The 1911 National Insurance Act

1912 – Clinics set up in schools to give children free treatment

The 1919 Housing Act

1948 – The NHS is established

1970s – Health care campaigns begin – for example, against smoking

What was the Big Picture of public health changes after 1800?

One of the problems students often have is that they get so involved in the details of each stage of the history of public health that they lose track of the overview – how the different pieces fitted together. This page and our 'swingometer' helps you get that Big Picture clear in your mind.

Public health – the headlines

1831

CHOLERA KILLS THOUSANDS
Filthy towns suffer most.
Councils refuse to tax for clean-up.

1842

CHADWICK'S REPORT PUBLISHED.
'Increase taxes, force councils to clean up.'
Government refuses to force councils to
improve sewers and water supply.

1848

PUBLIC HEALTH ACT PASSED!
Councils encouraged to improve
water supply and sewers.
Only very worst to be forced to change.

1858

THE GREAT STINK!
London's sewer system to be built.

1878

ANOTHER PUBLIC HEALTH ACT
Government hopes to win over new voters.
Sewers and water supplies compulsory.

1901

ROWNTREE REPORT
Over a quarter live in poverty.

1901

BOER WAR FIGHTING
38% of recruits unfit to serve.

1907

BRING OUT YOUR BABIES!
Health visitors to check health of every
baby. Drive to reduce infant deaths.

1911

NATIONAL INSURANCE ACT PASSED
Medical help and sick pay for unemployed.
Liberals help those who can't
help themselves.

1920s

HOMES FOR HEROES!
Infant deaths increasing.
Millions cannot afford to see doctor.

1942

ALLIED VICTORY AT EL-ALAMEIN
Beveridge Report published.
Promises attack on poverty and sickness.

1948

FREE HEALTH CARE FOR ALL!
National Health Service begins today.

Activities

Your teacher will give you a copy of this swingometer.

1 Write on each of the five sections of the swingometer the dates when the pendulum settled there.

2 Add brief notes in blue identifying the events that support your choice. Use the information opposite, but also look back in this section for more evidence.

3 Add brief notes in red explaining why the pendulum was in that section at that time. Try to do this without looking back through the book, then check back to see if you are right.

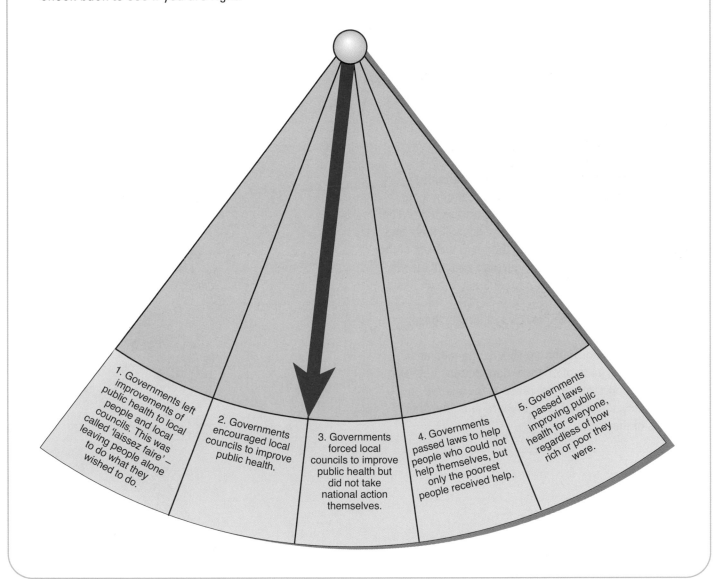

1. Governments left improvements of public health to local people and local councils. This was called 'laissez faire' – leaving people alone to do what they wished to do.

2. Governments encouraged local councils to improve public health.

3. Governments forced local councils to improve public health but did not take national action themselves.

4. Governments passed laws to help people who could not help themselves, but only the poorest people received help.

5. Governments passed laws improving public health for everyone, regardless of how rich or poor they were.

10.1 The road to Bacteria-ville – using road maps to revise key themes

This final section helps you look back across your whole course and make sense of the overall pictures of the history of medicine and health. The activities will help you revise effectively.

Activities

Creating a road map is an excellent way of summarising developments across a long period of time. We have created this example for you as a guide. Can you use your living graphs to help complete road maps for other important themes?

1 This road map summarises the story of changing ideas about the causes of disease across time. Work with a partner or in a small group. You will have **one minute** to tell the story of this theme to the rest of the class. Use the map to help you plan and tell the story.

2 Create your own road map for at least one of these themes across time:

   a methods of treating and preventing disease
   b public health.

Think about how your map shows changes and continuities, pace of change, connections between topics, important people, reasons for change and continuity, ideas that got nowhere and any other parts of the story.

10.2 What was so special about each period of medical history?

Now it's time to think about each period of medical history – what made each period special and can you sum up each period by identifying its key features in just FIVE words or phrases? Dig out those memory maps and make sure you can remember the key developments in each period.

Activities

The period cards opposite sum up medical knowledge and methods in each period.

1 Create a new Word file or start a sheet of A4 paper for each of the five periods.
2 Put down the period name and the five headings below. Then note down the major features of medicine in the period under each heading, adding your own examples and details to support the outline on the cards.
   • Understanding of the cause of disease
   • Treating and preventing illness
   • Hospitals
   • Training doctors and nurses
   • Public health
3 At the foot of each page, write down:
   a the names of key individuals from this period
   b key features of life in the period that affected medicine.

4 Across the top of the page, write down up to five single words, names or short phrases that sum up medicine in the period. To choose your words, names or phrases think about:
   a what makes this period different from others
   b whether this was a time of continuity or change (if change, how rapid was it?)
   c the overall significance of the period in the history of medicine.
5 Compare your five words, names or phrases with the rest of the class. For each period, pick out the best five words, names or phrases from the ideas put forward by the class.

Medicine in Roman Britain

1 Some important, long-lasting aspects of medicine had already begun by the Roman period. These included the idea that gods and spirits caused diseases, and the use of herbal remedies. While most people in Britain prayed to the gods to help them recover from illness, specialist doctors believed that sickness had natural causes, following Hippocrates' Theory of the Four Humours which was further developed by Galen. Treatments included herbal remedies, prayer, bleeding, purging and rest, exercise and diet. Most people had to look after their own health and hygiene, but the Romans made a major effort to improve public health in military forts and towns by building aqueducts, sewers and public baths.

Medieval medicine

The destruction of the Roman Empire led to the collapse of Roman public health systems and the destruction of many books containing medical knowledge. However, everyday medicine for ordinary people continued unchanged, based on prayers and herbal remedies. In the 1200s, universities were set up and physicians were trained, reading the works of Galen and Arab doctors. Their methods were based on Greek and Roman ideas and so they believed that illness was caused when the humours were out of balance. Some attempts were made to clean up towns, especially after the Black Death in 1348. Hospitals looked after the elderly and poor but did not treat the sick. Overall, new ideas were discouraged by the Christian Church.

2

Renaissance medicine

The Renaissance saw a battle between old and new ideas. There were some important new discoveries – Vesalius improved knowledge of anatomy and Harvey discovered that the blood circulates round the body. These discoveries (and the invention of the microscope) provided the basis for later developments but did not make people healthier. Many doctors were still hostile to new ideas and people still believed that God or bad air caused diseases. Governments did not think it was their responsibility to improve public health. However, during the later 1600s, the idea of science being based on experiments and challenging old ideas became much stronger, providing the essential background for later breakthroughs. By 1750, some doctors were being trained on hospital wards.

3

Medicine in the 1800s

The major breakthroughs began. First came Jenner's use of vaccination against smallpox, which showed that opposition to new ideas was still strong but could be beaten. Epidemics of diseases such as cholera in the filthy, over-populated industrial towns forced governments to begin to improve public health. Then came Pasteur's germ theory which at last explained the true cause of disease. From this came more vaccines to prevent diseases and major improvements in public health, which also benefited from improved engineering methods. Hospitals became places to go to get well instead of places to go to die, with nurses being much better trained by 1900. Life expectancy was finally beginning to increase, but there was still a huge gap between the health of rich and poor and there was very high infant mortality. Patent medicines, 'cure-alls', were still very popular despite the changes in scientific medicine.

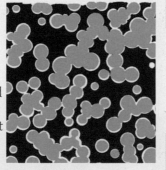

4

Medicine since 1900

The 1900s continued the stories begun in the 1800s. Developments in science and technology continued to improve surgery and to help find the first chemical and antibiotic cures for illnesses and infections. The pharmaceutical industry grew rapidly, making new treatments available in chemists' shops, although at a price before the introduction of the NHS. Wars also forced governments to invest more in these developments and to improve public health with better education, housing and public health provision, leading to the Beveridge Report in 1942 and the foundation of the National Health Service, providing free medical care. In the 1950s, scientists discovered the existence of DNA, the 'building bricks' of the human body, paving the way in the twenty-first century for the possibility of preventing inherited diseases – possibly an even bigger breakthrough than Pasteur's germ theory.

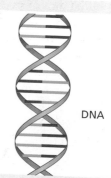

DNA

5

10.3 Which individuals were most significant?

One of the key factors has been the work of individuals so let's complete these revision tasks by deciding on the greatest medical pioneer of them all. And make yourself a set of Top Trumps cards to help revision while you're awarding the gold, silver and bronze medals.

Activities

Below you can see the awards ceremony at the Medical Olympics. Your task is to decide which medical pioneers get the medals. This is how you do it.

1   Work in a small group to create a Top Trumps card for key individuals in the history of medicine.
    a   Decide which people to have on your list. Use the group opposite to set you thinking but look for some famous names who are missing.
    b   Decide what score each person gets for each of the criteria below and reach a decision about their overall score.

2   As a class compare your results. Add up the class totals and see who comes top of the league table and wins the medals.

3   Write short acceptance speeches for the winners, explaining why they won their medals.

Use your criteria carefully!

What do the criteria on the Top Trumps card mean?

Originality – the highest marks go to people who did or thought something that nobody had ever done or thought of before. Lower marks for building on someone else's idea even if it was a great success.

Impact – how many people were helped or hindered by this individual's work? High marks for a world-wide impact, lower marks for a local impact.

Correctness – the highest marks go to ideas that were not only correct but people understood why they were correct. Good marks for correct ideas or methods when the individual knew it worked but didn't know how. And low marks for ideas that turned out to be wrong even if they lasted a long time!

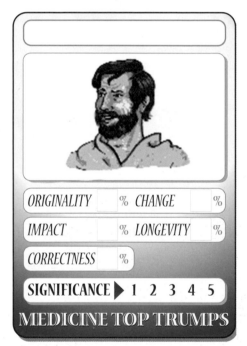

ORIGINALITY   %   CHANGE   %

IMPACT   %   LONGEVITY   %

CORRECTNESS   %

SIGNIFICANCE ▶ 1   2   3   4   5

MEDICINE TOP TRUMPS

Change – did this individual's work just affect one aspect of medicine (e.g. surgery) or did they influence a variety of aspects of medicine?

Longevity – how long did someone's impact last? The idea might be wrong but a wrong idea that lasted a long time was still very influential. What about a modern discovery that's not been around long? Do you think it will last? If so, then give it a high mark.

Overall significance – use half marks if you wish – it might help separate all these star performers.

10.4 What do we owe our lives to?

Finally, let's go back to the very first question we asked – why do we live much healthier and longer lives than in the past? Which factors do you think have been most important?

'History is not the story of strangers, aliens from another universe; it is the story of us had we been born a little earlier.'

This is a wonderful quotation. It reminds us that we aren't any different from people who lived many years ago – after all, they were our ancestors. Way back in time – in the 1800s, 1400s, the Roman Empire – there were people with our DNA, people who looked like us, had the same colour hair or eyes, the same way of walking, the same energy or laziness!

But what if you'd been born in their time?

You now know that there is one very important way in which we are different from our ancestors. On average, we live much longer, healthier lives. Let's take the example of one real family – John and Margaret Pepys and their children from the 1600s. John was an ordinary working man, a tailor who worked in London. They had eleven children, born between 1627 and 1641, shown below at their time of death.

Mary
Died aged 13

Paulina
Died aged 3

John
Died aged 8

Ester
Died aged 1

Samuel
Died aged 70

Thomas
Died aged 30

Sarah
Died aged 6

Jacob
Died aged 6 months

Robert
Died aged about 15

Paulina
Died aged 49

John
Died aged 36

Activities

Now decide which of the factors below have been most important in improving medicine and health. This will not only help you revise, but develop that very important skill – working as a team. It's amazing how a group of people working together can spark a whole host of good ideas that a person working by him or herself would have missed.

1   As a class, decide what criteria you will use to decide which factors have been most important.
2   Divide into groups and take one factor for each group. Make a list of the beneficial effects of your factor. There are clues below but you should be able to think of some more. Then use the class criteria to decide how important your factor has been.
3   Feed back your results to the rest of the class. Which factor or factors have been most important in improving medicine and health?

Get busy! What about the Romans and their Empire, blood transfusions, the Boer War and World War Two, penicillin and plastic surgery, and the NHS?

Pasteur said germs cause disease. So that means I can …

Check up on how Fleming discovered penicillin.

Think about opposition to Harvey, Jenner, Simpson and Lister – and those good people who opposed public health reform. Long live vested interests!

What about the people who bravely tried new ideas – Vesalius, Snow, Pasteur and all those people you listed who fought against those selfish vested interests?

The Romans and their army, kings and the Black Death, making vaccination compulsory, Public Health Acts, Liberal government reforms, funding research (or not!).

Lots of research here – Roman engineering, printing, Renaissance inventions, Pasteur's industrial research, stopping the Great Stink, chemicals, the pharmaceutical industry, X-rays and all kinds of modern developments.

Source Enquiry:

The transformation of surgery c.1845–c.1918

You are now entering a different course unit.

This Unit looks as if it is part of your Development Study on medicine – BUT IT IS NOT!

This Unit is about developing your enquiry skills by using sources as evidence.

Surgery is the case study that provides examples for you to use when developing your source skills.

REMEMBER – SOURCES first, SURGERY second.

Activity

Think back over your work in History at Key Stage 3 or GCSE. Identify one enquiry you have carried out. In what ways was it similar to the approach being used by the ex-History student in this picture?

191

The transformation of surgery – what actually happened between 1845 and 1918?

This source enquiry is investigating which surgical breakthrough between 1845 and 1918 was the most significant. We will focus on improving your skills in using sources but first you need to know what those breakthroughs were. As this is an investigation, we're not going to tell you the answers. You're going to find them yourselves. So let's begin!

How did we get from this ...

▲ A drawing published in 1793 of surgery taking place.

... to this?

◀ A surgical operation taking place in the early twenty-first century.

Activity

1 Make a list of the differences between the two operations in these pictures.
   a Start by identifying differences you can see.
   b Then add to your list any differences you can infer from the pictures or think took place.

Activities

2 Read the news headlines below about developments in surgery.

   a Which of them do you think happened between 1845 and 1918? (Think about what else you know happened at that time.)

   b Check your answers by going on an information hunt through this section. Note down the dates of the developments that did happen between 1845 and 1918.

3 Create a timeline showing the main changes in surgery between 1845 and 1918.

4 You have **one minute**. Explain out loud the ways in which surgery was transformed. Your teacher will tell you how long you have to prepare your explanation.

---

1. First heart transplant

Dr Christiaan Barnard performs revolutionary heart surgery in South Africa.

2. Blood comes in different groups

Karl Landsteiner discovers three different blood groups. Safe blood transfusions now possible.

3. Chloroform – the first effective anaesthetic

James Simpson pioneers use of chloroform to save patients from pain. Chloroform used world-wide within a year.

4. Keyhole surgery a great step forward

Surgeons can operate without making long cuts. Surgery aided by computers and miniature instruments.

5. X-ray machines help surgeons

First X-ray machines used in hospitals. Help for surgeons in identifying problems.

6. Antiseptics cut deaths from infection

Joseph Lister uses carbolic acid to kill bacteria in wounds and operating theatres. Big reduction in deaths from infection after surgery.

7. Blood stored for future transfusions

Chemicals added to blood to stop it clotting. Possibility of building up blood banks for future use.

8. Rubber gloves used during surgery

William Halstead, an American surgeon, had rubber gloves made for his nursing assistant. Gloves and surgical masks reduce chances of infection.

---

smarter revision

These features will help you think through the issues and prepare your revision notes thoroughly.

Factors chart – helps you record how different factors affected surgery. See page 203.

Hypothesis triangle – helps you draw and revise your hypothesis. See page 194.

SMARTER REVISION TOOLKIT

Timeline – helps you see the order in which things happened and how each breakthrough related to the others. See page 204.

Breakthrough chart – helps you record the key features of each breakthrough. See page 211.

Your hypothesis: Which surgical breakthrough was the most significant?

This enquiry asks you to decide which of three surgical breakthroughs – anaesthetics, antiseptics or blood transfusions – was the most important. The sources on the opposite page help you create your hypothesis, your first thoughts on what the answer might be. As you work on the sources on later pages you can amend it. This way you won't lose track of the main focus of the enquiry.

Activities

1   Read Sources 1–6. Think about whether they are all useful for your enquiry. Explain whether you think they are or whether any can be discarded because they aren't helpful.

2   a   **Hypothesis triangle:** Record your hypothesis by placing a cross on your own copy of the triangle to show which breakthrough you think is most important. If you're certain place your cross in one corner. If you're uncertain place it near a corner or between the corners you think is most important. (It's OK to be uncertain at this stage!)

   b   Write out your hypothesis. Think carefully about which words to use to show how certain or uncertain you are at this stage.

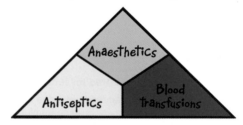

Which surgical breakthrough was the most significant?

Source 1

An account of a blood transfusion between a calf and a man, Antoine Mauray, in 1668:

'As soon as the blood entered his veins, he felt the heat along his arm and under his armpits. His pulse rose and soon after we observed a plentiful sweat over all his face. His pulse varied extremely at this instant and he complained of great pains in his kidneys, and that he was not well in his stomach, and that he was ready to choke. He was made to lie down and fell asleep, and slept all night without awakening until morning. When he awakened he made a great glass full of urine, of a colour as black as if it had been mixed with the soot of chimneys.'*

* This describes what happens when a patient receives blood which reacts badly with their own blood group.

Source 2

The verdict of Sir Clifford Albutt (1836–1925), Professor of Medicine, quoted by David Zuck, president of the History of Anaesthesia Society, 2007:

'When I was a boy … the best surgeon was he who broke the three-minute record for amputation. What place could there be in record-breaking operations for the fiddle-faddle of antiseptic precautions? The obvious benefit of freedom from pain was the benefit of time. With anaesthesia ended slapdash surgery; anaesthesia gave the necessary time for the theories of Pasteur and Lister to be adopted in practice.'

Source 4

Professor David Leaper, writing in the *European Wound Management Journal*, 2007:

'[Lister's use of carbolic meant that] the operating theatre in Glasgow was witnessing the introduction of carbolic hand washing, skin preparation and of course the famous carbolic spray. The success of these measures was spectacular. Between 1864–1866 there had been 16 deaths after 35 amputations (a 46 per cent mortality) and between 1867–1870, after the introduction of antiseptic surgery, there were 6 deaths after 40 operations (a 15 per cent mortality). Lord Lister also left us with the memorable surgical statement that "success depends on attention to detail".'

Source 3

A description of surgery in St Thomas's Hospital, London in 1871, written by John Leeson, a medical student:

'Ovariotomy was becoming common and one of our surgeons was keen on it. His mortality was round about 80 per cent. I used to dread seeing a notice of the operation, as I knew that in a few days the patient would probably be lying on the post-mortem table.

'I remember the house-surgeon in the operating theatre with his threaded needles dangling from the front flap of his coat. One of our surgeons lectured on anatomy in an old frock-coat buttoned up to the chin. I see him now, pawing the dissection as he lectured on it. When the coat was past even this work he took it up to the operating theatre. An operation was a dirty job and an outworn old coat was a suitable garment! I see it now, faded with age, stained with blood and spotted with pus.'

Source 6

The novelist Fanny Burney wrote this account of her mastectomy operation in 1811:

'… when the dreadful steel was plunged into the breast – cutting through veins, arteries, flesh, nerves – I began a scream that lasted during the whole time of the incision – I almost marvel that it does not ring in my ears still! So excruciating was the agony. When the wound was made, and the knife was withdrawn, the pain seemed undiminished, for the air that suddenly rushed into those delicate parts felt like a mass of small but sharp and forked poignards [daggers], that were tearing at the edges of the wound.'

Source 5

An extract from 'A short history of blood transfusion' by Phil Learoyd, 2006:

'By the end of the 19th Century, the practical use of blood transfusion was only slightly less primitive than it had been two and a half centuries earlier. The principle accomplishment during this period was the recognition, by the majority of people in the field of transfusion, of the inappropriateness of the use of animal blood for human transfusion. The discovery (in 1900) of the human ABO blood groups by Dr Karl Landsteiner in Vienna was the major step (forward).'

Activities

3 What else do you want to find out to continue your investigation?

4 Which skills have you used so far in this enquiry?

Now that you have a hypothesis, it's almost time to begin your enquiry in detail – and develop the skills you need to do well in your Source Enquiry exam at the same time. As you'll see below, the exam tests the skills you'd need if you really were sifting through files of evidence and reaching a conclusion for the boss!

The Source Enquiry is an important exam, worth 25 per cent of your final mark – the same percentage as the Development Study. The Source Enquiry exam consists of six to eight sources and five questions testing your skills in using sources as evidence. This exam paper and the sources booklet on the next page show you what the 'real thing' will look like.

> ## Unit 3: Schools History Project Source Enquiry
> ### Option 3A: The transformation of surgery, c.1845–c.1918
> Time: 1 hour 15 minutes
> The total mark for this paper is 50.

TIMING

The marks for **each** question are shown in brackets. Use this as a guide to how much time to spend on each question.

It is important to time yourself carefully. Some students run out of time because they spend too long on the first two questions and don't have time for the higher mark questions that come later. So stick to a time plan like this:

- Approx. 5 minutes: Read all the questions, the background information and scan the sources so that you pick up the theme of the paper and how the questions and the sources relate to each other.

- No more than 20 minutes: Questions 1 and 2 (14 marks)

- Approx. 25 minutes: Questions 3 and 4 (20 marks)

- Approx. 20 minutes: Question 5 (16 marks)

- Approx. 5 minutes: Check your answers. If time is really short check your answer to Question 5 first. This is where the examiner will be looking particularly closely at your spelling, punctuation and grammar.

Answer all questions.

Look carefully at Sources A to F in the sources booklet and then answer Questions 1 to 5 which follow.

1 Study Source A.

What can you learn from Source A about how operations were carried out before the nineteenth century? **[6 marks]**

2 Study Source B and use your own knowledge.

What was the purpose of this representation?

Explain your answer, using Source B and your own knowledge. **[8 marks]**

3 Study Source C and use your own knowledge.

Why was there so much opposition to the introduction of anaesthetics?

Explain your answer, using Source C and your own knowledge. **[10 marks]**

4 Study Sources D and E and use your own knowledge.

How reliable are Sources D and E as evidence of the success of Lister's antiseptic?

Explain your answer, using Sources D and E and your own knowledge. **[10 marks]**

*5 Study Sources D, E and F and use your own knowledge.

Spelling, punctuation and grammar will be assessed in this question.

Source F suggests that anaesthetics were the major surgical breakthrough of the period 1845–1918.

How far do you agree with this interpretation?

Explain your answer, using your own knowledge, Sources D, E and F and any other sources you find helpful. **[16 marks]**

(Total for spelling, punctuation and grammar = 3 marks)

(Total for Question 5 = 19 marks)

DEVELOPING **INFERENCES** FROM A SOURCE

The first question will usually be an inference question. You need to go beyond the obvious clues in the source and explain what you can learn from the source. The advice on pages 200–201 helps you tackle 'inference questions' effectively.

ANALYSING **REPRESENTATIONS** OF HISTORY

The emphasis in this question is on how a person, event or discovery has been represented by the person who produced the source. You need to explore the purpose of the representation and the message it is intending to get across. Advice on how to tackle this type of question can be found on pages 206–208.

DEVELOPING **EXPLANATIONS** FROM SOURCES AND OWN KNOWLEDGE

This question is asking you to use the source **and** your own knowledge to explain why something happened. The advice on pages 210–211 helps you write developed explanations.

EVALUATING THE **RELIABILITY** OF SOURCES

For this type of question you need to explore the reliability of two sources for a particular enquiry. You need to explore the strengths and weaknesses of each source before reaching an overall judgement. The advice on pages 216–217 helps you tackle this type of question effectively.

EVALUATING **INTERPRETATIONS** OF HISTORY

The final question asks you to use your own knowledge **and** the sources to evaluate an interpretation or point of view. You must decide the **extent** to which agree or disagree with the interpretation. The advice on pages 222–223 will help you.

Although the question directs you to use sources D, E and F, you can use any source on the paper to support your argument. Before you answer this question, a good tip is to go through the sources and place a tick or a cross in the margin when you find evidence that either supports or contradicts the statement.

Make sure you check your answer for spelling, punctuation and grammar. This question carries 3 additional marks for the quality of your written communication. It could make the difference between a grade!

SOURCES BOOKLET

Source A

▲ A drawing published in 1793 of a surgical operation at that time.

Source B

▲ A cartoon called 'Operation madness' published in 1870.

Source C

From the *London Medical Gazette*, 1848, describing Hannah Greener's operation:

'The inhalation was done from a handkerchief on which a teaspoonful of chloroform had been poured. In about half a minute I requested Mr Lloyd to begin the operation. She gave a kick which caused me to think that the chloroform had not had sufficient effect. I started to apply more when her lips became suddenly balanced and she spluttered at the mouth. I threw down the handkerchief, dashed cold water in her face but this had no effect. The whole process of inhalation, operation and death could not have occupied more than two minutes.'

Source D

From Lister's own record of amputations:

	Total amputations	Died	% who died
1864–66 (without antiseptics)	35	16	45.7
1867–70 (with antiseptic)	40	6	15.0

Source E

An operation taking place while a carbolic spray disinfects the area. One assistant is using chloroform to anaesthetise the patient, another is mopping up blood with a sponge:

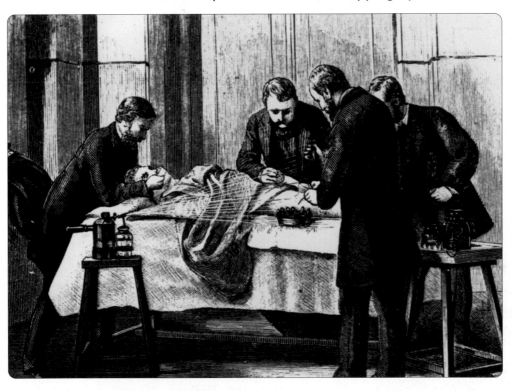

Source F

The verdict of Sir Clifford Albutt (1836–1925), Professor of Medicine, quoted by David Zuck, president of the History of Anaesthesia Society, 2007:

'When I was a boy … the best surgeon was he who broke the three-minute record for amputation. What place could there be in record-breaking operations for the fiddle-faddle of antiseptic precautions? The obvious benefit of freedom from pain was the benefit of time. With anaesthesia ended slapdash surgery; anaesthesia gave the necessary time for the theories of Pasteur and Lister to be adopted in practice.'

What was surgery like in the early 1800s?

You can begin your detailed enquiry by investigating surgery in the early 1800s. Patients faced many dangers and discomforts. Surgeons had to battle three major problems. Use the sources and your inference skills to find out more.

How to – annotate and infer from sources

When you use a source it is a good idea to annotate it, particularly for drawing inferences. (An inference is something you work out from a source even if the source does not explicitly say it or show it.) So … what do Sources 1 and 2 tell you about surgery in the 1800s?

- **Step 1:** annotate the source to spot the obvious clues. In the inner box write about the obvious details – the things you can see.
- **Step 2:** draw inferences. What do these clues *suggest* about surgery in the early 1800s? Write your inferences in the outer box.

Activity

1   In the example below the student has labelled the key details then used those key details to develop inferences. Now complete the annotation on your own copy of Sources 1 and 2.

2   Use the obvious clues in each source to develop your own inferences about surgery in the early 1800s.

Inference

This suggests that surgeons at the time did not use anaesthetics and that patients were conscious during operations.

Obvious clues

The patient is clearly in a lot of pain and is being held down by the surgeon's assistants.

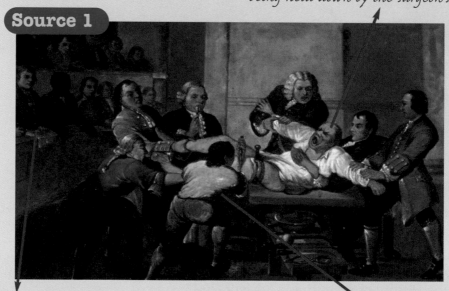

Source 1

Lots of people have been allowed in to watch the operation.

This suggests that …

The surgeon and his assistants are wearing normal clothes for the time. They are not wearing gloves.

This would spread infection. The source suggests that surgeons did not realise the importance of antiseptics.

▲ A painting from the early 1800s showing an operation taking place at that time.

Inference

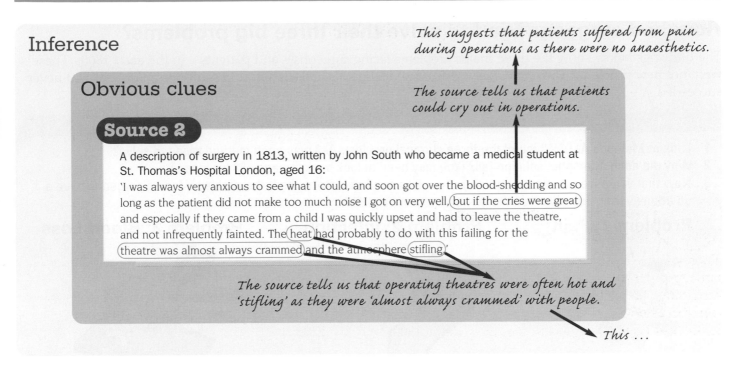

Obvious clues

This suggests that patients suffered from pain during operations as there were no anaesthetics.

The source tells us that patients could cry out in operations.

Source 2

A description of surgery in 1813, written by John South who became a medical student at St. Thomas's Hospital London, aged 16:

'I was always very anxious to see what I could, and soon got over the blood-shedding and so long as the patient did not make too much noise I got on very well, but if the cries were great and especially if they came from a child I was quickly upset and had to leave the theatre, and not infrequently fainted. The heat had probably to do with this failing for the theatre was almost always crammed and the atmosphere stifling.'

The source tells us that operating theatres were often hot and 'stifling' as they were 'almost always crammed' with people.

This ...

Answering 'inference questions' in the exam

The first question on the Source Enquiry exam paper will usually be an inference question. Look at the exam question below:

> What can you learn from Source 1 about surgery in the early 1800s?　　　　　**[6 marks]**

The source suggests that surgery in the early nineteenth century was painful and dangerous. — **Inference**

For example, the expression on the patient's face shows that they are in a lot of pain. No anaesthetics appear to have been used and the patient clearly has to be held down. — **Reference to the source**

You can also see that the surgeon and his assistants seem to be wearing their normal clothes and are not wearing protective gloves. — **Reference to the source**

This suggests ... — **Inference**

 WARNING

Inference questions are usually worth six marks so you should not spend too long on these questions. One paragraph should be enough for full marks.

The key things to remember are:

- **Stick to the focus of the question** … Stick to what you can learn from the source. There is no need to evaluate how trustworthy the source is. You will waste valuable time and pick up no extra marks.
- **Support the inferences you make with references to the source**. It is better to make two supported inferences than it is to make five or six inferences that you do not back up by referring to details in the source.

Activity

Read the student answer above. Note how the student **uses the key details** in the source **to develop inferences** about what surgery was like in the early 1800s. Each inference is **supported by a specific reference** to the source. Now complete the answer.

How had surgeons tried to solve their three big problems?

The drawings below show the three major problems facing surgeons – and patients – in the early 1800s. These were not new problems. They had always existed and surgeons had tried to find solutions before but had never succeeded.

Activities

1 Look at Methods A–D. Which of the three surgical problems 1–3 was each method trying to solve?
2 Why did each attempted solution fail? (You may need to look back to page 193 for ideas.)
3 Now that you have practised your inference skills and know more about the problems facing surgeons have a go at answering question 1 on the exam paper on page 197.

Problem 1: Pain

Problem 2: Infection

Problem 3: Blood Loss

Method

A

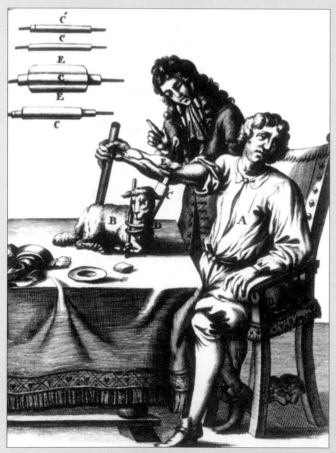

▲This picture shows an experiment in 1665.

B

A fourteenth-century medical book contains this recipe:

'To make a drink that men call dwale, to make a man sleep during an operation.

'Take the gall of a boar, three spoonfuls of the juice of hemlock and three spoonfuls of wild briony, lettuce, opium poppy, henbane and vinegar. Mix them well together and then let the man sit by a good fire and make him drink of the potion until he falls asleep. Then he may safely be operated upon.'

C

In the 1500s, gunpowder in gunshot wounds was thought to be poisonous so boiling oil was poured onto wounds to kill the poison. The great French surgeon Ambroise Paré replaced the use of boiling oil with his own mixture of egg yolks, oil of roses and turpentine. This was much less painful, but did not deal with the problems caused by surgery on open wounds or bullets carrying fragments of uniform deep into the body.

D

Paré also used ligatures (silk threads tied around individual blood vessels) to stop bleeding, but the thread could carry infection deep into a wound, causing death.

Why were the problems of surgery overcome?

In your enquiry you are not only thinking about *how* the problems of pain, infection and bleeding were overcome but also *why* they were overcome. So, meet the factors that helped or hindered the transformation of surgery.

1 Factor	2 Evidence of factor helping development of surgery	3 Evidence of factor hindering development of surgery	4 Assessment – Did it do more to help or hinder development?
War			
Science and technology			
Attitudes and beliefs in society		*Anaesthetics – opposed by ...*	
Individuals			
Communications			
Chance			

Breakthrough 1: Anaesthetics – how was pain overcome?

The first breakthrough came in the 1840s with the discovery of the first effective anaesthetics. Pain-free surgery became possible. Bud did this breakthrough solve the surgeons' problems?

▲ James Simpson, who first used and publicised chloroform as an anaesthetic.

Activities

1 **Timeline:** Create your own timeline showing the stages in the development of anaesthetics.
2 Look at the reasons for opposition to chloroform opposite. Which of these headings would you give to each reason?

- Pain is good!
- It's God's choice
- Is it safe?
- Shock death!
- More operations, more deaths
- Old skill no longer important

Step 1: 'Laughing gas' (nitrous oxide)

Anaesthetics developed partly because of improved knowledge of chemistry. In 1799 Sir Humphry Davy discovered that laughing gas (nitrous oxide) reduced pain. He suggested that it could be used in surgery and by dentists.

BUT

1 It did not make patients completely unconscious so was not a complete answer to the problem of pain.
2 An American dentist, Horace Wells, became convinced of the value of laughing gas after inhaling it at a fair. However, when he used it in a public demonstration his patient was in agony. This killed confidence in laughing gas as an anaesthetic.

Step 2: Ether

In 1846 John Collins Warren, an American surgeon, removed a neck tumour using ether as an anaesthetic. A year later, a famous English surgeon, Robert Liston, used ether to anaesthetise a patient during a leg amputation.

BUT

Ether irritated the eyes and lungs, causing coughing and sickness. It could catch fire if close to a flame and had a vile, clinging smell that took ages to go. Ether also came in a large, heavy bottle that was difficult to carry around.

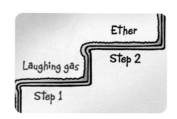

Step 3: Chloroform

James Simpson, a Professor at Edinburgh University had used ether but was searching for a better anaesthetic. One evening in 1847, he and several colleagues experimented with different chemicals to see what anaesthetic effects they had. Simpson wrote 'I poured some of the chloroform fluid into tumblers in front of my assistants, Dr Keith and Dr Duncan and myself. Before sitting down to supper we all inhaled the fluid, and were all "under the table" in a minute or two, to my wife's consternation and alarm.'

Simpson realised that chloroform was very effective and within days started using it to help women in childbirth and in operations. He wrote articles to tell doctors about his discovery and other surgeons started to use it in their operations.

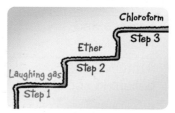

Why did some people oppose the use of chloroform to kill pain?

Chloroform was the most effective anaesthetic yet discovered, but that didn't mean it was problem-free or, astonishingly to us, that everyone was enthusiastic about pain-free surgery.

1. In the early 1800s, surgeons prided themselves on how quickly they could operate because speed was the only way of reducing pain. Anaesthetics meant that speed was no longer so important.

2. Chloroform was untested. No one knew if there would be long-term side effects on the bodies or minds of patients. They did not know what dose to give different patients.

3. In 1848, Hannah Greener died whilst being given chloroform during an operation to remove her toenail (see *Source D*, page 12). This first death from the use of chloroform scared surgeons.

Why did people oppose using chloroform?

4. With patients asleep, doctors attempted more complex operations, thus carrying infections deeper into the body and causing more blood loss. The 1870s were known as surgery's Black Period because of the high death rate. Some surgeons returned to using ether mixed with nitrous oxide.

5. Letter to the medical journal *The Lancet* in 1849: 'The infliction [of pain] has been invented by Almighty God. Pain may even be considered a blessing of the Gospel.'

6. Letter to the medical journal *The Lancet* in 1853: '[Anaesthesia] is most unnatural. The pain and sorrow of child-birth exert a most powerful and useful influence upon the religious and moral character of women.'

What impact did the new anaesthetics have on surgery?

Despite such opposition many surgeons followed Simpson's example in using chloroform. At least some of this opposition weakened in 1853 when Queen Victoria accepted the use of chloroform during the birth of her eighth child. She publicly praised 'that blessed chloroform'. There were still many improvements to make, but Simpson's use of chloroform was the turning point on the way to pain-free surgery.

When Simpson died, flags were flown at half-mast throughout Britain and a plaque dedicated to him in Westminster Abbey says:

To whose genius and benevolence (kindness) The world owes the blessing derived From the use of chloroform for The relief of suffering Praise be to God

BUT ... DON'T EXAGGERATE

1 It took time for surgeons to find the right dosages.

2 Chloroform made many patients vomit.

3 Surgeons still operated at high speed at first. Liston still took only 30 seconds to amputate a leg!

4 With patients asleep, surgeons tried more risky operations, leading to more deaths.

5 The problems of infection and blood-loss continued so surgery was still very dangerous.

Stepping stones to the future

1. Surgery was pain free. This also meant that fewer patients died of shock.

2. Surgeons began to take more time over operations and were able to work deeper inside the body, developing new operations that saved more lives.

3. Research began into using chloroform more safely and effectively.

4. Research led to better anaesthetics that relaxed muscles as well as simply putting patients to sleep and had fewer side effects than chloroform.

5. Local anaesthetics were developed.

Improved surgery

How did people portray developments in anaesthetics?

The use of anaesthetics was big news in the 1840s. Newspapers and magazines reported on the first operations using ether and chloroform. Artists painted their versions of great breakthroughs. Surgeons wrote letters and made speeches recording their work, while other surgeons and individuals wrote about their opposition to anaesthetics. This page helps you think about how those first experiments in using anaesthesia were portrayed in pictures and words. In order to do this, you will need to develop your source handling skills and learn how to spot how an artist or a writer can create a specific impression of an event.

How to ... analyse representations of history

Your Source Enquiry exam paper will include a question asking you to analyse the way in which a source represents an individual, discovery or event. You need to work out the message the person who produced the source is trying to get across and **explain the purpose of the source**.

Step 1: Annotate the source – spot the obvious clues in the source.

You can approach 'portrayal questions' such as the one opposite in a similar way to how you approached 'inference questions' on pages 200–201. Start by spotting obvious clues in the source.

Step 2: Explain how the artist/writer is aiming to create a specific impression by including these details.

The difference between portrayal and inference questions is that for portrayal questions the focus of your answer should be on how the artist or writer has deliberately set out to create a specific impression and put across a message.

Artists and writers can create strong messages by:
- **what** they choose to include (the details they deliberately choose to include)
- **how** they portray an event (through the use of specific words or the use of colour).

Step 3: Use your own knowledge to explain the purpose of the representation.

Explain why the source was produced.
- Why did the artist produce this source?
- Why did they want to get across a particular message at that particular time? Your knowledge of the historical context really helps here. The source was produced at the time in which anaesthetics were first being used. The artist has set out to show that the first use of ether was an important event and a major breakthrough.

DON'T WANDER OFF THE POINT

The emphasis in portrayal questions is on how an impression was deliberately created; there are no marks allocated for a discussion of how reliable the source is or how useful it is for a specific enquiry.

The key things to remember are:
- **Stick to the focus of the question.** Stick to explaining how the artist or the writer has set out to create a specific impression. There is no need to evaluate how trustworthy the source is. You will waste valuable time and pick up no extra marks.
- **Support the points you make with references to the source**. Aim to make two or three supported and developed points. Use the details in the source to support the points you make.

Study Source 1 and use your own knowledge.
What was the purpose of this representation?
Explain your answer, using Source 1 and your own
knowledge.

[8 marks]

Activity

Finish annotating the source and
then answer the question.

Explanation

The artist is aiming to show that this was an important event. He has not just focussed on the operation; he has included the crowd to show that it was a significant event that captured the interest of people. The use of anaesthetics such as ether was big news in the 1840s. Ether was seen as a big breakthrough and artists such as Robert Hinckley aimed to portray how important it was to the wider public.

The artist is putting across the message that ether was effective. There was some opposition to anaesthetics at the time. Some people lacked confidence in whether they worked effectively, paintings such as this reassured people that it was safe and the patient felt no pain.

Obvious clues

This is a large crowd watching the operation and some people are standing up to get a better view.

You can clearly see that the patient is unconscious and not in any pain.

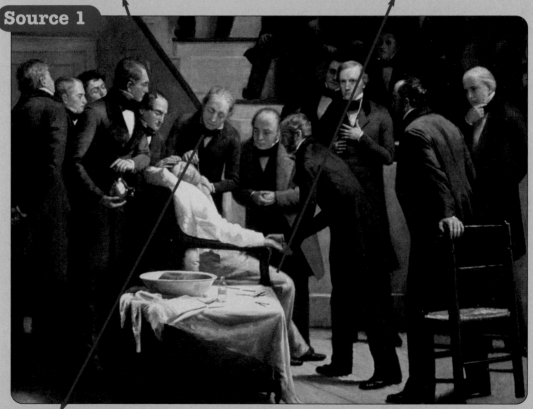

Source 1

The expressions on people's faces and their body language show that they are really taking notice of what is happening.

▲ A painting by Robert Hinckley of the first use of ether as an anaesthetic. It shows an operation carried out in the USA by Dr Warren and Dr Morton in 1846.

The aim of Robert Hinckley is to ...

Analysing representations: practise your skills

As you have seen, some people opposed anaesthetics. The struggle to persuade people to change their attitudes continued with anaesthetics gradually winning wider acceptance. James Simpson continued to play a leading role, presenting a powerful case for the use of chloroform as an anaesthetic. He brought the example of Ambroise Paré to his defence. He also used language very cleverly to make his case and persuade people that anaesthetics were a good thing.

Activities

1   Study Source 2.

> **2   Study Source 2 and use your own knowledge.**
> What was the purpose of this representation?
> Explain your answer, using Source 2 and your own knowledge.   **[8 marks]**

Finish the answer below. You can use the sentence starters provided or develop your own. Note how the student supports each point they make with specific references to the source.

2   Attempt the purpose question from the practice exam paper (see Question 2 on page 197).

Source 2

James Simpson speaking to a meeting of doctors in Edinburgh in 1847:

'Before the sixteenth century surgeons had no way of stemming the flow of blood after amputation of a limb other than by scorching with a red hot iron or boiling pitch. The great suggestion of Ambroise Paré, to shut up the bleeding vessels by tying them, was a vast improvement. It saved the sufferings of the patient while adding to their safety. But the practice was new, and like all innovations in medical practice, it was at first and for long, bitterly decried... attacked ... suppressed.

'We look back with sorrow on the opponents of Paré. Our successors in years to come will look back with similar feelings. They will marvel at the idea of humane men confessing that they prefer operating on their patients in a waking instead of an anaesthetic state, and that the fearful agonies that they inflict should be endured quietly. All pain is destructive and even fatal in its effects.'

James Simpson creates a very positive impression of anaesthetics by comparing it to the developments made by Paré. He states that Paré 'saved the sufferings of the patient' and made surgery safer. Simpson points out that at first Paré faced opposition but that people living in the middle of the nineteenth century now 'look back with sorrow on the opponents of Paré'. He then suggests that the same will happen to the opponents of anaesthetics and that their opposition will seem ridiculous to people in the future.

Simpson is very critical of those people who refuse to use anesthetics. Simpson uses powerful words to describe operations without anaesthetics. For example ...

Simpson's aim is to persuade other doctors that anaesthetics are a positive development. He achieves this purpose by ...

What do sources tell us about how people at the time reacted to the introduction of chloroform?

Look at Source 1. Given how horrific operations were before anaesthetics you could assume that everybody was as positive as the person who wrote the letter about the introduction of chloroform. This was not the case.

Activity

Study the sources below. List the reasons why some people opposed anaesthetics.

Source 1

An extract from a letter to Sir James Simpson, written by someone who had had an operation without anaesthetic:
'Several years ago I was required to prepare for the loss of a limb by amputation. Suffering so great as I underwent cannot be expressed in words.

'Before the days of anaesthetics a patient preparing for an operation was like a condemned criminal preparing for execution.

'I still recall the spreading out of the instruments, the first incision, and the bloody limb lying on the floor. From all of this I should have been saved by chloroform.

'When I first heard that anaesthetics had been discovered I could not believe it. I have since thanked God that he has put into our heart to devise so simple and safe a way of lessening pain.'

Source 2

From the *London Medical Gazette*, 1848, describing Hannah Greener's operation:
'The inhalation was done from a handkerchief on which a teaspoonful of chloroform had been poured. In about half a minute I requested Mr Lloyd to begin the operation. She gave a kick which caused me to think that the chloroform had not had sufficient effect. I started to apply more when her lips became suddenly balanced and she spluttered at the mouth. I threw down the handkerchief, dashed cold water in her face but this had no effect. The whole process of inhalation, operation and death could not have occupied more than two minutes.'

Source 3

An extract from a letter to the medical journal *The Lancet* in 1853, opposing the easing of the pain of childbirth:
'It is a most unnatural practice. The pain and sorrow of labour exert a most powerful and useful influence upon the religious and moral character of women upon all their future relations in life.'

Source 4

A quotation from Army Chief of Medical Staff, 1854:
'… the smart use of the knife is a powerful stimulant and it is much better to hear a man bawl lustily than to see him sink silently into the grave.'

Using sources effectively: Developing explanations from sources and own knowledge

In your Source Enquiry you will need to explain why something happened using a source **and** your own knowledge. The source will provide a useful starting point but you must **extend your answer** using your own knowledge.

Activity

1   Use the advice on this page to answer the question below.

Study Source 1 and use your own knowledge.
Why was there so much opposition to the introduction of anaesthetics?
Explain your answer, using Source 1 and your own knowledge.   **[10 marks]**

Source 1

An extract from a letter to the medical journal *The Lancet* in 1849:
'The infliction [of pain] has been invented by the Almighty God. Pain may even be considered a blessing of the Gospel, and being blessed admits to being made either well or ill.'

Step 1: Start with what the source tells you.

Highlight key phrases in the source and note down any reasons why there was opposition to the introduction of anaesthetics.

Here the reason is because of people's religious beliefs. Pain was seen as something that was 'invented' by God.

Step 2: Build on this starting point with your own knowledge.

Religious beliefs were not the only reason why anaesthetics were opposed.

- Look at the list of reasons you produced after looking at the sources on page 209.
- See also the diagram on page 205.
- Aim to **link events together** like the student has in the example below:

Anaesthetics <u>led to</u> longer and more complex operations. <u>This meant</u> a great risk of infection and blood loss. <u>As a result</u>, death rates increased and the 1870s were known as the 'Black Period' of surgery.'

Activity

2   Apply the skills that you have learned to the question on the practice exam paper on page 197.

3   Study Source C and use your own knowledge.
Why was there so much opposition to the introduction of anaesthetics?
Explain your answer, using Source C and your own knowledge.   **[10 marks]**

Anaesthetics – your breakthrough chart

A chart like this will help you record the key features of each breakthrough.

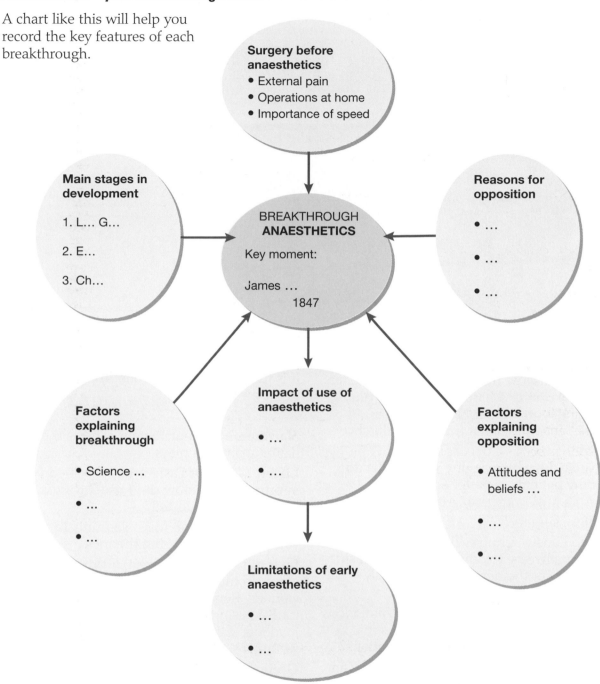

Surgery before anaesthetics
- External pain
- Operations at home
- Importance of speed

Main stages in development

1. L... G...

2. E...

3. Ch...

BREAKTHROUGH
ANAESTHETICS

Key moment:

James ...
1847

Reasons for opposition
- ...
- ...
- ...

Factors explaining breakthrough
- Science ...
- ...
- ...

Impact of use of anaesthetics
- ...
- ...

Factors explaining opposition
- Attitudes and beliefs ...
- ...
- ...

Limitations of early anaesthetics
- ...
- ...

Activities

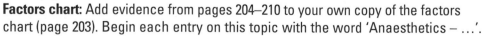

1 Complete this breakthrough chart for anaesthetics, using the information on pages 204–210 to help you.

2 **Factors chart:** Add evidence from pages 204–210 to your own copy of the factors chart (page 203). Begin each entry on this topic with the word 'Anaesthetics – ...'.

3 **Hypothesis triangle:** Review your hypothesis triangle (page 194) for the main enquiry question 'Which surgical breakthrough was the most significant?' Now you have studied anaesthetics do you think your original hypothesis is looking right? Add notes around your triangle to explain where you have placed your cross at this stage.

Breakthrough 2: Antiseptics

The second breakthrough to investigate is the discovery of antiseptics which killed infections. As you've been working hard, we'll start with some fun – this play is complete fiction but you'll learn a lot from it!

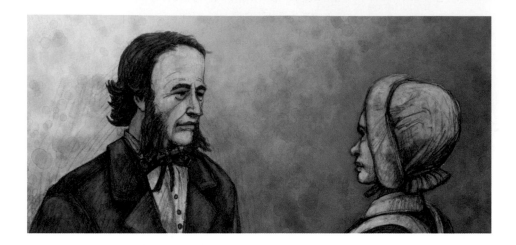

Narrator: In Glasgow Infirmary, Dr Joseph Lister is trying to relax after a hard day's surgery but he has a nagging worry. Enter Nurse Greig, a formidable Scottish woman trained by Florence Nightingale.

Lister: Nurse, I have a nagging worry. Why do over half my patients die after operations?

Greig: Good question, doctor. Do you wash your hands before surgery?

Lister: Good answer, nurse. That Hungarian doctor, Semmelweiss, told his students to wash their hands. It cut the death rate to virtually nothing.

Greig: Yes, but the other doctors hated him! Now, have you noticed that greenish black pus that grows out of patients' wounds after operations?

Lister: Of course. I was taught that infections are caused by worms and maggots growing out of dead flesh, but that doesn't seem right. We need new evidence!

Narrator: The sound of clanking glass bottles and boiling water. Monsieur Pasteur appears.

Monsieur Pasteur: Bonjour, I bring the magic of science! In my left hand I hold a flask from the beautiful mountains. It is crystal clear! In my right hand I hold a flask from the filthy streets of Paris. It is full of bacteria. Eh voila! It proves that germs in the air cause decay.

Narrator: Monsieur Pasteur exits as the French national anthem plays.

Lister: Monsieur Pasteur has provided vital information but how can I use it to stop my patients being infected?

Greig: Aye, Doctor. Miss Nightingale says it's what you do that matters, not theories.

Lister: If Pasteur is correct, maybe I can stop germs in the air getting into and infecting open wounds. Remember – we saw sewage workers in Carlisle using carbolic acid to clean up the stench. I wonder if carbolic would stop germs infecting wounds?

Greig: Try it out, man. We have a young boy with a broken leg – run over by a cart. The bone's out through the skin. Either amputate or try your new idea.

Lister: Perfect! I'll dip some bandages in carbolic acid and see if that stops Pasteur's germs. I could even invent an ingenious, but clumsy, carbolic spray to keep the whole operating theatre infection free.

Greig: The rest of the surgeons won't like that, but when did they ever like something new!

THE END

How was the problem of infection overcome?

Chloroform changed surgery in some ways, but the surgeons using this wonderful discovery in the 1850s were still operating wearing old, pus-stained clothes. They did not wash their hands, nor sterilise equipment before operations. Why? They knew that operation wounds often got infected and patients died. But they did not know why. They did not know that bacteria cause infections in open wounds. The man who began to change all this was Joseph Lister.

Joseph Lister and science

Lister was an outstanding surgeon but also had a keen interest in the application of science to medicine. He researched infection and knew all about Pasteur's germ theory, sparking the idea for his own discovery.

There are bacteria in the air which cause rotting and infections such as gangrene.
Pasteur

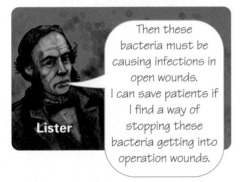

Lister
Then these bacteria must be causing infections in open wounds. I can save patients if I find a way of stopping these bacteria getting into operation wounds.

Where did the idea of using carbolic come from?

Sewage! Lister wrote, 'In 1864 I was struck by an account of the remarkable effects of using carbolic acid upon the sewage of Carlisle. It prevented all smell from the lands covered by the sewage and destroyed the parasites that usually infest cattle feeding on such land. The idea of using carbolic acid for the treatment of open fractures naturally occurred to me.'

What did Lister do?

- He first experimented by treating people with compound fractures where the bone breaks through the skin. Infection often developed in these open wounds. Lister applied carbolic acid to the wound and used bandages soaked in carbolic. He found that the wounds healed and did not develop gangrene, saving many lives.

- He then did the same with amputations, covering the wound with carbolic soaked bandages.

The impact of these changes was spectacular. Between 1864 and 1866 (before carbolic), there had been 16 deaths after 35 amputations – a death-rate of 46 per cent. Between 1867 and 1870, after the introduction of antiseptic surgery, there were six deaths after 40 operations – a death-rate of 15 per cent.

In 1867, Lister published his ideas and results, showing the value of the use of carbolic acid. At the same time he worked at improving his methods in three ways:

Improvement 1
Handwashing with carbolic before operations to avoid the surgeon introducing infections into wounds.

Improvement 2
A carbolic spray to kill germs in the air around the operating table.

Improvement 3
An antiseptic ligature to tie up blood vessels and prevent blood loss.

Activities

1 **Timeline:** Add the main developments in antiseptics to the timeline you began on page 204.

2 Why was Lister's work an important breakthrough in surgery?

3 **Factors chart:** Which factors helped him make his discovery? Add details to your factors chart from page 203.

Why did surgeons oppose such a good idea?

Just as there had been opposition to the introduction of anaesthetics, so there was opposition to antiseptics.

1   Lister's carbolic spray seemed very extreme. It soaked the operating theatre, cracked the surgeon's skin and made everything smell. The new precautions caused extra work, making operations more expensive and less pleasant for surgeons. One doctor wrote 'The whole scene of an operation was covered in carbolic spray which dispersed its globules into every nook and cranny of the wound. Our faces and coat-sleeves often dripped with it. It was a relief to us all when the spray was abandoned. It was costly and cumbersome and often broke down.'

2   Despite anaesthetics, surgeons were still convinced that speed was essential. Lister's antiseptic methods just seemed to slow operations down.

3   When some surgeons copied Lister's methods, they did not achieve the same results. This was usually because they were less systematic but they still criticised Lister. Others argued that antiseptics actually prevented the body's own defence mechanisms from working effectively.

4   Pasteur's ideas had spread very slowly. Even trained surgeons found it difficult to accept that tiny micro-organisms caused disease. One surgeon regularly joked with his assistants to shut the door of the operating theatre in case one of 'Mr Lister's microbes flew in'.

5   For centuries, surgeons had lived with the fact that many patients died. When Lister said he achieved good results, their first reaction was disbelief. The next reaction was defensive, feeling that Lister was criticising them for letting patients down.

6   Lister was not a showman giving impressive public displays. Indeed, he appeared cold, arrogant and aloof and was sometimes critical of other surgeons. Many surgeons regarded him as a fanatic.

7   Lister constantly changed his techniques to find a substance that would work equally as well as carbolic, but without the corrosion it caused. His critics said he was changing his methods because they did not work.

How did Lister and antiseptics change surgery?

Antiseptic surgery

There are germs in the operating theatre but surgeons use methods, such as carbolic spray, to stop open wounds being infected.

Aseptic surgery

Cleaning and sterilising methods prevent there being any germs in the operating theatre to infect wounds.

Lister's methods marked a turning point in surgery. By the late 1890s Lister's antiseptic methods (killing germs on the wound) had developed into aseptic surgery (removing germs from the operating theatre). To ensure absolute cleanliness:

- Operating theatres and hospitals were rigorously cleaned.
- From 1887, all instruments were steam-sterilised.
- Surgeons stopped operating in their ordinary clothes and wore surgical gowns and face masks.
- In 1894, sterilised rubber gloves were used for the first time. Because however well surgeons' hands were scrubbed, they could still hold bacteria in the folds of skin and under the nails.

These improvements reflected Lister's belief that 'success depends on attention to detail'.

With two of the basic problems of surgery (pain and infection) now solved, surgeons attempted more ambitious operations. The first successful operation to remove an infected appendix came in the 1880s. The first heart operation was carried out in 1896 when surgeons repaired a heart damaged by a stab wound.

And there's a love story linked to that last bullet point!

In 1889 Caroline Hampton, an operating theatre nurse in America, developed a skin infection from the chemicals used to disinfect hands before operations. She showed her hands to the chief surgeon, William Halsted, and he arranged for the Goodyear Rubber Company to make a pair of thin rubber gloves to protect Caroline's hands. Within a year the nurse and the surgeon were married – and Halsted spread the idea of wearing rubber gloves during operations. He went on to become one of America's most famous surgeons, responsible for many new developments.

aaaah!

How to … evaluate the reliability of sources

In your exam paper you will be asked a question which aims to test your ability to evaluate the reliability of two sources. The advice below shows you how you need to approach this type of question. It provides a good opportunity to practise evaluating the reliability of a source for a specific enquiry.

Study Source 1.
How reliable is Source 1 as evidence of how surgical operations were performed in the 1880s?

Source 1

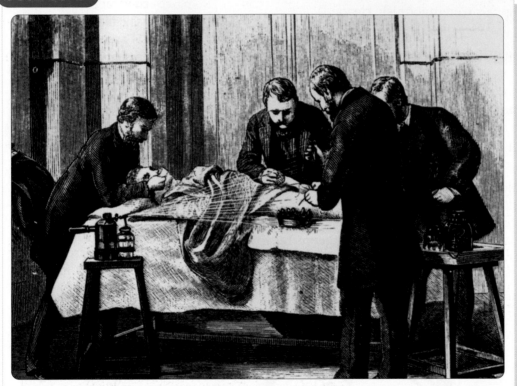

Note the distance of the spray from the wound and the position of the surgeon and the assistant. The surgeon should always have his hands in the spray and the assistant should hand the instrument to the surgeon through the spray.

▲ An illustration and caption showing an operation taking place while a carbolic spray disinfects the area. One assistant is using chloroform to anaesthetise the patient, another is mopping up blood with a sponge. It appeared in *Antiseptic Surgery*, published in 1882 and written by one of Lister's assistants.

Advice

- Keep the specific enquiry in mind at all times. Here the focus of the enquiry is on 'how surgical operations were performed in the 1880s'. You must evaluate the source on its reliability for this particular enquiry.
- As you go through the steps below try to consider both the **strengths and limitations** of the source.

Step 1: Consider the nature, origins and purpose of the source (What? Who? When? Why?).

Nature

WHAT type of source is it? This source is an illustration. It is not a photograph of what was actually happening during an operation. It is a representation of an operation. How does this affect reliability?

Origins

WHEN and WHO produced the source? The source was produced in the 1880s and appeared in a book produced by one of Lister's assistants. What are the advantages and disadvantages of this? It is written by someone who witnessed operations; however, he may want to show Lister in a good light.

Purpose

WHY was the source produced? The information in the picture and the caption is very precise. The purpose is to make sure that Lister's methods are followed very carefully. Bring in your own knowledge of surgery at the time to explain the context of the source. Remember that many surgeons at the time struggled to follow Lister's methods. Some were impatient and did not carry out operations carefully enough to reduce the risk of infection.

Step 2: Use your own knowledge to judge HOW typical the source is.

Think carefully about what happened after Lister's introduction of antiseptics. Did all surgeons start to use his methods? Was there opposition to his methods?

Remember that this is just a representation of **one** operation. How typical was it of other operations at the time? Were they all carried out with this amount of care and precision? Remember to focus on the question, which asks you to consider how reliable the source is of evidence of surgical operations in the 1880s. While the source might be very good evidence of how operations were performed by Lister and his team it might not be typical of **all** operations at the time.

Activity

Now you have practised evaluating the reliability of one source have a go at attempting the exam question below. Aim to cover both sources in a similar amount of detail. You may want to draw comparisons between the two sources and reach a judgement as to which source is the most reliable in your conclusion.

3 Study Sources D and E and use your own knowledge.
How reliable are Sources D and E as evidence of the success of Lister's antiseptic?
Explain your answer, using Sources D and E and your own knowledge. **[10 marks]**

Source D

From Lister's own record of amputations:

	Total amputations	Died	% who died
1864–66 (without antiseptics)	35	16	45.7
1867–70 (with antiseptic)	40	6	15.0

Source E

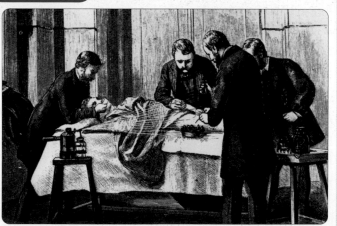

▲ An operation taking place while a carbolic spray disinfects the area. One assistant is using chloroform to anaesthetise the patient, another is mopping up blood with a sponge.

Breakthrough 3: Blood transfusions

Blood is so ordinary that this breakthrough probably does not seem either as dramatic or important as the others. However, your opinion might change if you had an accident and needed blood. Nowadays a blood transfusion is as normal as pain-free surgery, but only a hundred years ago the story was very different.

Doctors first attempted to give blood to humans from dogs, sheep and cows until this practice was banned in the 1670s. The first human-to-human transfusions started in the 1790s in America. A British doctor, James Blundell, did a lot of work trying to solve the problem of blood loss in the 1800s. He did not keep a diary – as far as we know – but if he had his notes might have looked like those below.

Activities

Why did Henry die, but Annie survive?
A mystery
1. From the diary entries below, can you work out why some patients survived a blood transfusion but others died?
2. What was needed to prevent the patients from dying?

▲ James Blundell

28 April 1818

A young boy, John, suffering from anaemia (not enough red blood cells). I was able to pass 12 ounces of blood from the artery of the lamb into the boy's vein in his arm. He immediately complained of a great heat in his arm.

3 May 1818

John's pulse has increased rapidly, and there is a plentiful sweat over his whole body. His urine is as black as if mixed with soot and he has great pains in his kidneys and liver.

John passed away in the early hours of the morning.

21 October 1819

Reading the work of Dr Leacock from Edinburgh has convinced me of the need to perform human-to-human transfusion. In the ward a 35-year-old man, Henry, was bleeding heavily as a result of gastric carcinoma (stomach cancer). I gave him 14 ounces of blood by a syringe at intervals of 5 to 6 minutes.

22 October 1819

Henry is making a small improvement, but I fear that it is too little.

23 October 1819

Henry passed away during the night.

8 September 1826

A woman called Annie bleeding heavily after giving birth. I administered 8 ounces of blood from my assistant over a period of three hours. The patient expresses herself very strongly on the benefits from the injection of the blood; she felt as if life were infused into her body.

4 June 1827

A young man called David lost a lot of blood after being trapped in a machine. His twin brother Daniel was with him and it was decided to transfer blood directly between them. I transfused about 12 ounces of blood. The operation was a great success.

How was the problem of blood loss overcome?

Stage 1: Landsteiner identifies blood groups

The first breakthrough came with the discovery of the different blood groups in 1900. Karl Landsteiner (a doctor from Austria) identified the blood groups and demonstrated that some blood groups were incompatible with others – you cannot give a person blood from someone whose blood group is incompatible. Landsteiner showed that each blood cell had antibodies which would react with those from a different blood group, meaning that blood transfusions could only work if there was no reaction.

In 1907 in New York, Reuben Ottenberg performed the first blood transfusion using blood typing. However, although blood transfusions were now possible, the patient and the donor had to be in the same place. When doctors tried to store blood for later use it clotted and could not be used for transfusions.

Stage 2: Storing blood for later transfusions

So blood transfusion was possible, but it needed an emergency to make it much more commonly used and to solve the problem of storing blood for later transfusion. That emergency was war – World War One. Casualty rates were huge, far greater than in any previous conflict and the impact of high explosives and machine gun bullets made the need for blood transfusion even more desperate.

Two discoveries solved the problem of storing blood.

1 Scientists discovered that sodium citrate could be added to blood to prevent it clotting. They also realised that a citrate glucose solution allowed blood to be stored for several days after it had been collected. This led to the first blood banks being set up by the British for use during the war.

2 Scientists also discovered how to separate and store the crucial blood cells. The cells could be bottled, packed in ice and stored where they were needed. The cells only had to be diluted with a warm saline solution and then usable blood was ready. This discovery helped save many lives both in the trenches and on the operating table and made possible the huge blood banks that supply today.

Activities

3 **Breakthrough chart:** Complete a breakthrough chart for blood transfusion, using the chart on page 211 as a model.

4 **Factors chart:** Continue building up your factors chart (page 203). Begin each entry on this topic with the word 'Blood – …'.

5 **Hypothesis triangle:** Review your hypothesis triangle for our main question 'Which surgical breakthrough was the most significant?' Add notes around your triangle to explain where you have your cross at this stage of the investigation.

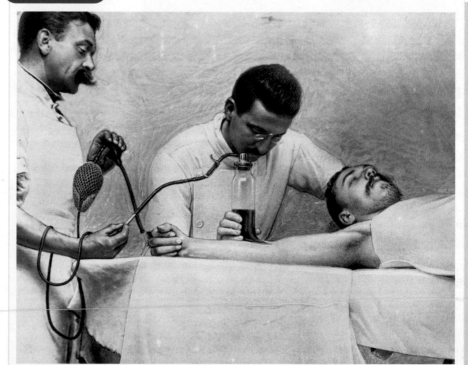

▲ Early use of human-to-human blood transfusions. A photo taken in the early 1900s.

How did World War One change surgery?

1 Effective blood transfusions

During the war casualty rates were far greater than they had been in any previous conflict. In the early years many soldiers bled to death because there was no store of blood to use. When doctors tried to store blood it clotted and could not be used for transfusions.

As you saw on the previous page the war helped speed up two breakthroughs (sodium citrate and the discovery of how to separate and store blood cells) which solved this problem. This led to the first blood banks being set up by the British for use during the war and as a result many lives were saved.

Source 1

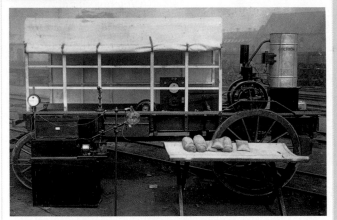

▲ A portable X-ray machine developed during World War One.

2 The development of X-rays

A German scientist, Wilhelm Röntgen, was carrying out experiments in 1895 when he realised that rays of light in a covered tube were lighting up a far wall. They could pass through black paper, wood and flesh. He did not know what they were so he called them X-rays. Within months of Röntgen publishing his discovery the news had spread world-wide and the first X-ray machines were being used in hospitals.

World War One had a major impact on the common use of X-rays. Surgeons needed to locate bullets and shrapnel lodged deep within wounded men and X-rays provided the answer. Governments ordered the making of many more X-ray machines and they were installed in all major hospitals on the Western Front.

3 Fighting infection

Lister had begun the fight against infection but wartime wounds caused problems that needed new solutions. Many wounds were very deep and bullets carried fragments of clothing, carrying bacteria deep inside the body. This caused deep infections. Gradually, through practice and trying out new methods during the war, surgeons learned how to cut away the infected tissue and protect it with a saline solution.

4 The development of plastic surgery

Plastic surgery had been carried out in India centuries earlier but was always limited by pain and the danger of infection. The terrible injuries in World War One led to a rapid improvement in techniques, especially the use of skin grafts. Injuries were mostly from bullet and shell damage. Surgeons carried out over 11,000 plastic surgery operations, increasing their experience and learning from each other.

5 The development of brain surgery

At the start of the war, a serious head wound was rarely operated on. However, as the war progressed, new treatments such as use of saline for shock and blood transfusions kept the patients alive and it became possible to tackle severe head injuries. Surgeons developed new techniques and improved their skills as they were faced with large numbers of casualties suffering from serious head wounds. For example, **Harvey Cushing** developed a surgical magnet during World War I to extract bullets from the heads of wounded soldiers.

The work of Harold Gillies – father of plastic surgery?

Harold Gillies was a pioneer plastic surgeon in the First World War. Gillies was born in New Zealand and served in the Royal Army Medical Corps during the war. In France he met the renowned surgeon Hippolyte Morestin. He saw him remove a tumour on a patient's face, and cover it with jaw skin taken from the patient. When Gillies returned to England he persuaded the army's chief surgeon that a facial injury ward should be established at the Military Hospital in Aldershot.

In 1917 a new hospital (The Queen's Hospital) specialising in repairing facial injuries was set up at Sidcup. Gillies and his colleagues developed many techniques of plastic surgery. More than 11,000 operations were performed on over 5,000 men (mostly soldiers with facial injuries).

Which factors played the biggest parts in the transformation of surgery?

It's time to borrow an idea from Maths – one of the interesting ones. Now you're nearly at the end of your investigation you can use a Venn diagram along with your factors chart to work out why surgery changed so much in the late 1800s.

Activities

By now you should have completed your factors chart from page 203 with examples of the impact of the factors you can see opposite. Here's how to use the Venn diagram to assess the importance of the factors – you could do this physically in your classroom rather than using pieces of paper.
Work in pairs or groups of three.

1 Time to complete your **Factors chart**. Read the information on page 220 about how surgery changed as a result of World War One. Add examples to your factors chart.

2 Use the information in your factors chart to suggest whether we have placed war and communications in the correct places. If we're wrong, move them to where you think they should go.

3 Now create cards like those below to show the evidence for your placing of the factors. You may need more than one card for each factor.

4 Decide where you think each of the other factors goes on the diagram and create evidence cards for them.

5 The most important factors ought to be in the very middle of the diagram. Compare your results with those of another group and revise or add new evidence to your diagram as a result of your discussion.

Simpson publicised use of chloroform in letters and medical lectures.	Lister read a report of use of carbolic acid at sewage works in Carlisle.	Landsteiner's research led to the identification of blood groups.

6 **Hypothesis triangle**. It is judgement time. On page 194 you made you hypothesis as to which was the key breakthrough. Do you want to change that in the light of all that you have studied?

How to ... evaluate interpretations

The last question on the exam paper is not just another individual question on one or two sources. Instead, it is an overall conclusion to the whole exam paper, asking you to use the sources and your own knowledge to reach an overall conclusion on the theme of the exam paper. You are expected to produce an extended piece of writing to make your judgement, worth 16 marks, the highest value question in the exam.

The final question asks you to use your own knowledge **and** the sources to evaluate an interpretation or point of view. You must decide the **extent** to which you agree or disagree with the interpretation. The advice on pages 223–225 will help you.

The question below is a typical example of a big question that ends the Source Enquiry exam paper. The question is taken from the practice exam paper on page 197.

---

*5 Study Sources D, E and F and use your own knowledge.

Spelling, punctuation and grammar will be assessed in this question.

Source F suggests that anaesthetics were the major surgical breakthrough of the period 1845–1918.

How far do you agree with this interpretation?

Explain your answer, using your own knowledge, Sources D, E and F and any other sources you find helpful.   **[16 marks]**

(Total for spelling, punctuation and grammar = 3 marks)

(Total for Question 5 = 19 marks)

For questions such as this you need to evaluate the relative importance of a development in surgery before coming to a conclusion. This means weighing up the evidence for and against the interpretation before you reach a conclusion about the relative importance of anaesthetics. There will not usually be a preferred answer. The marks are available for:

- the clarity of your arguments
- how well you explain your arguments
- how effectively you support your arguments from the sources and your own knowledge
- the clarity of your final conclusion.

Activity

Now have a go at question 5 using the sources booklet on page 197. Use the tips on the next three pages to help you.

Tip 1: Plan your approach to the question

It is not simply a case of saying whether you agree or disagree with the statement. There are 16 marks available, so the examiner will expect you to **explore both sides of the argument** before you reach a conclusion.

Plan to include three paragraphs.

- **Paragraph 1** should explore the evidence that supports the interpretation. Why could anaesthetics be seen as a significant breakthrough? Use the sources and your own knowledge to show how anaesthetics changed surgery.
- **Paragraph 2** should explore evidence against the interpretation. What evidence could you use from the sources and your own knowledge to argue against the interpretation? What were the limitations of anaesthetics? What other developments were important?
- **Paragraph 3** is your conclusion. You need to reach an overall judgement. To what extent do you agree or disagree with the

Tip 2: Use the sources *and* your own knowledge to support your answer

Try to avoid making general points without fully explaining them and backing them up with specific examples from your own knowledge and the sources.

Look at the following student answer.

> *Anaesthetics were a very important breakthrough in surgery. During the nineteenth century anaesthetics such as ether and chloroform were introduced.*

The student starts by making a general point. They would score just 1 mark if they stopped here. They are simply saying something, they are not proving anything!

> *This meant that surgery became pain free. This also resulted in fewer patients dying from shock. The introduction of anaesthetics such as chloroform also led to surgeons being able to take more time over operations and work deeper inside the body. New operations could be developed that saved more lives.*

However, the student goes on to score extra marks by <u>proving their point</u>. They use connectives like 'this meant that', 'this led to' and 'this resulted in' to prove their point and show how anaesthetics had a major impact on surgery.

Tip 3: Refer to specific sources

You <u>must</u> base your answer on the sources on the exam paper. You will not achieve a good grade if you ignore the sources and simply write an answer to this final question based on your own knowledge. You do not have to use all the sources, but you should try to use most of them in your answer.

Make sure you refer to the source that you are using by letter so that the examiner can see which sources you are using to support your answer.

Tip 4: use connectives to tie what you know to the question

Phrases like: This meant that …, This resulted in …, This led to … will help you avoid general low level answers but instead help you show you understand specific things that resulted from each of the breakthroughs. For example:

Tip 5: Think carefully about your concluding paragraph

This is a crucial part of your answer. It is usually the part that pupils forget or answer poorly. Just producing a balanced answer is not enough. You have been asked to **evaluate** the extent to which you agree or disagree with the interpretation **'Anaesthetics were the most significant surgical breakthrough of the period 1845–1918'**. It would be easy to sit on the fence and avoid reaching a final conclusion. Sitting on the fence is a dangerous position. Your answer collapses and you lose marks!

Instead, you need to be confident and reach an **overall judgement**.

Activities

We have put some evidence on the scales for you already. Which side would you put the following:

- The 'benefit of time' (Source F) – led to longer and more complex operations.
- End of 'slapdash surgery' (Source F) – theories of Pasteur and Lister could be put into practice.
- Blood transfusions and developments in the First World War were also very important (e.g. development of X-rays and plastic surgery).

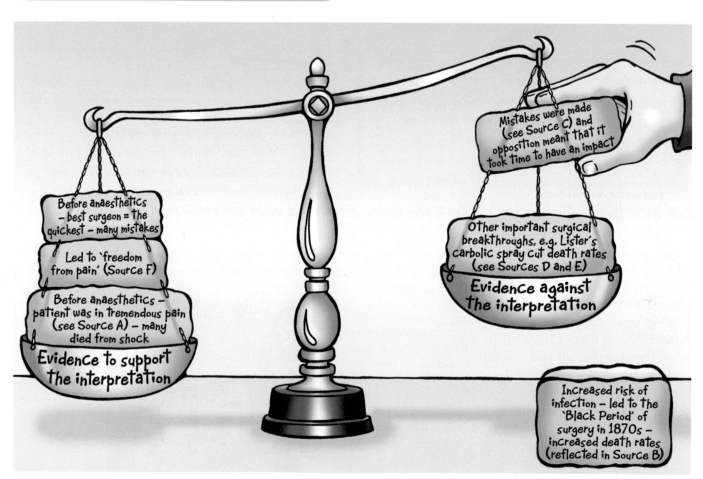

Advice

What makes an effective concluding paragraph?

Things to avoid:

- A detailed summary of everything that has already been said.
- A one sentence conclusion that reaches an overall judgement but does not explain it or show that there are two sides to the argument.
- A weak conclusion that sits on the fence and does not reach an overall judgement.

Things to do:

- Focus on the question. You could use words or phrases from the question in your final paragraph.
- Show that you recognise that there is evidence that agrees and disagrees with the interpretation.
- Come to a strong overall judgement.
- Explain your main reason for reaching this judgement.

 How to structure a concluding paragraph

Start with what you regard as the weaker argument and concede that it still has some strengths.

↓

Give an example.

↓

Then make it clear that you think the other argument is stronger.

↓

Provide your main piece(s) of evidence that supports this.

↓

Try to end with a memorable final sentence.

Example 1

The introduction of anaesthetics was an important breakthrough in Surgery.

↓

For example …

↓

However, overall I disagree with the statement.

↓

This is because …

↓

The key breakthrough in surgery was still to happen.

Example 2

The development of anaesthetics was not the only important breakthrough in surgery between 1845 and 1918.

↓

For example …

↓

However, the introduction of safe and effective anaesthetics was the key turning point.

↓

This is because …

↓

Anaesthetics changed surgery forever and opened up the door to new possibilities.

Medical terms

ailment an illness that is not serious

amputation the removal of a limb by surgery

amulet a charm that the wearer believes gives protection from disease

anaesthetic a drug or drugs given to produce unconsciousness before and during surgery

anatomy the science of understanding the structure and make-up of the body

antibiotics a group of drugs used to treat infections caused by bacteria, e.g. penicillin

antisepsis the prevention of infection by stopping the growth of bacteria by the use of antiseptics

antiseptics chemicals used to destroy bacteria and prevent infection

apothecary a pharmacist or chemist

arteries blood vessels that carry blood away from the heart

arthritis the painful swelling of joints

Asclepion temple of the Greek god of healing Asclepius (or Askiepios)

astrology the study of the planets and how they might influence the lives of people

bacterium (pl. bacteria) see **germ**

bezoar stone a ball of indigestible material found in goats' stomachs

biochemist a scientist who studies the make-up of living things

Black Death a phrase used in the Middle Ages to describe bubonic plague. (The 'blackness' was caused by bleeding under the skin. Over 50 per cent of all cases were fatal)

bleed/bleeding the treatment of opening a vein or applying leeches to draw blood from the patient. Also means the loss of blood caused by damage to the blood vessels

buboes black swellings in armpits and groin that were symptoms of the Black Death

cauterise using a hot iron to burn body tissue. This seals a wound and stops bleeding

cell the basic unit of life that makes up the bodies of plants, animals and humans. Billions of cells are contained in the human body

cesspool/cesspit a place for collecting and storing sewage

charlatans people pretending to have a skill or knowledge that they don't really have

chemotherapy treatment of a disease such as cancer by the use of chemicals

chilblains painful swellings on feet and hands caused by exposure to cold and wet

chirurgery/chirurgeons surgery/surgeons

chloroform a liquid whose vapour acts as an anaesthetic and produces unconsciousness

chromosomes thread-like structures in the cells of the body that contain genetic information

consumption/consumptive fever tuberculosis which was observed as the wasting away of the body

contagion the passing of disease from one person to another

contaminated/contamination something that is infected

court an enclosed area of housing, often with little daylight and heavily over-populated

culture/culturing the growth of micro-organisms in the laboratory

diarrhoea a symptom of a disease; frequent, fluid bowel movements

dissection the cutting up and examination of a body

DNA Deoxyribonucleic acid, the molecule that genes are made of. See **gene**

dysentery a severe infection causing frequent, fluid bowel movements

effluvia/effluvial unpleasant smells from waste matter. Blamed for disease in the eighteenth and nineteenth centuries

embalm the treatment of a dead body to preserve it

endoscope an instrument used to view inside the body

faeces waste material from the stomach and digestive system

gangrene (gas gangrene) the infection of dead tissue causing, in the case of gas gangrene, foul smelling gas

gene part of a cell that determines how our bodies look and work. Genes are passed from parents to children

genetic engineering the investigation of genes and how they can be used to change how the body works

germ a micro-organism that causes disease

germ theory the theory that germs cause disease, often by infection through the air

Health Authority the people controlling NHS health care in the regions

herbal remedy a medicine made up from a mixture of plants, often containing beneficial ingredients

high-tech surgery surgery using the most modern techniques, including computers, new skills and new drugs

Hippocratic Oath the principles by which doctors work, for the best health of the patient and to do no harm, named after Hippocrates who wrote it

humours the Ancient Greeks believed the body contained four humours of liquids – blood, phlegm, black bile and yellow bile

immune protected against a disease

immunise the process of giving protection from disease through the body's own immune system

immunity protection against disease through the body's own defences or immune system

incision a cut made with a knife during surgery

infection the formation of disease-causing germs or micro-organisms

infirmary a place where the sick are treated, a hospital

inoculation putting a low dose of a disease into the body to help it fight against a more serious attack of the disease

King's Evil see **scrofula**

laissez-faire belief that governments should not interfere in people's lives. It prevented public health schemes getting underway in the nineteenth century

leeches blood-sucking worms used to drain blood from a wound

leper someone suffering from leprosy, an infection that causes damage to the nerves and skin

ligament tough elastic tissue that holds joints of the body together

ligatures a thread used to tie a blood vessel during an operation

lunatic an old-fashioned word for someone who is insane

malady see **ailment**

maternity concerning motherhood and looking after children

medical officer a person appointed to look after the public health of an area

melancholy part of the Theory of Four Humours, brought on by excess of gloominess

miasma smells from decomposing material that were believed to cause disease

microbe another name for a micro-organism

micro-organism a tiny single-celled living organism too small to be seen by the naked eye. Disease-causing micro-organisms are called bacteria

osteoarthritis see **arthritis**

papyrus early 'paper' made from the papyrus plant

patent remedy a medicine usually sold for a profit. In the nineteenth century patent medicines were often made from a mix of ingredients that had no medical benefits. They were also known as 'cure-alls'

penicillin the first antibiotic drug produced from the mould penicillium to treat infections

physic a medicine or the skill of healing

physician a doctor of medicine who trained at university

physiology the study of how the body works

plague a serious infectious disease spread to humans by fleas from rats and mice

pneumonia the inflammation of the lungs due to an infection

Poor Law Commission three commissioners who controlled the work of parishes which provided help for the poor. They were influential in public health reforms

poultice a warm dressing made of layers of fabric and moist paste

prognosis medical judgement about the probable course and result of a disease

public health refers to the well-being of the whole community

pus a pale yellow or green fluid found where there is an infection in the body

putrid decomposing

quack a person who falsely claims to have medical ability or qualifications

quinine the drug treatment for malaria

radiotherapy treatment of a disease such as cancer by the use of radium

radium a metallic chemical element discovered by Marie Curie in 1898 (see radiotherapy)

remedy a drug or treatment that cures or controls the symptoms of a disease

rheumatism a term describing stiffness in muscles or joints

rickets a disease caused by a poor diet resulting in a misshapen skeleton

sanatorium a place where people who are chronically (very) ill can be cared for

scrofula sometimes known as the King's Evil. It is tuberculosis of a gland in the neck. At one time it was believed that being touched by the king could cure the disease

septicaemia blood poisoning caused by the spread of bacteria from an infected area

sinew a tendon or fibrous cord that joins a muscle to a bone

spontaneous generation the theory that decaying matter turns into germs

staphylococci bacteria found on the skin that can cause infection if the bacteria become trapped

sterilise to destroy all living micro-organisms from surfaces and surgical instruments, e.g. on a scalpel before an operation

stye a small pus-filled abscess near the eyelashes caused by infection

sulphonamide an antibacterial drug used to treat bronchitis and pneumonia

superbugs bacteria that have developed immunity to treatment by antibiotics or methods of destroying them by cleaning

supernatural something that cannot be given an ordinary explanation

superstition an unreasonable belief based on ignorance and sometimes fear

suppuration the formation and/or discharge of pus

suture the closing of a cut or wound by the use of stitches (sutures)

syphilis a sexually-transmitted disease that was common from the late fifteenth century until the introduction of penicillin

thalidomide a drug to help morning sickness that was withdrawn in 1961 after it was found to cause limb deformities in babies born to women who had taken it

therapy the treatment of either a physical or mental disease

transfusion the use of blood given by one person to another when a patient has suffered severe blood loss

trephining the drilling of a hole in the skull (also called trepanning)

tumour a swelling caused by cells reproducing at an increased rate/an abnormal growth of cells that may or may not be cancerous

ulcer an open sore on the skin

unpasteurised food or drink that has not been pasteurised. Pasteurisation is a process of heating that destroys harmful bacteria

uroscopy diagnosing illness by examining the patient's urine

vaccination the injection into the body of killed or weakened organisms to give the body resistance against disease

virus a tiny micro-organism, smaller than bacteria, responsible for infections such as colds, flu, polio and chicken pox

wise woman a person believed to be skilled in magic or local customs

witch/witchcraft a person who practises magic and is believed to have dealings with evil spirits

worms an infestation where worms live as parasites in the human body

Index

Acknowledgements

Photo credits

p.2 The Art Archive/Anagni Cathedral Italy/Dagli Orti (A); **p.3** t Topfoto/AP, b Eric Draper/AP Photo/Press Association Images; **p.24** l © Chris Warren/Loop Images/Corbis, r © English Heritage Photo Library; **p.25** t © English Heritage Photo Library, b The Oxford Archaeological Unit ltd; **p.27** The Art Archive/National Archaeological Museum Athens/Dagli Orti; **p.28** akg-images/Rabatti – Domingie; **p.32** © 2006 Topfoto; **p.33** The Art Archive/Anagni Cathedral Italy/Dagli Orti (A); **p.34** Peter Smith; **p.38** © Canterbury City Council Museums; **p.39** geogphotos/Alamy; **p.40** The Art Archive/Victoria and Albert Museum London/Eileen Tweedy; **p.41** The Art Archive/Bibliothèque Universitaire de Médecine, Montpellier/Dagli Orti; **p.43** Mary Evans Picture Library; **p.46** l The Art Archive/University Library Prague/Dagli Orti, r The Art Archive/Bodleian Library Oxford/The Bodleian Library; **p.47** akg-images/British Library; **p.49** Trinity College, Cambridge, UK/The Bridgeman Art Library; **p.55** rt Topfoto/AP, l By permission of the British Library (MS Egerton, f53), rb Rischgitz/Hulton Archive/Getty Images; **p.56** l Bodleian Library MS Rawlings B124f 197v Oxford, r Hulton Archive/Getty Images; **p.58** l Musee Conde, Chantilly, France/The Bridgeman Art Library, r akg-images; **p.60** l Wellcome Library, London, r www.topfoto.co.uk; **p.61** www.topfoto.co.uk; **p.68** Ann Ronan Picture Library/HIP/TopFoto; **p.70** Mary Evans Picture Library; **p.71** www.topfoto.co.uk; **p.73** l Getty Images/The Bridgeman Art Library, r © Corbis; **p.74** t The Art Archive/Victoria and Albert Museum London/Eileen Tweedy; b Wellcome Library, London. Wellcome Images; **p.75** Wellcome Library, London. Wellcome Images; **p.77** The Art Archive/Palazzo del Te Mantua/Dagli Orti (A); **p.78** Wellcome Library, London. Wellcome Images; **p.79** t © Charles Walker/TopFoto, b Wellcome Library, London. Wellcome Images; **p.92** Science Museum; **p.93** tl Wellcome Library, London, tr © Bettmann/Corbis, bl Hulton Archive/Getty Images, br © Bettmann/Corbis; **p.96** Wellcome Library, London; **p.99** Wellcome Library, London; **p.100** © Bettmann/Corbis; **p.101** l&r Hulton Archive/Getty Images; **p.106** t Warner Bros/DC Comics/The Kobal Collection, b Eric Draper/AP Photo/Press Association Images; **p.110** Getty Images/The Bridgeman Art Library; **p.113** t Wellcome Library, London. Wellcome Images, b Science Museum, London. Wellcome Images; **p.117** lt Kurt Hutton/Picture Post/Getty Images, rt © Bettmann/Corbis, lb Wellcome Library, London; **p.119** BMJ, 15 August 2009, 339:355–410 No 7717; reproduced with permission from the BMJ Publishing Group; **p.120** l © Bettmann/Corbis, r Chris Ware/Keystone Features/Getty Images; **p.121** t World History Archive/TopFoto, b © Hulton-Deutsch Collection/Corbis; **p.122** t © Jochen Tack/Alamy, b Popperfoto/Getty Images; **p.123** tl © Eyewire, tr © NHS Cancer Screening Programmes, www.cancerscreening.nhs.uk, b Barros & Barros/Photographer's Choice/Getty Images; **p.126** t Mary Evans Picture Library, b © Trevor Smith/Alamy; **p.128** Hulton Archive/Getty Images; **p.129** Greater London Council, UK/The Bridgeman Art Library; **p.130** St Bartholomew's Hospital/Science Photo Library; **p.132** © graficart.net/Alamy; **p.133** © Maximilian Stock LTD/Phototake/Alamy; **p.134** t Museum of the City of New York/Getty Images, b Hulton Archive/Getty Images; **p.136** National Library of Medicine/Science Photo Library; **p.137** National Library of Medicine/Science Photo Library; **p.144** Wellcome Library, London; **p.147** t The Art Archive/Science Museum London/Eileen Tweedy, b Museum of London/HIP/TopFoto; **p.149** © Punch Limited/TopFoto; **p.150** British Museum, London, UK/The Bridgeman Art Library; **p.151** Punch Limited/Topfoto; **p.155** Hulton Archive/Getty Images; **p.159** t Wellcome Library, London, b The Granger Collection/TopFoto; **p.160** HIP/TopFoto; **p.162** l Courtesy of Newham Heritage and Archives Service, r © Hulton-Deutsch Collection/Corbis; **p.163** bl Science Museum, br © Mary Evans Picture Library/Alamy, t Popperfoto/Getty Images; **p.164** © The Granger Collection/TopFoto; **p.171** t © Hulton Archive/Getty Images, b © Punch Limited/Topham Picturepoint/TopFoto; **p.169** t Mansell/Time & Life Pictures/Getty Images, b The Art Archive/Private Collection MD; **p.170** l Wellcome Library, London, r Topical Press Agency/Getty Images; **p.173** t&b Mirrorpix; **p.174** Reg Speller/Fox Photos/Getty Images; **p.176** l Wellcome Library, London. Wellcome Images, r © Crown Copyright; **p.186** Peter Smith; **p.190** Royal College of Surgeons, London, UK/The Bridgeman Art Library; **p.192** t The Art Archive/British Museum/Eileen Tweedy, b Mark Harmel/Stone/Getty Images; **p.198** l The Art Archive/British Museum/Eileen Tweedy; **p.199** Hulton Archive/Getty Images; **p.200** Royal College of Surgeons, London, UK/The Bridgeman Art Library; **p.202** l © Corbis; **p.204** © Hulton-Deutsch Collection/Corbis; **p.207** akg-images; **p.216** Hulton Archive/Getty Images; **p.217** Hulton Archive/Getty Images; **p.218** Mary Evans Picture Library; **p.219** l © Bettmann/Corbis, © Corbis; **p.220** Imperial War Museum, image ref. Q52408.

Text acknowledgements

The Publishers would also like to thank the following:

Lindsay Allason-Jones: extract from *Women in Roman Britain* (British Museum Press, 1989); inscriptions from Roman altars found in Britain; Galen: extract from *On Anatomy* (c.AD190); Geoffrey Chaucer: extract from *The Canterbury Tales*; extract from the rules of the hospital of St John, Bridgwater (1219); Brother John Clynn: extract from his account of the plague; Petrarch: letter to a friend (1350); Swedish bishop: extract from his writings on the plague; Prior of Christchurch Abbey, Canterbury: extract from a letter to the Bishop of London (September 1348); John of Burgundy: extract from his writings on the plague (1365); John of Burgundy: extract from his advice on the plague (1365); fourteenth-century writer: extract from a report on a method people used to avoid the Black Death; Samuel Pepys: extract from his diaries (3 July 1668); James Woodforde: extracts from his diary (1778, 1779, 1791); suggestions on how to help plague sufferers (1660s); extract from *The New London Dispensary* (1682); Thomas Jefferson, President of the USA: extract from a letter to Dr Edward Jenner (1808); Dr Jenner: extracts from his casebook (1798); Pasteur: extract from his lecture at the University of Paris (1864); F.B. Smith: extract from The People's Health (1971); traditional home remedies used in the nineteenth century; Lt Colonel Pulvertaft: account of the first use of penicillin in the British army (1943); Charles Dickens: extract from *Martin Chuzzlewit* (1844); report in the *Suffolk Times and Mercury* (16 December 1892); memorials put up to women healers (1629, 1643, 1689); Thomas Huxley: extract from his writings on women (1851); Dr H. Bennett, writing about women in the medical journal *The Lancet* (1870); Sophia Jex-Blake: extract from *Medical Education of Women* (1878); Ian Mortimer: *The Time Traveller's Guide to Medieval England* (The Bodley Head Ltd, 2008); Edward III: extract from a letter to the city of York (1332); A traveller's description of Leeds, *The Morning Chronicle* (1848); James Smith; extract from 'Report on the Condition of the Town of Leeds' (1844); extracts from a letter on cholera, *The Times* (1 August 1854); John Snow: extract from 'On the Mode of Communication of Cholera' (1854); letter on cholera, *The Times* (1 August 1854); Mrs John Brown: extract from her memoirs describing a visit in the late 1800s; extract from an article in *The Times* on plans to provide free school meals for the poorest children (2 January 1905); extract from an interview with Kathleen Davys on home cures; extract from a speech by Aneurin Bevan introducing the National Health Service to Parliament (1946); Alice Law: recollections of 5 July 1948, the first day of the NHS; account of a blood transfusion (1668); David Zuck, quoting the verdict of Sir Clifford Albutt (2007); John Leeson: account of surgery in St Thomas's Hospital, London (1871); David Leaper: extract from an article in the *European Wound Management Journal* (2007); Phil Learoyd: extracts from *A Short History of Blood Transfusion* (2006); Fanny Burney: account of her mastectomy operation (1811); extract from anonymous letter to Sir James Simpson; extract from an article in the *London Medical Gazette* (1848); Professor David Leaper: extract from an article in the *European Wound Management* Journal (2007); John South: description of surgery (1815); James Simpson: extract from a speech to a meeting of doctors in Edinburgh (1847).

Every effort has been made to trace all copyright holders, but if any have been inadvertently overlooked the Publishers will be pleased to make the necessary arrangements at the first opportunity.